Sheila Petersen-Lowary

A FIRESIDE BOOK PUBLISHED BY SIMON & SCHUSTER INC.
NEW YORK   LONDON   TORONTO   SYDNEY   TOKYO

THE 5th DIMENSION

CHANNELS TO A NEW REALITY

Fireside
Simon & Schuster Building
Rockefeller Center
1230 Avenue of the Americas
New York, New York 10020

Copyright © 1988 by Sheila Petersen-Lowary

Designed by Barbara Marks Graphic Design
Manufactured in the United States of America

3   5   7   9   10   8   6   4   2

Library of Congress Cataloging in Publication Data

Petersen-Lowary, Sheila.
The 5th dimension: channels to a new reality/Sheila Petersen-Lowary.
p. cm.
"A Fireside book."
ISBN 0-671-65873-5
1. Petersen-Lowary, Sheila.   2. Mediums—United States—
Biography.   3. New Age movement.   I. Title.
BF1283.P44A3 1988   88-20105
133.9'3—dc19   CIP

ISBN 0-671-65873-5

To my children,

Stephanie,

Jeff,

and Cathy

ACKNOWLEDGMENTS

MY SPECIAL THANKS GO TO Raymond van Over for his many hours of help on this book and for his support and friendship. I would also like to thank Barbara Gess for her support as my editor, Judith Cameron, Rogue Simpson, Stevi Deer, Connie Cory, Elizabeth Backman, and Raleigh Pinskey.

Thanks to all my clients who have participated in groups or solo with Theo and, finally, to my family, who have given me their loving support and encouragement.

C O N T E N T S

I

CHANNELS

TO

A

NEW

REALITY

*The heart of humankind asks
to become a part of this 5th
Dimension transformation, to
become a part of your planet's
spiritual evolution.*

1

The 5th Dimension

I CAN FEEL THE TRANCE START AS a tingling sensation moving up through my neck and into my head; the large muscle on the right side of my neck seems to thicken and tighten. A sensation of fullness moves up and gathers at the back of my skull before it fills the whole of my head. Often there is a feeling that my skull is expanding. I know, of course, that this is not physically happening, but the impression is powerful. Yet soon after my head, neck, and upper body seem engorged with this tingling electrical charge, a peace unlike any I have ever experienced before overcomes me and I find myself drifting into an indefinite world that isn't the least bit frightening. On the contrary, I experience an atmosphere of love and caring building around me.

As I sit cross-legged in my comfortable beige armchair breathing gently and rhythmically, and opening myself to the coming of

Theo, there is none of the fear or panic at losing control of myself
that I once felt. By now, after eighteen years of going into a trance,
of offering myself to strange powers wishing to channel information to our world, I have become used to the experience—as
bizarre as it may appear to others. In fact, it has become a familiar
splendor that nourishes me in untold ways.

My psychic life began in earnest one morning while having
coffee with a friend at her breakfast nook. We were sitting on high
stools chatting when she suddenly said, "You want to try some
automatic writing?"

"Sure," I said, not really sure at all.

We got some paper and pencils and she said, "You just ask
for a spirit to speak through you."

I asked for my grandmother, who I had been very close to. I
don't know what I expected to happen—probably nothing—but
clearly not what then occurred.

My pen began scribbling, "I am here, can you feel me?" I
wasn't sure whether I was unconsciously writing this or something weird was happening. Then I got the surprise of my life. The
chair under me began moving, vibrating and shaking like an
earthquake had just started.

After I calmed down and could breathe again, I became tre-
mendously excited. I thought, I've got to do this again, this is
really neat.

So I did it again . . . and again . . . and again. Then I started
hearing messages, voices whispering in my head. At first I was a
bit scared, concerned that I was going crazy. This was an incredible experience for a housewife and mother of three living in Car-
bondale, Colorado.

But then an incredibly intense energy began flowing through
my body. It felt electric and warming, peaceful and exciting, all at
the same time. On the third day I went into a trance for the first
time in my life—and began "channeling." It went that quickly,
yet I realize now that the awakening had been building for the
whole of the previous year since my "near-death" experience.
And with the coming of Theo four years later I knew that a major
spiritual change had occurred and a new, powerful momentum
had entered my life.

• • •

The first time Theo channeled through me it was like putting my finger into an electric light socket. My body was jolted with a tingling, rushing electrical current that was unlike anything I had ever experienced before.

This is the beginning, is it not!

Indeed, it was. This is how the Theo group first channeled through me. And each session since that sunny winter afternoon in February of 1976, Theo has opened with the same greeting.

Even though I had been channeling for six years by then, the first time Theo came through was overpowering. I came out of the trance in tears.

I had been prepared for a new level of trance and a new teacher-guide by Orlos, a soft-spoken, loving entity who was my first experience with channeling. Orlos had told me in previous sessions over a three-year period that my body was slowly being prepared for higher teachers to come through. I had no idea that it would be such an intense experience. Nor did I realize the surprising message about a "5th Dimension" that would be coming from Theo.

When Theo first came through, I was at home in my living room. I expected this to be a normal channeling session with Orlos, where we would answer some personal questions from clients' letters. The trance began as usual, and Orlos entered, but he immediately stated, "It is now time for the exchange; the higher teachers are here. I bid you good-bye. . . ."

It was that abrupt. Then, I was told later, a new voice came through.

This is the beginning, is it not!

And the Theo group was present.

I was later told that tears were running down my cheeks throughout the trance session. When Theo came through the energy—for those in the room—it was enormously powerful. The voice was loud and distinctly different from Orlos's. When I came out of the trance, my upper body, especially my head and face, was tingling with an electric charge—a very similar feeling to when my arm or leg would go to sleep from lack of circulation.

I felt sad at the departure of Orlos yet fascinated by these new and powerful personalities.

*Theo is a group and not to be thought of as one person-
ality. You can identify this energy by the word "Theo."*

*Theo is the name of a group of entities, a collective
consciousness that has come forth from what you might
term angelic form to assist the progress of humankind in
the changes that are happening in this world now. It is a
change of energy, a change of dimensions . . . it is a 5th
Dimension!*

*To open the mind and heart of the people, to open
the world to the vibrations of this energy, is our work.*

*The 4th Dimension began with the Christ teachings,
to honor and love the self and others, but humankind did
not want to listen. The vibrational increase into the 5th
Dimension is a higher frequency for human beings. It is a
time of balance within individuals. It is a time of truth, of
light and spirit, of enlightenment. You cannot avoid it; do
you understand?*

At first I was shocked when I heard this new message of a 5th Dimension; then I became intrigued, and finally fascinated, as the details became clearer. The more I heard about the 5th Dimension the more important it seemed. I suddenly understood that we were moving into a new age, into a period of dramatic change that was going to have a stronger impact upon our world than anything we have every known before.

In the many channeling sessions that followed, Theo was often asked about the 5th Dimension—what was it? What did it mean for the people of Earth? What was going to happen in the future? How were the cataclysmic changes going to affect our lives? What did the 5th Dimension mean to us personally, and what could we do to prepare ourselves for its coming?

The questions seemed endless, and through it all Theo pa-tiently communicated to us the full impact of the changes that we were going to witness in the coming years.

I can still remember one of the early channeling sessions where Theo's comments sent a chill up my spine.

A cycle has been completed upon this planet that has lasted twenty-six thousand years. It was an experience necessary for the evolution of mankind. Know that this 5th Dimension energy is a shift within humankind as well as within the physical structure of the planet—and the reason for this is that the planet has come to a point of annihilation!

Annihilation! My God, I thought, what is going on? Was the earth going to be annihilated? At first I couldn't believe it, but as the channeling sessions progressed I realized—and Theo clearly confirmed—that this did not mean a nuclear holocaust, but rather a continuing and slow erosion of the earth's ecology.

There are many people on your planet, yes? And you are witnessing the destruction of your planet's habitat. You have disease now, and many more will depart with the death of your planet.

Will this be through cataclysm or disease? Both! The apathy can no longer be, and the new consciousness being brought about by the 5th Dimension will assist humankind in preserving the earth.

The 5th Dimensional shift brings about a greater attunement to the earth. The shift allows a greater and finer attunement to the universal energy. It will change the consciousness of humankind . . . bring about an appreciation of balance and harmony, create new thought patterns that will alter the destructive path your world is now moving down.

To the channeler, the psychic, the mystic, these states of consciousness Theo speaks about are not so unusual. That is why so many psychics and channelers often make the same points and raise the same issues. For the nonpsychic, however, this higher state of consciousness is usually a fleeting experience—if had at all.

But as the 5th Dimension energies expand their influence, more and more people will find themselves perceiving the world through these higher states of consciousness. To a degree this is already happening, for many people seem to be more sensitive to the mystical or psychic world than most of us have realized.

People are noticing the difference. That awareness is the influence of the 5th Dimension. A finer attunement, an awareness of change happening. The energy grids of the planet have already shifted and changed—and the energy grids in the physical body as well. A fine-tuning of all physical structures is happening. Many will feel a buzzing sensation in the cells of their bodies. But they need not be alarmed about that. Some will feel a spiraling effect as if they were leaving the body now and again—a light-headedness. That is part of the 5th Dimension attunement. A vibrational alignment of the cells, you could say.

At first I did not understand just exactly *what* the 5th Dimension was—a higher state of consciousness, a period of time the world was entering, or a spiritual process involving some form of subtle cosmic energy. As it turned out, all three ideas were true.

Over the years many others have been puzzled over the precise definition of the 5th Dimension. Consequently, a question about what the 5th Dimension was often came up during channeling sessions.

There is much change coming in the world as you know it. In the year 1986 there was the completion of a twenty-six-thousand-year cycle and the bringing forth of the 5th Dimension energy of this planet. The energy grids of your planet have shifted and changed—as well as the energy grids within the physical structure of humankind. This cannot be seen by the eye or the microscope, but it has occurred.

There has been a raising up of the energy-vibrational levels. Many have been feeling this . . . and it has strongly affected the emotions. Now is a time for emotional re-

lease, for a greater refinement of the energy affecting your life. This shift will bring into balance the wholeness of your being.

The old thought patterns, the old forms of interacting with the world, can no longer be. There will be the creation of the new within your thinking processes. For it is the shift of intention and attitude within each mind that is important now. It is a shift of consciousness, of thought. That is what is happening in the presence of this 5th Dimensional energy—it is enlightenment and light, which brings about a shift of thought patterning for humankind. For the old processes have come out of fear and destruction. The 5th Dimensional shift brings about a greater strength, with greater attunement to the earth. That is what this energy is about.

The 5th Dimension allows a greater and finer attunement to the universal energy. It will change the consciousness of humankind.

It is brought about by an alignment of harmonic vibrations that will bring forth a finer attunement within the physical world as well as the mental and spiritual.

The patterns of the past that have worked on this planet will no longer be a part of the patterns now coming about. To bring about a unification of this planet, and to change the thinking patterns of mankind, is of great necessity at this time.

It is important to change the thought patterns of human beings, for much of the 5th Dimension change comes from "thought"—which is the creative force of the universe. There is always some effect created by thought —there is a universal impact. The beings upon this planet have great influence, and there is a continual shift and change within the structures of the universe that allows the planets to change as well. These changes are wrought, to a large degree, by the attitudes and intentions, by the consciousness, of the beings on the planet.

Realize that all thought is but energy—energy that is held within the personalities of human beings. You are a

receptor, a holder of that energy, and you act upon it.
That is why it must change at this time, for there has been
much upheaval on the emotional level of humankind.

You must understand that thought is the creative
force of your universe. Be clear about this. It is the energy
within—and around—you. It is the same as you think of
an aura—electric and a part of your being. It is the energy
form of your being and is involved in the thinking processes of your conscious mind. Therefore you have the
power to alter its patterns. Its energy is available for your
use. And with its power humankind can influence the
universe.

Through thought you have built the past, in thought
you exist in the present, within thought you build your
future.

**How will the coming of the 5th Dimension energy af-
fect our lives?**

The 5th Dimension is what brings harmony, a global
unity to the world: a unification of religion, of humankind; not divisions in politics, but a healing and a common thread that leads to an honoring of one another.

This changing of Dimensions is a powerful time. All
the dimensional shifts have been important. But know
that in this time the planet is in such a state that there
needs to be a balancing: of the body, mind, and spirit.
And that is the 5th Dimension energy.

This is a time to become aware of—and acknowledge
—the uniqueness and beauty of your spirit upon this
planet. Many seek the sensational rather than the truth.
But many will accept the gift of becoming attuned to the
spirit, the soul, the essence of their being, that the 5th
Dimension shift of energy offers. The heart of humankind
asks to become a part of this 5th Dimension transformation, to become a part of the process of spiritual evolution.
And for the many who open themselves to this process,

they will become a gift unto the planet. In such a way the 5th Dimension reality becomes the truth of your being.

Those who deny or resist the spiritual changes that are offered will go another way. Those who resist will experience anger and frustration. That is because the spirit that has been repressed, that has been hidden away, comes forth now with ever greater power. The energy of the spirit bubbles up into consciousness, demanding to be realized.

Those who embrace the energy will feel release; the individual will feel freer. Those who resist will create negative feelings. To know the difference is an important action at this time; trust the self during this process of the 5th Dimension shift.

Not only was I fascinated by these revelations from Theo, but I began looking at the world in an entirely new way. I saw people differently. I began to identify with their conflicts. For example, when Theo said "those who resist the 5th Dimension energy changes will create negative feelings," I wasn't exactly sure what they meant. It became clear later with more questioning and thinking. It took me a while, but I eventually understood that the "negative feelings" meant fear, frustration, and even anger, which would be created in those people who resisted the urge of their inner spirit to come forward and respond to the 5th Dimension energies.

The inner conflict became clear: How painful it would be for those whose spirits responded to the call of the 5th Dimension shift but whose old patterns were too strong. The old habits of egotism, self-interest, greed and materialism, violent confrontation and competition in these people would just be too hard to overcome. These people would stay isolated, islands unto themselves and their old patterns instead of seeing themselves as part of a universal theme, as part of a dramatic shift in Earth's history —the 5th Dimension.

The ideas that have channeled through me during these last years are so exciting, and so complex, that I want to let the Theo group speak for themselves. The questions and answers are from many sessions conducted over many years involving clients, re-seachers, and friends.

When is the end of the 4th Dimension and the beginning of the 5th Dimension?

It is happening now. In this time. The completion of the cycle is in the year 1988. The transition began seven years ago and there has been a great intensity during the two years of 1986 and 1987. But with the year of 1987 the full alignment of the transition is at hand. The 5th Dimension is upon your planet now.

You will notice it more in 1988 and 1989 and 1990. By the end of this century, as you call it, the year 2000, the full power and expression of the 5th Dimension will be in your experience. Many of you already notice that there is upheaval now within the beings. There is rapid movement of the spirit now . . . and it will accelerate.

How will the 5th Dimension energies affect human beings?

The people will become more sensitive to the psychic world and will be in contact, in one form or another, with our level of energies through meditation and prayer. With the coming of this enlightenment of mind—if it is accepted by people—there will be a unifying force of thought on the earth plane.

Thought is the most important thing in any existence, for through thought you build your spiritual being; through thought you build your world; through thought you influence the universe. Thought is the totality of soul, of mind, of personality. Understand that through thought you find your total being. Thought is your path to enlightenment.

Understand that time is also built through thought. And time is passing—quickly or slowly—in your mind. This is also the power of thought. Time is infinite, eternal, as is thought. We deal with time only through thought—

so understand you build your past, present, and future
with thought.

Humankind will notice a change in the attunement
to spirit. All are now feeling its power. Many will leave
the planet during this time; they will depart the physical
plane. For there is great intensity within those beings that
have chosen to be present during the 5th Dimension en-
ergy shift—for they have chosen to help the growth and
learning of this time. Those that wish to grow in different
ways will wish to go into other dimensions: those that
have chosen not to be a part of this 5th Dimension energy
will be leaving the planet.

It is now that each individual, each personality, will
need to take responsibility for his or her experience and
the thoughts that have created them. For it is within the
power of each personality, within each being of this
world, that the constructive changes will come about. It
will occur on an inner level first, within the "thoughts"
of people, and then be expressed outwardly. Understand
that the expression outside the self is but an expression of
change within.

Theo, those who have chosen not to continue [that is,
to die] during the 5th Dimension changes, can they
suddenly wake up one morning and say they would
like to stay? Can they change inside and thereby
change their destiny?

They can, yes. The will of man is strong and each, through
thought, creates his or her own destiny. Each individual
is the creator of his or her own experience and determines
his or her own path into the future.

This time of the 5th Dimension offers an opportunity
for people to alter their paths. This is a time for clearing
of the past, yes? Millennia of karma, as you call it, is
clearing away now within the lives of many people. There
is no longer any time for superficialities, for the trivialities
of the past. Such diversions can no longer serve. Relation-
ships between males and females will be changing dra-

matically. It is now a time for the creation of trust and unconditional, nonjudgmental love between individuals. It is a time of unification, of a sharing between independent individuals coming together to share their strength and knowing.

The 5th Dimension energy allows each person to attune him- or herself with the universal power, to open him- or herself to changes in their thought and to move on to a higher state of consciousness. In that way you can become the creator of your own experience and create your own future.

You must understand that each entity is the fullest expression of spirit; each is divinity. Each person has the full potential to create his or her experience using this inner power. Have you not seen those that have been downtrodden come forth to be leaders of their land? This power comes from the attitude and intention within the mind of man; each person in any circumstance has the power to create his or her own experience. Together, it becomes a mass energy that brings forth a higher consciousness of humankind; that is the purpose, the reason, for the coming of the 5th Dimension.

Understand that you are a reflection in physical form of the energy of the God-source of the Creator and that the power of <u>thought</u> is the creative force that acts in the world. Know that harsh judgments are but a reflection of the self and the nonacceptance of your own inner being.

Accepting the responsibility for your actions and what you create in your experience changes the world. You are the creator of it all. For as one man changes, becomes enlightened, all are affected. Do you understand?

Theo, does the 5th Dimension have anything to do with the Age of Aquarius, and does the 4th Dimension have anything to do with the Age of Pisces?

We find these terms . . . interesting. The 4th Dimension has been more a preparation, an alignment, for the Aquarian Age, to use your words. The 5th Dimension is a continuum, a further coming into the fullest power and energy of the planet and humankind, do you understand?

The 4th Dimension has been preparatory. It has been the teaching of balance, of openness. It has been a continuance of the Christ learning. The 4th Dimension has also been a time of the intellect, incorporating what you call the "Industrial Age." But now is time for the spirit to come forth, for the balance of both sides of the brain to work in harmonious action.

If we are moving from the 4th into the 5th Dimension, what were the other three Dimensions?

The changing of Dimensions is a powerful time, and all the Dimensional shifts have been important. There should be an acceptance of all the facets of change, not giving more attention to one period or another. But know that in this time of the 5th Dimension energy, there needs to be a change, a rebalancing of the body, mind, and spirit because the planet is in such a dangerous time.

The other Dimensionary experiences have also been shifts of vibrational frequencies, brought about by universal alignments of the planets, or the stars, if you would. During every shift there have been changes within the structures of this planet. Know that the 1st Dimension was the creation of the planet.

Know that the 1st Dimension brought in the plants and the animals, but no human beings during this period.

When did the human being arrive on the earth?

The 2nd Dimension brought forth the humans.

Did human beings come from the apes, as evolution states?

In similar form to an ape, yes. But not an ape. But know that the human spirit or soul, that energy, came from other dimensions in the universe.

So we did not evolve from an apelike creature as evolutionary theory says?

The human form evolved into its own form, do you understand? The spirit or energy that inhabited this planet needed to have a physical form that worked well upon this world, see?

What was the 3rd Dimension?

The 3rd Dimension brings in civilization, as you know it, as expressed in the history of humankind. But before that there was another civilization . . . the Atlantean.

Were the Atlanteans the beginning of human civilization?

They helped bring forth the 3rd Dimension upon the planet.

Then where did prehistoric man fit in?

That was in the 2nd Dimension, the ending of that energy.

And the dinosaurs and other prehistoric animals?

The great reptiles, plants, and animals began in the 1st Dimension, and ended in the 2nd.

What caused the massive destruction of the dinosaurs during that period?

There was a transition, a shift on the planet similar to what is happening now. There has been a shift at the end of every Dimensional change.

Then the 3rd Dimension was the beginning of the Atlantean and Lemurian civilizations?

*Yes, they existed at the same time in order to bring forth
a higher consciousness. Each of the Dimensional shifts
moved the consciousness of humankind; the 3rd and 4th
Dimensional shifts had a definite effect on humankind's
thinking and attunement to the spiritual. The 3rd Dimension was a part of when Christ came forth, as well as
Atlantis and Lemuria, do you understand?*

What form was Christ during the 3rd Dimension?

*The Christ energy has incarnated on Earth many times. In
the 3rd Dimension experience he was called Genlanier.
The Christ energy had experience in both Atlantis and
Lemuria. In Lemuria the energy was a being named Veon.*

How long was the 3rd Dimension, and why did it end?

*The 3rd Dimension was five thousand years, and it ended
because of the shift in the alignment of the universe. Also,
a greater learning on this planet was needed, so that the
beings would become more attuned, and move on
through the material to higher realms. Evolution of the
spirit, see?*

What was the significance of the 4th Dimension?

*The 4th Dimension began humankind's spiritual attune-
ment. What is surfacing now as humankind moves from
the 4th Dimension is a clearing of all the emotions that
have been repressed as the spirit began to manifest itself.
Remember, the 4th Dimension began in the Atlantean
and Lemurian period and shifted forward through the
Christian period. Now it is time for another realignment,
for a finer attunement to the spirit . . . and that is the
purpose of the 5th Dimension, to continue the evolution,
see? That is what the 5th Dimension is about . . . it is
light, enlightenment. But it has been the preference of
humankind to become more attached to the physical, to
the material world, rather than to the spirit. Know that*

*you are all born with perfection, and all choose their ex-
perience in order to achieve higher learning. Emotion is
the great teacher on the earth plane. At its lowest it is
involvement in the physical; at its highest it is unconditional love. Do you see?*

**Does all the fear, confusion, and anger arising now
come from experiences in the previous Dimensions?**

*Yes. It is surfacing from all areas, from all periods. Millen-
nia of karma, yes. It is being expressed now, rising to the
surface from within each personality, do you see?*

**Theo, what makes the interest in psychic phenomena
seem to wax and wane? Why does it come in waves or
cycles like this?**

*It has only seemed to be cyclic in expression on this
planet. But your world is now in a twenty-six-thousand-
year cycle just completed in the year 1986. This galactic
energy now present upon your planet has given the earth
an opportunity. New highways to the universe have been
opened for the people of Earth.*

*The completion of this twenty-six-thousand-year
cycle brings forth the 5th Dimensional energy, or what
you have called the "New Age." The 5th Dimensional
energy brings forth a vibrational condition that will open
humankind's consciousness; and the Christ energy will
again be present after a 2100-year cycle. This 5th Dimension energy will raise consciousness, but its effect will be
to create a greater attunement of the spirit, the opening of
the human heart, to the universe.*

*There is much upheaval now, is there not? Many feel
anger and frustration. What has been hidden away, repressed, will now come forward. It is now a time for the
emotions to be released. It is necessary for the refinement
of the energy, to bring the energy into balance both on
the planet and within each person. But the changes to
come forth are good, and you all have chosen to partici-*

pate in this time of high transformation. Those who experience the 5th Dimension raise in consciousness will learn to utilize the energy of the universe.

Understand that the earth plane is one of balance, of a positive and negative energy. Realize that each being is the creator of experience and energy upon your planet, and if each one takes full responsibility for the energy he or she creates, the earth will become balanced and you will have the peace you seek.

Peace does not come from politics or politicians; each personality changes and shifts the attitudes of the world. That is what this 5th Dimensional energy is about— heightened consciousness, if you will. This rebalancing, unification, is necessary to save the planet. Many fear that war and nuclear bombs will destroy the earth. But a nuclear holocaust is not to be feared; there is more to fear from the ecological changes on your planet. Fear the apathetic individual who will not open the self to the God-source or take responsibility for his actions. Thought is the creative power of your world.

Many of us feel a great sadness of spirit, Theo. What is the purpose of this black feeling?

It is much easier to think in the negative than the positive, so many feel the impact of sadness. They sense the imbalance. But it would be better not to allow the negative to control the thinking or feeling, for then you cannot be effective in controlling your own mind or creative energy, do you understand? There is a rebirth, if you would, of this planet. Many of you can achieve that balance, an attunement within yourselves. Do this first, and then the energy is radiated out to others, which assists in the growth of humankind. Each being counts in this 5th Dimension change.

The urgency, the anxiousness, that many of you feel is caused by the vibration that is creating the changes. The energy that is making an impact on, and activating the planet now, has been opened up from the universe. It has to do with what you call astrological alignments, with bringing the energy of the universe forth. Your conscious mind cannot perceive all that is happening in this period of time. But the human being, the human experience, the soul or the spirit, or the electromagnetic field that you are, is finely attuned to these vibrations. What is happening now is that you are sensing the shifts and changes and the urgency of the period.

But this does not mean you should have fear. Be clear within your own being. Being fully present with your self creates a peacefulness, a balance within, a nonatttachment, a nonjudgment in which you can continue to live your life and interact with others in an unconditional, loving way.

Theo, you said that you have come to assist humankind during this time of transition into the 5th Dimension. What is it about humans that makes us worthy of this help?

There is a oneness of all energy. Know that humans are also part of the energy of the angels. Human energy is part of the universe, is it not? Each soul is important to the wholeness of the universe. Each spirit and its relationship to the whole moves God's plan toward completion.

What is God's plan? Many people ask this, but no one can know the fullness of God's design. Even we in the 6th Dimension see but a small part, infinitesimal segments, individual cells, that make up the whole body of the divine.

We, the Theo group, are in service to humanity, one unto the other. Do you see? By being of service to you, we are assisted in our own evolution.

Theo, are you also angelic energy?

We are not limited to physical expression, no? Understand that we are of the angelic force, yes. We are messen-

*gers and teachers from the God-source of the Creator,
come to assist you along the way. We are not limited
physically; our vibrations are electric and finely tuned.*

*We are the same source of energy as humans, only
more finely attuned to the God-source. Remember that
when one is embodied and physical, it does not mean that
one is less angelic. Energy is constant. It is only the form
that changes. And coming into a finer attunement, into a
higher form of consciousness, is moving closer to this angelic energy. It is this angelic energy that is being focused
during this 5th Dimension period. This is to allow humans
to achieve that finer attunement and have their consciousness blossom forth. As each of you move into a
higher Dimensional vibration, your gifts will be used to
help the earth survive. This is the 5th Dimension energy,
understand?*

**Theo, if everything in the universe is evolving into a
higher vibrational energy—what is the purpose of
that?**

*It brings about a heightened enlightenment, a heightened
receptivity. Each individual then becomes what you
might term "perfect energy."*

**What is the purpose of achieving perfect energy? What
is perfect energy? God?**

*We can describe it in terms of "electric" energy, which
would be more acceptable to your scientists. It is more
difficult to give a complete explanation because your language and experience have no references, see? Your conscious mind does not have the vision, the symbols, for this
form of energy. It is a fine attunement to all knowing, to
all experience, to all expressions of life. It is also a knowledge within each of you that a oneness exists in all things.
It is a condition that is unlimited, and the words we give
you here limit your perceptions. Do you understand?*

What will come of this upheaval during the 5th Dimension? What will happen on Earth over the next century?

The world as you know it will no longer be. There will be a rejuvenation, a rebirth, of the physical planet. And the consciousness of humankind will be—and is now being —raised. The energy systems for the human being will be much more refined. Political forms will change; economic systems will change—the old forms will no longer be. But this will happen more quickly, in the more immediate time frame, as you would call it, the next five years.

What will happen to the physical planet?

There will be changes of landmasses. There will be more active volcanoes, earthquakes. This has already begun. The ring of fire that began six years ago has been speeded up. There is a shifting of the axis of the planet now. The plates under the surface of the earth are moving. There are masses of land surfacing now where the civilizations of Atlantis and Lemuria existed. You will see these changes soon.

Where are Atlantis and Lemuria emerging?

Off the southeast coast of the North American continent, close to the islands of Bahama. The Lemuria landmass rises off the coastal regions of Japan. There will be changes in the atmosphere. And the areas of land that have been dry will become wet; and those that have been wet will become dry. This is occurring because the land has been abused and misused. This is a cleansing, a rebirth, a rejuvenation, of the planet.

Theo, you've spoken of famine, earth changes, and that a nuclear holocaust is not to be feared. What, then, are the greatest dangers the modern world faces?

It is the ecological destruction of the planet. To prevent this, humankind must take responsibility for both thought and action that have harmed the planet. You must honor the gift of this world, respect its balance—as you would honor the physical structure of its vehicle, as you honor your own body, do you understand? A shift of consciousness is needed, which is why the 5th Dimension is here.

So the ecological destruction will continue until this shift of humankind's consciousness occurs? But what if the change of consciousness moves so slowly that the ecological destruction begins to harm all life on the planet?

It is already that great. The imbalance exists now, and life is in danger. The destruction of the ozone above your planet is one such imbalance. But there is also rapid movement and change in the consciousness of humankind. You will bear witness to this change. Yet there is no longer time for the trivial, or the superficialities of the past. Time is short for the planet. It is now a time of depth, of openness and understanding—truth on all levels of experience.

Understand that when one takes responsibility for what one has created in the life experience, then one takes responsibility for the planet itself, see?

Will we see these changes immediately or further down the path of our evolution?

One does not heal the wound with a bandage. The healing comes from the depths, does it not? What you would call, from the inside to the outside. That is how the consciousness changes. The 5th Dimension frequency shift is allowing the electromagnetic body to change on its cellular level, which brings forth chaos from within, and then from the chaos comes understanding, yes?

Will these earth changes have a major or destructive impact on agriculture in our country?

There is much change in everything at this time. You will see weather patterns changing. There will be shifts in climate. Places with much moisture will become drier, and those that have been dry will become moist. This is part of the process of the 5th Dimension shift.

Yes, it is important to be aware of foodstuffs. There will be problems of sufficiency in many places. There are many changes coming, but do not fear, for this is part of honoring the earth, of allowing the lands that have been exhausted and abused to rejuvenate. Lands that have not been used for growing things for many thousands of years will be utilized for food.

It is necessary for this planet to rejuvenate itself, for there has been much destruction of the land. You should see this as a positive expression rather than be upset about it.

Theo, you speak of having sufficient foods. Do you suggest that we put foods away? And if so, what diet do you suggest that we follow in order to raise our bodies into a higher state?

To put foods away? Yes, you should use freezing and canning to preserve foods. But one should have fun with this as well, enjoy the experience of handling food. Preparing the food with joy also enhances the food when it is eaten, enhances the cells, yes? But you are to rotate your foodstocks—that is, use them in the order in which they were prepared. They are not to be kept for great periods of time.

Diet? Yes, fresh fruits and vegetables. Food from the sea is extremely important for balance—kelp, fish, and fowl, for instance. Grains are extremely important as well. But everything in moderation, yes?

Self-sufficiency in growing your own food is impor-

tant. *Eating foods that are of the area where you live is also valuable.*

Theo, I would like to know what will the government of the United States be like over the next four or five years while the 5th Dimension energy shift is being felt?

Political factors are shifting. The governments of the world are changing as well. The political factors can no longer rule the world in the old ways, for what has happened is a great manipulation of resources and peoples. There has not been a proper direction toward unity and brotherhood. It is important for this planet that the scientific and artistic worlds speak out more directly; they will be instrumental in stopping the destruction and saving the world. There will be a unification of your planet through the people. The arts and sciences will have more influence and control than politics. This must be, for the planet is now in self-destruction. The planet itself cannot withstand the destruction any longer. Humankind will have to unify its thinking to save the planet and not be so limited by boundaries, see? It will happen worldwide, not just in the United States. The divisions, the limitations, can no longer work if the planet is to be saved. You will bear witness to these forces in the immediate future. There will be a meeting of minds, of individuals, not only politicians, for the world is becoming dissatisfied with politics and governments. You will see this in your lifetime.

But how can this happen globally when the world is so divided by different attitudes, political systems, languages, and religions?

There is a knowledge of this sharing from the past. The Christ energy was here 2000 years ago and gave the knowledge. Today is a rebirth of that spirit.
    The survival instinct of the human being is also now coming forth. Survival recognizes the necessity of coming

together, of communicating, and of the exchange of infor-
mation. That begins in the scientific and artistic worlds.
Individuals feeling these things will begin to speak out,
will come forward. It has already begun to happen. In
your country you see individuals speaking out. But the
same is happening in smaller countries of Europe, in
countries not dominated and controlled by their gov-
ernments. The speaking out begins because there is
this sense, this upheaval in the heart of humankind, that
seeks unification of the earth and return to the God-
source.

The Christ spirit has slowly evolved on the planet and,
cyclically, is now again coming forth fully with the 5th
Dimension consciousness. The earlier Dimensions were
preparation to bring forth this consciousness more fully
now, do you see?

Like-minded entities will come together and will be
placed in positions of authority. The political systems are
shifting rapidly throughout the world. Many of you who
are knowing, sense that the leadership needs restructuring
and that these changes are coming soon. You are aware
that the world at this time is self-destructing on many
levels. Many of you know it is time for each being to
create a new and positive expression in the world, not to
put it on the shoulders of a few government officials.
Many understand that it is necessary for all beings to re-
member that they are body, mind, and spirit, that they
are embodied on the planet Earth in one mind.

Many of you already speak of the second coming of
the Christ spirit, do you not? It is here. It is now. The 5th
Dimension opens the way. This knowledge is in your ex-
perience, for each one of you is of that Christ energy. The
confusion that is felt now in the physical body is but a
catalyst for moving forward, an affirmation for accepting
that energy within you. Out of the chaos comes light,
yes?

You speak of the Christ energy and the second coming.
What is the Christ energy?

The Christ energy, or vibration, is upon the planet now. Many speak of the Christ as a being, but the coming of the Christ energy is manifesting itself in each and every spirit. It is unconditional love and is the vibration that we speak about happening now. It is the raising and elevation of consciousness. Some may need the manifestation of a figure, a physical form that they can recognize, but it is within each being—and is already at hand. The Christ energy is part of this cycle of the 5th Dimension. The energy that gives you life, the expression of your awareness, the centeredness, the unconditional love that radiates—that is the Christ, or the coming, that many speak about.

Now, in the time of the 5th Dimension experience, you will begin to utilize your own energies. Many of you will learn from this experience and achieve higher levels of consciousness. There are many beings who have chosen to be present now to assist this evolution.

But there will be those who resist, who do not take full responsibility for their experience and will find the transition period painful. For what you resist continues, it persists, does it not? When you accept your own power, accept responsibility and realize that you have created your own experience, the transition into 5th Dimension consciousness is not difficult. There is an excitement in the shift, in the changing of Dimensions. The evolution of consciousness, of thought, of enlightenment, is a powerful experience. Have fun with it.

2

The Coming of Theo

IT MAY SEEM STRANGE, BUT IT took my nearly dying to wake me up and force me to redirect my life. I still clearly remember the wintery Colorado day in 1969 when I stomped out of the house, angry at my husband. Like a spiteful child I began shoveling the heavy, wet snow off the walks and driveway, which would have been all right—except that I was eight months pregnant. Panting and cursing like a mad-woman, I sweated and whipped the snow in every direction. I was a fat, angry one-woman snow machine blasting the walks clean.

In my fury I felt I had the strength of ten men, but the snow must have been at least seven inches deep. I pushed the shovel under the heavy snow . . . lift, turn, throw . . . I can do it. The nerve of him . . . lift, turn, throw. . . . Boy, will he be sorry if this makes me have the baby early. Then he'll be sorry.

These were the childish thoughts running through my mind.

Spiteful, willful, and silly. Not surprisingly, I went into labor that night and my husband, Ed, took me to the hospital at 11:00 P.M. The labor stopped, but the doctor decided to keep me overnight for observation. I suppose he wasn't quite sure what I would do next after he heard about the snow-shoveling episode.

The next morning I showered and was getting ready to go home when it hit me: I started coughing up large globs of bright red blood. For some godforsaken reason I decided not to mention it to anyone. The doctor came in for a final examination and decided against letting me leave because I was still dilating. That decision may have saved my life.

At 4:30 that afternoon, with light delicate flakes of snow drifting past my hospital window, I went into heavy labor. My daughter, Cathy, was born a half hour later, but she was so premature that she was taken to the preemie ward at the University of Colorado Medical Center later that night.

After the birth and my secret coughing up of blood, I felt surprisingly well. In fact, I felt wonderful and wanted to go home as soon as possible. But the next morning I went into the bathroom and suddenly doubled over with an explosion of coughing. Blood again gushed out, and as the coughing continued I could barely breathe. I truly thought I was going to die a violent and bloody death right there.

I remember a flurry of white coats and stethoscopes . . . snatches of scattered words and images.

"Are you all right?"

"More oxygen!"

"Yes, ICU, stat!"

"Are you sure you're all right?"

Pokes with fingers and hands, fleeting faces and white coats, a spinning chaotic world, and I seemed to have no part of it even though I was somehow the focus of all the activity.

Thoughts of death ran through my mind, and I silently prayed.

More snatches of disjointed words and ideas. "Sheila, we're taking you to the Intensive Care Unit. You've thrown blood clots from your lungs, and we need to keep a closer eye on you."

"Can you hear me, Sheila?"

I nodded my head weakly—at least I think I did. Everything

was going so fast, so rushed. I knew that something terrible had happened because I was coughing up bright red blood again. It was so violent, it hurt my chest.

Ed was holding my hand, I remember, as we spun off down the hall on a gurney. He looked very pale and drawn. He was talking to me, trying to calm me. "Listen, honey, everything's going to be all right. While you were in the lung scan more blood clots released and went into your lungs. I won't lie to you; it's serious, but don't be scared. Everything'll be all right."

I remember rushing through some large doors with a sign in large letters—ICU. It seemed dark . . . and deathly quiet.

"Sheila," one of the nurses said as they moved the gurney closer to the bed, "are you all right?"

I nodded my head again.

"If you can help us, slowly slide yourself over . . . be careful of the tubes. That's it. Okay, there you go . . . good."

Then everything slowed down. The room was small, about the size of a bathroom in a normal house. The walls were regular till halfway up and then glass to the ceiling. Suddenly the nurse closed the drapes around the bed. The only vision to the outer world was the open door. I could see the corner of the nurses' station and another little cubicle room similar to the one I was in across the hall. The drapes in the little room were open and I could see an elderly man stretched out unmoving in the bed.

The nurses' station looked like the control panel of a spaceship with monitors and flashing lights. I learned later that most people in ICU are heavily sedated. I could not be sedated because other medications would alter the anticoagulant medication I was given, so I was completely conscious.

Time drifted in that yellow, small, and airless room, until bells suddenly started going off. Two nurses ran into the little cubicle room across the hall. The old man was having problems. One of the nurses checked the monitor above his bed. I could see the nurses' lips moving and hear the commotion in the hall. People were flooding into the little room, some pushing a square machine. The old man was lying flat, his pale, bony rib cage showing as they tore open his pajama top. I could hear the voice of the doctor yelling, "Hurry, bring in the defibrillator."

I watched breathlessly, half knowing it was hopeless, as the doctor placed the paddles on the poor pale chest, turned his head, and nodded to the other doctor running the machine. Everyone else stepped back as the current snapped through the paddles and the frail body leaped several inches off the bed. They did it again and again . . . at least five times. But each time the old man's limp body fell back onto the bed like a corpse. Nothing happened. The old man didn't move. The doctors and nurses looked at one another, and the paddles were placed back on the machine. All but two nurses, who closed the old man's pajama top and pulled the sheet up, filed out of the room. It was deathly quiet. No one said a word.

In a matter of minutes everything was normal again. The old man was removed from the cubicle, and the bed was remade. The room looked as if it had never been occupied.

I don't mind admitting I was terrified. The death of the old man shook me. One of the nurses came into the room to adjust the heparin drip through the intravenous tube stuck in the back of my hand. As she started to leave she straightened my pillow and whispered, "Do try to close your eyes. You need sleep."

I couldn't understand why they kept telling me to sleep when I dared not close my eyes. I was sure that if I fell asleep, I would never wake up again. The pain in my chest was excruciating, shooting through me every time I breathed. I didn't have the strength or will to lift my head from the pillow. Again, time drifted in the small room, and I seemed to move listlessly with it. My only connection to my body was the painful labor of breathing.

In those lonely hours I began praying. I knew I was dying, and I prayed, "Please, God, let me live, let me stay and raise my children. Give me a job, please, God, I'll do anything. Please." I repeated the simple prayer. When nurses came into the room to check the medication and monitor the machines attached to my exhausted body, I continued my silent prayer. I felt as if I were hanging on to life with every fiber of my body, but it all amounted to nothing more than a thin thread that could snap at any time.

I don't know how long I prayed but it seemed forever, when suddenly the room exploded in a starlike burst of light—similar to abruptly turning your head and staring directly into the sun. I blinked back tears and squinted at the incredible brightness that hung above the end of my bed. I blinked several times, trying to clear my vision. The whole room had become miraculously bright, but I could make out a tall figure standing at the end of the bed. I was mesmerized by the figure. It was Christ, but unlike any picture or image of Him that I had ever seen. Everything had become crystal-clear, and I could see details as if through a magnifying glass. The robe He wore was of a heavy, coarse natural fabric.

The clarity of my vision surprised me, for I could see incredible details. His eyes were hazel and His hair darker than I had imagined. I could not take my eyes off Him.

Moments seemed to pass, and He didn't say anything. Then He slowly raised His hands and, crossing His arms, tucked them into the large sleeves of His robe. This simple movement seemed to take forever; time seemed to stop, and I was suspended in this miracle of light. His hazel eyes were staring at me with great love and compassion. He smiled, a sweet, gentle smile. And the thought came to me, His voice resonating in my mind: Remember, my child, you are loved. Ask and you will receive.

I didn't hear the words out loud. It was an inner hearing; I knew that they were not my thoughts but coming directly from Christ. It was a distinctly male voice, gentle and warm.

I felt tears burning down my cheeks, tears of joy. I had never felt so full of love, never felt so secure, so safe and confident, in my life. My body suddenly relaxed completely. I hadn't realized how hard I had been hanging on, and the abrupt release of tension made me feel as if I were melting into the bed. Christ continued to smile at me, sending waves of understanding and acceptance to me. It seemed that the crown of my head opened up and warm honey had been poured in. The warm sweetness ran slowly down through my body, into every cell, filling me with a wonderful peace. Because my lungs were full of fluid and blood it had hurt me to breathe, but suddenly I could again take a deep breath without pain.

Then I knew I could close my eyes, and I wouldn't die. My prayer had been answered. I didn't know why, or how, but I knew I would live and had been given a job to do.

Then He was gone, the light vanished, and the room returned to normal. I was in shock; an awsome power had touched me, and I suddenly felt whole. I could sleep now. . . . Everything would be all right.

• • •

I remained in the ICU for one week. The doctors were amazed at how fast I recovered. They commented on it daily; young interns would come in and stare at me quizzically. I stared back, smiling. I knew I had been healed by my visitor.

I grew stronger by the moment, and the doctors filled me in on my problem. The trauma of the birth had caused my entire abdominal area to become one mass of blood clots. As these clots broke up they filled my lungs and caused pulmonary embolism. I was told later that they used my lung scans and X rays in training new radiologists at St. Luke's Hospital. The students were asked whether the patient whose X rays they were examining had lived or died, and the answers given were always yes, the patient died. I'm sure that they were right: I would have died except for the miraculous healing I had been given.

I was in the hospital for another week and then released. I didn't tell anyone about my near-death experience and my bright visitor for the simple reason that I couldn't talk about it. Every time I even thought about it I became so emotional I couldn't speak. In fact, it's been only in the last two years that I've been able to talk objectively about it. It was so intense that I would dissolve in tears every time I tried to describe it.

But the effect of the experience was immediate. As soon as I got home I realized how changed I was. I had no fear—no anxiety about the future, no fear of death or pain. My values went through a radical alteration: I had always believed in traditional American values of hard work, thrift, and charity, but I now felt—with a deep conviction—that it wasn't important whether I lived in a one-room shack or a mansion; the most important thing in life was love, the love of life. Friends, family, animals, even the leaves on the trees and grass under my feet, became objects of love for me, partners in living. When I walked in the sun, I felt solar-powered. Colors were brighter, almost iridescent with the vitality of life. Sprouts on the bare winter trees sparkled as spring approached. I felt awe for all the things that I had once taken for granted. I loved life with an intensity that shocked me. I never realized I could feel so deeply about all the small things surrounding me. More than a miraculous healing had taken place in that hospital room—I was a completely different person.

My vision of religion, and of God, became that bright light I had seen. Before that day I had thought of religion as what I did on Sunday when I went to church with everyone else. But now God had become for me that brilliant light of warmth and compassion I'd felt healing me; God was not a physical being but a light encompassing everything, radiating an energy imbuing each thing it touched with a divine essence, a spark having a universal power, a force of life that ran the cosmos.

At its core the feeling I now had about God was not unlike the sense I had about myself. At first I was confused and began asking questions like "Why me?" But I eventually came to realize that when I acknowledged myself completely and accepted myself as a whole being, I became a balance of forces, a unity of the many aspects of myself that began to come together after that day. When I am in that place of centeredness, I am filled with a feeling of being finely attuned to that universal energy, that bright power Christ showed me. To put it simply, I came to see this unifying force as a powerful source of creation, of individual choice, of freedom. But these feelings of wholeness didn't come immediately. Soon after I returned from the hospital and got back into the routines of normal life, I fell into old habits. I hadn't yet learned some important lessons. That had to wait for the coming of Theo.

Transformation! That seemed to summarize much of what happened after I left the hospital—moving from one condition to another, from one state of "being" to another as I opened myself to the universal powers I had experienced in the hospital. But it wasn't an easy transition; I went struggling every step of the way. But I went!

What I call the first opening (after the Christ vision) came while I was having coffee with a friend. My grandmother's name had been Catherine Majors, and when my friend and I started fooling with the automatic writing, I asked, "Catherine Majors, please talk to me."

I held the pen as lightly as I could without dropping it so I knew I wouldn't create any pressure. The pen started moving in a circular motion, around and around in circles. Then it began to create letters, and then recognizable words.

"I'm here, can you feel me?" The first words scribbled loosely across the page. That I could read a message—which I was sure I hadn't written—scared me silly. I jumped off the chair and put the pen down. My teeth were literally chattering. My knees felt like Jell-O, and I was afraid I would faint. I calmed myself down, took some deep breaths, and then realized that this was exciting. Fun. I wanted to do it again.

I was still scared, and doubted what was happening, but I tried to relax and open myself to allowing a message to come through my hand. I mentally asked her to give me a sign, a confirmation that it was really she. The message scratched out: "Where are all my white flowers?"

That didn't mean a thing to me, but it was all I could get, so we ended the session.

When I got home, I called my mother and told her about the automatic writing. I thought it would amuse her, but when I mentioned the white flowers, she pulled me up short.

"Well, of course," she said matter-of-factly, "those were the Easter lilies that were in her rose garden. Every year we children would give her an Easter lily at Eastertime. She would plant the bulbs in her garden. It was her favorite garden."

While the confirmation was nice, I really didn't need any particular reason to continue experimenting with the psychic: I became fascinated; I began to "play" with it every chance I got.

Another confirmation came soon after I began. My friend Karen, who had started me on the automatic writing, called and invited my husband and me over for dinner. We had never met her husband, John, but both men were in the construction business and very down-to-earth types. It seemed like a good idea.

After supper we began talking about what had happened to me with the automatic writing, and both men were, to say the least, skeptical. But I got out a pencil and paper, and, in the spirit of a game, John asked about his father, who had died years before.

After a few moments a message began coming through. "It was an accident; it was an accident" kept returning. Then the name of a town in France, a date during World War II, and the word "bomb" was scratched out. Ed and I had no idea what all this meant, but John had gone white. He told us that his father had been killed in France during the war by a bomb. The name of the town and the date given were correct.

After that evening nothing could stop me. I became almost obsessed with the psychic, and Ed began to pull away with comments like "Don't do it anymore. . . . You can't talk to spirits. . . . That's crazy." On and on the tension grew between us. What was frightening to me was that I was losing control. I began to get material about something called "Watergate." This was two years before the scandal broke in Washington. And then psychokinetic energies began manifesting. When I sat down, chairs would move. I would wake up in the middle of the night, the bed shaking beneath me. Ed slept through it all, but I became concerned about this peculiar energy that was constantly flowing through me. I couldn't control it. I couldn't stop it even if I wanted to. On the one hand I was appalled, scared out of my mind with the power I was sensing; on the other hand I was fascinated—it seemed doorways into the universe were being opened up to me. I felt special, different, even unique and chosen. It was an ego trip I eventually had to conquer, a double-edged sword.

As the automatic writing became easier I found that I began to hear voices speaking the words as they were being written down. Then, within only a few days after the original incident with my grandmother, I didn't need to write anything—I was simply hearing the voices.

I was clearly playing with powers beyond my ability to control, but I couldn't stop. The voices began to tell me "Call Jennie; call Jennie." It was then that I met a woman who introduced me to a group that held regular meetings on the psychic. Jennie was part of this group. It was the first time I began to feel not so alone.

I continued to work with the group for a while and to experiment by myself with my rapidly expanding psychic powers. When the break with Ed came, it was an accumulation of many pressures that had built up over the years, but my involvement with the psychic played a major role. At the end his comment was "Well, something's wrong with you. . . . I think you're acting crazy with all this psychic mumbo jumbo. . . ."

After my divorce my sense of isolation became even sharper. Even with those few people who were sympathetic, like my parapsychology group friends, my mother, and a few others, none could actually empathize with the intensity of the changes—both emotionally and physically—that I was going through.

During the first few weeks of my obsession with this "other" world, I lost twelve pounds in three days. I didn't even realize it myself until someone pointed out that my arms looked like toothpicks. The energy was consuming me. It was a power I didn't know how to use. I was feeling a strong vibration running through my body, as if all my cells were buzzing.

I began reading everything on the subject I could get my hands on—the history of psychic phenomena, books on parapsychology and the scientific experimentation going on. In 1973 a group of us formed a parapsychology organization called Psi Group to bring in speakers to our area. We also conducted little experiments on Kirlian photography, seeing auras, clairvoyance, and all the other phenomena I had read about and experienced.

My own channeling, which I date from the third day after my grandmother came through, continued without stop. The voices never identified themselves by name, and their personalities now seem somewhat pale to me.

Then in 1974 a new voice came through, a stronger but quiet and kind voice. It was Orlos. For two years Orlos channeled through me and would often mention that he was simply preparing me for "higher teachers." In February 1976, the Theo group first introduced themselves.

This is the beginning, is it not? This is a group, not to be thought of as one personality, not to think of us as one.

After the first session I looked up Theo in the dictionary because I didn't think it was a real word. It said: "Theo, the beginning." Another meaning was connected to God or divine force.

We are teachers, messengers from the God-source of the Creator. We come to assist you along the way. We are not limited to physical expression; our vibrations are electric and finely tuned. They can be manifested in visual form if necessary, but it's not necessary, do you understand? We exist in a 6th Dimension when communicating with your world.

We have been assisting this planet before the Christ was present; we have assisted the planet at the time when the pyramids were built, at the time of the Atlantean civilization. We have assisted during the Crusades and what you call your World Wars. And we have returned to assist now during this change. We are here again in this cycle. Today is a rebirth and the growth of a new understanding of spirit. It is the beginning of the 5th Dimension.

As I said earlier, the Theo trance was overwhelming; the energy and power seemed like a miniatomic bomb to me. For the first time that painful and acute sense of isolation left me, and I felt I had found the work that had been promised years before in that tiny hospital room.

By this time I had worked with some scientists. I had met Dr. Jules Eisenbud, a Colorado psychiatrist who had done much work in parapsychology. He had reassured me during those early years that I wasn't crazy. I worked with Dr. Evan Harris Walker and various other scientists in a further effort to find out what was going on. I had even created a two-day symposium and conference on parapsychology in Glenwood Springs, near Aspen, Colorado, in order to bring together experts in the field of parapsychology. And even though these scientists gave me encouragement, nothing clarified what was happening within my mind and body more than the information I began getting from Theo.

At first when I went into trance I was completely unconscious. I didn't remember a thing and had to read the transcripts of the tapes afterward to know what had been said. But as I channeled more subtle changes kept happening. I felt the electric energy moving in my body; I felt my emotions "cooling out," felt myself relaxing even when faced with dramatic or stressful life changes. But when Orlos came through, and then Theo, the trance changed even more. Now I can sometimes hear what is being said, almost as if I am eavesdropping. I'm not paying attention to the dialogue, or focusing on listening; it's just something that happens nearby. It isn't constant, however. Occasionally I have this awareness, but often I am still completely unconscious of what's going on.

There have been times when I am aware of incredibly powerful energy flows within my body during trances. I can see the color of the energy as it flows. I can see it spark as it comes off the palms of my hands. It is as if a part of me is above the physical self, still a part of the whole, but I am a separate consciousness observing another part of myself. Once I remember seeing a brilliant blue light coming off the ends of my fingers and orange lights covering the palms of my hands. My hands became hot, and I watched the energy flowing all through my body in different colors. It was indescribably beautiful—running over my skin, coming off my feet, off my toes, and the ends of my fingers. Most of the colors were green and blue, with some purple and orange cascading over my hands.

Basically what happens when Theo channels now is that I go into a meditation and the group begins to speak through me clairaudiently, a kind of inner-mind hearing. If I want to ask specific questions, or have questions from clients, my secretary usually asks them. When I first come out of a channeling session now it takes me a little time to get grounded. Sometimes I feel very energized and other times depleted, exhausted because I've absorbed the emotional turmoil of the people around me. I am still very vulnerable when I relax and go into trance.

Out of my near-death experience, and the long search that followed, I finally understood that an enormous power, a universal power, was available to anyone at any time. I had to go through a cauldron of confusion and learning; I had to wait until the vibratory level of my body had been altered so I could receive the guidance necessary from Orlos and Theo. But I also now understand that it is simpler than I thought. There are ways to open yourself to these powers without being burned out.

Many people say "Okay, so you open yourself to this great power, and this other psychic stuff comes in to you. So you're attuned." But it's not that at all. If that were the whole story, then everything would be over, your life would become passive. And I don't think life is passive; it's an active partnership with your own power source. This is the lesson my years of work have taught me. You have the power to make decisions, to choose which way to go, to choose what you really prefer, not what you've been taught to prefer—yes, you have the "power to prefer"; and that makes you a partner in the power of living, the cause rather than the effect.

In other words, I am not just a channel. No one is *just* a channel; the power manifests through you from one dimension and you influence it; you are the cause that changes its direction, flow, and impact.

One of the most important lessons Theo has taught me is that thought has the power to change reality. Your own thoughts can do so much that you would be shocked if you knew the full extent of it. In one way, changing your thought simply changes your perception of yourself by creating positive images; in another, it alters your internal energy patterns, which in turn alters your deeper psychological self. The change is real, not just a habit or the reinforcing of an illusion you've created. I know because the coming of Theo after eighteen years of work has confirmed it in my own life.

But to do all these things, to become your own channel to the universal powers within, as Theo calls them, you have to begin to accept—and acknowledge—powers greater than your normal everyday consciousness. This opens you to a whole new dimension of personal power—which describes better than anything else what is happening with the energy shifts of the 5th Dimension.

The obvious question, and the problem I struggled with for years before the coming of Theo, was—Okay, how do you do it? How do you attune yourself to this greater power source within? It obviously entailed more than just using some nicely phrased affirmations every day.

One of the greatest obstacles I had to surpass was to stop thinking of myself in limited terms. This is another of the great lessons Theo taught me. We all continually think of ourselves as limited by one thing or another. We are always creating barriers. If you can first accept that you have this power, that you can be the creator of your own reality, as Theo says, then the first stage is passed. Accept this truth if only for a moment, for an hour, for a day, and build on it. This means gaining acceptance of ourselves within, acknowledging that we can be the cause of the effect, that we can *cause* our own next moment to happen the way we want it to happen.

The next major obstacle I had before the coming of Theo was that I tended to think in spectacular terms. Probably most of us would want to start right off by altering physical reality a week after we begin to feel in tune with this greater power within. We want to feel powerful quickly so we can change things that displease us. Change my boyfriend's bad habits; change my boss's attitude toward me; change the way the old car runs; change the bottom line of the mortgage to read "paid." It can sometimes become just as silly as that.

In essence, I have worked with this all my life, but I've worked directly with it for almost twenty years, and I've learned it is a building process. We should learn to accept small daily manifestations first and not succumb to the hawkers in our society who sell instant gratification.

To think you can have spectacular results is missing the point: This path is a way of life, a spiritual acceptance of universal powers, not a cheap, instant "life fix-it" program. This path requires a commitment to a new way of life.

And besides, to move too quickly sometimes damages growth rather than helps it. This is another of the lessons Theo has taught me.

I had some friends who lived in the city and eventually bought a country home. They had seven acres of beautiful land, and they let their dog free to run around. But the dog went immediately crazy; he was whining and howling all day and night. It was too much, too quickly experienced. What they finally did was put the dog on a long chain attached to a large doghouse. The dog immediately calmed down, and in three days its appetite returned and it became its old, lovable, scruffy self. It needed the structure so it could become used to the new larger environment without becoming disoriented by the seemingly limitless freedom. We need to grow step-by-step so that we are comfortable with the changes. But once we get comfortable ("accepting" in Theo's terms), the boundaries can be taken away and we can enjoy our greater freedom. We need to take it in small doses so we can incorporate change comfortably both psychologically and physically.

If boundaries are suddenly eliminated, you may feel lost; you may feel that you no longer have any control over your life. This is what happened to me during the early phase of my channeling. Theo says that opening yourself to the universe is a process, and it is necessary to trust that process and let it evolve naturally. Enjoy whatever exists in the moment. Every step is full of joy if you just trust your inner awareness.

In other words, boundaries are guides that help us survive, but they are flexible not immutable. The ultimate condition is one of no boundaries, of limitlessness; that is our natural state. It is the state of our spirit: and is the purpose of the coming of Theo— to guide us through the dramatic changes coming during the 5th Dimension.

3

5th Dimension Transitions: Growing into the New Age

I AM NO STRANGER TO NEW AGE philosophies, but even I have become unsettled when I watch the selling of psychic wares in our modern spiritual supermarkets. Since the late 1960s I have been observing and participating in—for want of a better term—the counterculture questing movement. I've attended the "feel good" seminars, the "do-your-own-thing-at-any-cost" lectures, and wondered whether I was actually watching the dawning of a new age or a frightened culture's latest consumer fad. Or a bit of both. . . .

So even during those early days of confusion and self-seeking, I had my doubts—especially about the commercialization of what seemed to me a spiritual quest. In fact, the first entity to channel through me, Orlos, had to advise me directly to begin charging a "fee" for my time.

You must value what you do or others will not value the
information given here.

The commercialism of the psychic-supermarket approach has
always disturbed me. However, when I began devoting *all* of my
time to this work, I realized a certain degree of professionalism
was necessary. I found I couldn't spend all of my time doing
channeling and still pay my bills and survive. Hard choices followed, and I was thankful for the help of my guides during this
difficult period. In effect, I was learning to create a balance in my
life between the necessary demands of the physical world and the
internal quest for understanding.

Later, the necessity of balancing the inner and outer worlds
came to me more fully as Theo repeatedly made the same point.

We are assisting you in bringing forth the energy and
balancing within the physical structure. We are assisting
you with information. We are assisting you with oppor-
tunities for growth.

That is outer work, and now is inner work. It is to
honor the inner, allow that work, allow the vibrational
increase; for as this is achieved the productivity will be
enhanced in the outer world.

Yet it was clear to me the impulse underlying this quest, this
hunger for purpose in one's life, was real and necessary. To seek
meaning for one's existence in a culture where the social and
religious institutions did not answer basic spiritual longings
seemed the sanest thing I could do. And I was certainly not alone
during these past twenty years in seeking some sense in a society
where everything seemed disconnected and alienated from its natural origins. Nor is such questing unique to our disjointed, heart-
sick civilization; all societies, I have learned, try in one way or
another to provide religious organizations to satisfy these spiritual
longings. Yet cultural institutions have failed to answer, or even
ask, the significant questions for an individual's spiritual life. People continually question Theo about their spiritual growth, about
the evolution of their soul. One questioner recently asked:

I wonder why, Theo, it takes most of us a lifetime to learn how to be in tune with ourselves spiritually. Why can't we just be born with this knowledge, and why do we need you (or anyone else) to show us the way—and why do we have to go through such a struggle?

You are born with it: It is society that has told you you do not know the answer. The child within is well aware of these things. . . . It is the shift of attitude, the shift of thinking within societies, within civilization as you know it, that is necessary. This shift opens the mind, opens the heart, to the fullest expression. (It is simple, but society teaches the child it is difficult.) The child can breathe immediately when it is born. Yes, breathing is a necessity. But even in that natural form of breathing, the child grows up not understanding how to breathe properly.

Some social commentators I have read recently see the phenomenal renewed interest in the psychic and the growing fascination with things of the spirit as a way of questioning traditional values and beliefs that no longer work. Theo, on the other hand, talks about the necessity of changing "thought patterns" and places the responsibility on individuals—which in turn will change society into the 5th Dimensional world of the future.

It is intention and attitude that are important, for thought is the creative force, is it not? Know that all thought is but energy that is held within the personalities; know that each being is a recipient or receptor of that energy. Know that much of change comes from thought, which is the creative force, and the attitudes and intention of the beings on the planet. The beings on the planet have great influence as well. Do you see?

One of the most important changes in the 5th Dimensional world will be the development of psychic abilities. In the 5th Dimension everyone will be more psychic; the psychic will flourish in an atmosphere that is not as negative toward the spiritual world as today's is.

SOCIETY AND THE PSYCHIC

It seems that people living in this age suffer a split between wanting to accept what science tells us and an agonizing spiritual need. Millions of people are fascinated by the occult and mysterious, by the psychic and the new religions. These are not just personal impressions of my own, for research over the last decade has consistently shown that a surprising number of people have actually reported a wide range of psychic experiences (ESP, contact with the dead, mystical experiences, etc.). When millions of people believe in phenomena that their society rejects, there is obviously a lot going on under the surface that has escaped the sociologists and cultural commentators.

I am not overly impressed with statistics, but recent national surveys of people's attitudes toward the psychic are really overwhelming. In one poll, 67 percent of those surveyed say that they've experienced some form of ESP. The Gallup organization reports that 23 percent of Americans believe in reincarnation. And while millions say they've had mystical experiences, around 90 million report contact with the dead.

These numbers are surprising not only because of their size, but because they've occurred in a society that dismisses such experiences as delusionary, as the wishful thinking of crackpots and kooks, or the self-serving, simplistic theology of people yearning to escape their problems.

But this is not so, according to Andrew Greeley, the priest-novelist-sociologist who conducted the surveys with his colleagues at the University of Chicago. These psychic experiences are not signs of psychiatric disturbances, Greeley reported, but seem to have had a positive and lasting impact on the people who experienced them. Further, the experiences seemed to have improved the overall psychological health in most of the people.

The results puzzled Greeley and his associates. "Such paranormal experiences," he wrote, "are generally viewed as hallucinations or symptoms of mental disorder. But if these experiences were signs of mental illness, our numbers would show that the country is going nuts. It's even happening to elite scientists and physicians who insist that such things cannot possibly happen."

The researchers used what they called the "affect balance scale," a standard measure of psychological well-being and the healthy personality. "And the mystics scored at the top," Greeley said. "In any case, our studies show that people who've tasted the paranormal, whether they accept it intellectually or not, are anything but religious nuts or psychiatric cases. They are, for the most part, ordinary Americans, somewhat above the norm in education and intelligence and somewhat less than average in religious involvement."

And what happens to these ordinary people when they try to communicate these intense, highly significant experiences to others? They are met with blank stares, incredulity, and downright hostility. The antagonism toward the paranormal within the professional groups is withering for anyone involved in the psychic world like myself. In fact, I would not have believed the sense of isolation and rejection one suffers when one admits a belief in the paranormal if I hadn't experienced it myself. I remember how difficult it was to speak openly about my experiences when I started experiencing the psychic. I was so afraid people would think I was crazy. I felt a little crazy anyway because there was no one to talk to. Also, I was afraid I wouldn't be accepted. The old fear of abandonment was ever present.

I thought I was alone until I started reading and studying in parapsychology and discovered that many others had similar experiences.

Since that time Theo has clarified much for me—especially when they began putting these negative and destructive attitudes in the context of a world in change and the coming of the 5th Dimension.

Know that in the time of great teachers on your planet there was always scoffing, for it brings forth fear—fear of the change that comes about when the old ways can no longer work. There is an upheaval in the personal experience of those who scoff or do not wish to acknowledge the change. They are grasping for the past, do you understand? They do not want change. They are fearful of change and do not want the responsibility: For it is a responsibility to accept change, is it not?

And Theo has often said that there are those who will decide the change is not for them and will "leave the planet." This is not a terrible thing, Theo advised, but a choice made by the individual soul.

And those choosing not to participate will leave the planet. That is a statement not to be afraid of; it is simply knowledge of what is, do you understand? For all beings, all souls, all spirits, as you term them, choose their experience. Some have chosen to participate in the 5th Dimension and the 6th Dimension upon this planet, the evolution of Earth to a higher state of frequency. And there are those for whom the intensity is too much and they have chosen not to be present in the experience at this time, do you see?

Greeley's research uncovered evidence of this fear, particularly among the media, sciences, and the academic world. These professional groups mostly found it unthinkable that a sizable proportion of the people they see every day believed that they had had experiences outside the accepted limits of modern science.

"This discomfort," Greeley wrote, "has made it hard to carry on serious academic discussion about the mystical and paranormal experiences of ordinary Americans."

And, I might add, this discomfort has also contributed to the enormous chasm that now seems to exist between what the average individual is experiencing and what the professionals and leaders of our society will accept. Think how difficult such a situation must be for anyone having profoundly moving and often disturbing psychic experiences. Who can one turn to for comfort or advice?

In another study conducted by the University of North Carolina, none of the people questioned (widows who had communicated with their dead spouses) ever mentioned their paranormal experiences to their doctors—even though they had found the experiences powerful, personally significant, and helpful in adjusting to their loss. In fact, most reported that the contact with their dead spouse helped them in continuing with their everyday life.

I am aware through my work with death how comforting it is for survivors to know that a loved one is all right and happy.

Clearly, it is the sense that we will be laughed at, derided, scorned, and made to appear foolish that prevents us from mentioning such experiences to the establishment figures in our society.

What is even more fascinating is that the Greeley survey showed that the number of Americans experiencing the paranormal is *increasing*, not decreasing. In Greeley's latest (1983) survey, two-thirds of all adults (67 percent) report having experienced some form of ESP, while in an earlier 1973 survey the number was 58 percent. This expansion of the number of people experiencing the psychic is more evidence, I am sure, that we're moving into the 5th Dimension, where being psychic is "okay."

Nearly half the population now reports having had contact with the dead, while in the earlier survey only one-fourth reported the experience.

Other surveys tend to confirm Greeley's findings—and the trend seems to include all forms of psychic and spiritual phenomena, whether the most common forms of ESP or the rarest sort of mystical experience.

As the 5th Dimension energy comes forth, many will seek the sensational, but to become attuned to the spirit, to the soul, the essence of what you are is the gift of life. It is a time to see and acknowledge the uniqueness and the beauty of the spirit expression on this planet.

The reason these polls are important is that they confirm the gap between what people are experiencing and what the leaders of our society consider allowable. It is important that those 134 million people who've experienced the psychic world realize they are not alone, that they are not rejected, or merely a statistic, but are part of a spiritual revolution now overtaking our society. Changes are coming. What has been "paranormal" and ignored is not only rapidly becoming normal but, as Greeley pointed out, "may also be health-giving."

This is not welcome news to the traditionalists in our society.

The scientist, orthodox Church leader, physician stuck in his text-book, psychologists and teachers and other leaders of our society can no longer easily deny that the inner world of the spirit exists. They can no longer easily avoid seriously studying it.

In his summary of the survey report, Greeley wrote: "Despite years of attempts to study paranormal phenomena, there's been a scientific iron curtain raised against serious research on these ex-periences. But the data shows that these [paranormal phenom-ena] do exist, that great numbers of people experience them—and that they could even change the nature of our society."

The 5th Dimension! Change! It is one of the keys to Theo's message. The old ways are not going to work anymore. People are changing; their interest in psychic phenomena is changing. They are awakening, and their awarenesses are raising to new levels of insight; their fascination with spirituality and religion is all part of the 5th Dimension energy shift that Theo has predicted.

Each being is a teacher and a student; and to share that light, to acknowledge the wisdom within, is very impor-tant now, as the 5th Dimension changes continue.

How can people *not* change when profound spiritual experi-ences become commonplace, when they experience out-of-the-body trips, are bathed in light, speak or see loved ones who have died, or have other transforming moments light up their lives?

Clearly, when 20 million people undergo deeply moving reli-gious ecstasy, their consciousness and beliefs—the very structure of their lives—will surely be dramatically altered. People will be moving closer to a spiritual concept of life as the 5th Dimension shift occurs. And this is the central idea behind Theo's message: Humanity is moving closer to believing in a trusting and loving God, moving ever more toward a fulfilling, spiritually oriented life. The religious experience will no longer be an intellectual experience; rather it will be felt deep within each seeker.

As Theo has said, it is time to honor the spiritual self, for this will be the foundation of the 5th Dimension society.

It is time to honor the self in this 5th Dimensional change; and to acknowledge the change itself, to acknowledge what you have done and not so much what you haven't. Old patterns will die. Release the past—in essence to die and to be born again.

4

Life in the 5th Dimension

OVER THE YEARS THAT I HAVE BEEN channeling Theo a vision of the world of tomorrow, a world in which 5th Dimensional ideas will be a major influence, has become continually clearer. It is a world dramatically, even drastically, different than today. The vision of the Theo group has covered practically every aspect of society—political, world government, economics, earth changes and ecology, and even visits from aliens and UFOs.

Most of Theo's descriptions of the 5th Dimensional world of tomorrow have come spontaneously as the result of questions asked by clients during trance sessions. So even while the picture of the future is incomplete, it is also exciting and tantalizing, and, more often than not, relates to how people's personal lives will be affected by the 5th Dimensional world. There are also fascinating ideas on death and reincarnation, and how society's views will change toward these controversial subjects. For example, Theo describes how the physical body alters as it goes into an "electric mode" at the time of death. There is also insight into why the AIDS virus has spread so terrifyingly and the prediction of a cure by 1990. Reading Theo's comments, one thing becomes clear: the coming of the 5th Dimension will change the world dramatically.

ON SEEING INTO THE FUTURE

Theo, we have been curious regarding how you see the future. How do you have access to that information?

We speak futuristically for the truth of the moment. Understand that there are no absolutes, for the will of man is the creative force, the creator of what is to come about. So when we speak of the future it is truth seen for this particular time. As beings evolve and the direction of their will changes, they can alter the forward movement of events.

Then, does other people's free will alter the future, or are you taking all that into consideration?

We speak about personal choice. The future is seen for that moment; but as we have stated, individuals have the choice to continually create their own destiny. Given the way the energy is at any moment, there is a probable outcome, do you understand?

THE WORLD OF TOMORROW

Theo, what will our world be like in the next hundred years?

The world as you know it will not be. The consciousness of humankind is being raised, the energy is being more refined. There will be a rebirth, a rejuvenation of this planet. Political forms will change. Economic structures will change. The old forms will no longer be. This will happen in the near future . . . immediately . . . in your time frame, during the next five years.

What will the new forms be?

First, there will be great physical changes. This planet is formed on plates. . . . They will shift, and the landmasses will shift. The poles are shifting, and you will notice it in atmospheric or weather changes.

Some people have said that the North Pole is going to be where the South Pole is by the end of the century. Is this true?

It will not be that dramatic. Many people think of the changes as cataclysmic. There will be earthquakes and volcanic activity . . . and to those standing at the foot of the volcano it will indeed be cataclysmic, yes?

The volcanic activity has already begun. Masses of land are already shifting, especially those previously known as Atlantis and Lemuria. These are now surfacing. You will observe these changes soon.

Where are Atlantis and Lemuria surfacing?

Off the coast of North America, close to the islands of Bahama. Lemuria is emerging off the coastal waters of Japan.

A great deal has been written about the Atlantean and Lemurian civilizations. Is there anything about their disappearance that we should be aware of in this time of 5th Dimensional change?

The self-destruction, the self-annihilation. You are learning from it now, as the 5th Dimension brings a change in awareness. There is a deep awareness within the beings at this time. There is a growing awareness and concern for the earth and its care.

Is there going to be massive destruction of the earth?

Yes, in some areas there will be. There will be slippage of the coastal region's plates, yes. It will extend into the mountainous regions for some areas, others not so far.

In other areas the changes will not be volcanic but atmospheric. In Africa there are already many changes in weather. There will be a change in the living experience in these areas; some areas that have been dry will become wet, and others that have been wet will become dry.

The great devastation that has been spoken of has created much fear within the hearts of people. There will be destruction, yes; that is so. But the answer is not to rush about, move about, to seek out a place of safety. Understand that each being will be perfectly placed, will be exactly where he or she needs to be as the changes come about. Trust the choices you make within your heart, and do not hold fear of the change.

Theo, the rivers are polluted; wells and water are being filled with chemicals. And if the earth is going to be cleansed and purified with such violent change, what are people to do? Where should they go? Should they store foodstuffs?

Again, it is up to the individual. Each person should follow the knowing within the heart. Some will make moves, yes; but that is not as important as learning to nurture the place where you live. It is well to put up foodstuffs, to preserve, yes. But not out of fear.

Humankind will survive, and people will learn to help their brothers and sisters in disastrous situations. There will be those who will, out of fear, hold back. But know that in their fear they draw to themselves most of what they fear—and it will be created in their own experience. Those who have faith in the self; those who have faith in spirit and balance, who become open to the 5th Dimension changes, will have all they need from this earth. It is

*the learning to trust that comes forth now in this time of
the 5th Dimension.*

Theo, since we've already polluted the planet so badly
that even the government scientists have said the earth
is sick and if things don't change in twelve to fifteen
years it may be too late, my question is, since we're
destroying ourselves, why not simply let it happen?
Why help us?

*Each being, each soul, is important to the universe, to the
God-source. The changes and cleansing are necessary for
the evolution of both the planet and people. It is part of
God's plan.*

*It was the preference of humankind to become more
attached to the material than to the spirit. For all are given
to choose their experience, to go their own path to higher
learning. Many have to learn by experience. They have to
experience destruction and devastation in order to understand it, to learn from it. The point of destruction is a
catalyst to awaken to the spirit.*

*What is happening now is a great power is moving
and will bring about a balance within people. This shift
helps change the consciousness of man so that this new
awareness will bring about more change and the destruction of the earth will stop.*

*Healing, rebirth, rejuvenation, attunement to spirit—
there is a forward momentum now for these. This is a
positive message, yes? It is a cleansing, an adjustment for
the planet, not to be feared.*

*It is a time for nurturing of the self and for becoming
more attuned to what is the correct path for the self. It
is not a time to be intimidated by the changes but to
acknowledge trust in the self, to accept one's personal
strength and power and utilize it in the world. This is not
selfish, do you understand? It is selfless, for when you
love and accept the self completely, then you can be finely
attuned to others and assist in the healing, understand?*

It is now a time of acknowledgment of that universal

power within each person. Create this power within your experience, and do not feel fear, do you understand? Many start from fear, they hoard food, they hoard money, and it is out of fear. Know that one is sufficient unto one's self, and know that one can survive on the basic level, do you understand? Many view these changes as fearful prophecy. But doom will not come about as has been feared. The changes are to be blessed; and know that they are part of God's plan and will help many to the sharing of their heart, to an unconditional love and acknowledgment of self.

The lesson to learn from all this is trust, a trust in yourself.

Theo, it's very hard to tell those who have no home, have seven mouths to feed, or have just lost a loved one, that they must learn to trust their *self* more.

That is correct. But know that this has been a creation within their thought process, and that is why they have drawn the experience to themselves. It is the shift of intention and attitude within each mind that is important now. There will be a necessary shift of consciousness, of thought. That is what is happening in the presence of this 5th Dimensional energy. The enlightenment will bring about a shift of thought patterning for humankind.

Now is a rebirth and greater understanding of what is spirit. Know that you are a reflection in physical form of the energy of the God-source of the Creator. You are of Divinity, and you do a disservice in not accepting the worthiness of the self.

Theo, I was wondering how the more vulnerable groups in our society will be affected by the 5th Dimension changes. How will the lives of the elderly, for example, be affected?

There will be more elderly in your world and you will find that they will be more healthy, more active. As their life-

*times are expanded the elderly will want to be more pro-
ductive, do you see? They will take a more active role in
society, and many will have great wisdom to impart to
the world.*

**How will they become more active? Will the govern-
ment set up agencies to help them?**

*With more health and longer lives, they will come to-
gether in great numbers and demand more participation.
They will no longer accept being set aside in society as
they have in the past.*

When will these changes occur?

*Look for great changes coming within a ten-year period.
For the elderly will no longer be apathetic. They will band
together in great numbers and create a new voice. This
will be helpful, for they have great wisdom and power to
impart to your civilization.*

**Theo, can we change our thought about death? I mean,
can anyone decide not to die and by changing thought
and affirming longevity remain on Earth?**

*Yes, that is possible. It is in the commitment to self, to
being fully expressive and honoring the self, yes? It was
your Christ who first taught this clearly two thousand
years ago, was it not? Love the self first, and then your
neighbor as yourself. This teaching comes forth again
now.*

  *Know that the time and method of death is up to the
individual soul. You know when to die, how to die, and
where to die; you place yourself in the proper place when
you want to change your pathway to growth.*

**How will these 5th Dimension changes affect the indi-
vidual's personal life style?**

There will be a complete change in individual life patterns in every field. But it is necessary to see this as a rebirth, a rejuvenation and not something to be feared. The changes begin most intensely in 1988 as structures will be revised and changed. But life will go on. There will be oil, but it will not be controlled by one group as it has been. The banking structures, the exchange of monies and stocks, will all change but money will remain, you see? In the financial marketplace there will come agreements globally.

Theo does not predict stock market changes or give financial advice, but for those concerned about personal finances, can Theo give us a method, a visualization, that we can use in order to make ourselves more successful or to achieve financial abundance?

These things do not happen in spite of the individual, they happen because of what the individual is, do you understand? The wholeness of the person affects this. It is helpful to meditate on abundance, to see it in your experience. If you accept the beauty and uniqueness of your individual self, acknowledge and affirm your personal power, life's abundance will come to you. In meditation visualize success or abundance, even write down specific amounts, say them aloud, accept them as part of you and they will come. But it cannot happen if the attitude is negative, see? It is necessary to alter old thought patterns first.

Is there any affirmation that can help people change their attitudes?

Use the first person, the word "I," and then affirm with the words that you will deserve and create abundance on all levels in your experience now.

How often should you repeat that affirmation?

Daily, in the beginning of your meditation. Do not limit the thought to one area, but be open to all as the abun-

dance flows—no matter how small it may seem. Bless the abundance, no matter what it is, acknowledge it, accept it, and ask the universe for more, do you see?

Could you give us some insight into how money, attitude, and success relate to one another?

Attitude is how you feel about yourself, and the limitations that you place upon the self as not being worthy. If you feel unworthy in attitude, then abundance cannot flow toward you, can it? Then, there are many forms of abundance in life, are there not? Money is only one form, so be clear what kind of abundance it is you desire.

Success also may be judged on many different levels, and this also relates to attitude about the self. There is success in learning, in expansion of the self, success financially, success in life experience. Money, success, attitude, are all closely tied together, do you see; but they all relate to thought and how you see yourself, how you accept the self, do you see?

Do you have any advice for people who are confused and feel they are not successful because their attitude is wrong yet don't know how to change it?

Look into the depths of the heart. Have quiet moments to look inside to see where these patterns of thought were formed. Then look at the generational patterns that have affected your personality. Then meditate as we have described to change the thought pattern; do you understand?

In the same area, people are often confused about how they can find their place in the world and be successful in their career. Do you have any advice for these people?

To be successful in your career is to choose the right path; and that is found by work that resonates well within the heart. But understand, you draw to you what is important for your path and your learning. So it is important to take notice of each thing that you do on your life path, for each thing is a steppingstone to your wholeness of being. It is important not to let your intellect, or others', direct your life path. You must make the decisions. Sit quietly and listen to the inner self, the inner being, for that way you will see clearly.

Many speak of this inner self, this inner child of knowing, in psychological terms as your "personal myth." Pay attention and support this child within. Understand that as you find in your outer life experience, in utilizing your talents properly, the gifts that you have brought into the world will bring success and abundance —for these follow upon the joyful expenditure of time and energy.

Many people ask "What is my purpose in life?" It seems to be an effort to clearly understand their path. You tell us to listen to the heart, but how can we really recognize that our impressions are correct?

Again, sit quietly and listen. It does not help to question your inner wisdom and then ask where is it? Trust your inner voices; that is the way you will learn your purpose. Know that different things will be drawn to you during your life experience. You may be drawn to books, or drawn to expressing yourself with words but remain fearful about becoming a writer. Release the fear and accept what is happening in your experience. To release the fear, allow it to flow through you rather than intellectualizing it, or expressing it in negative thoughts: "I can't do this" or "I don't have enough talent." Sit quietly and center the self and allow the words to flow as they will. Accept the signs in your outer experience as resonances of your inner experience, see? This will clarify your life path, give you direction regarding career, and open you to receiving the abundance of the universe.

Usually in times of trouble people start to hoard money and valuable goods. Should people start to save their money?

Investments and property are important. Savings are good. But it should be done not out of fear but by honoring the self. Pay the self first, then divide what is left over. Many start to hoard or save money out of fear. But it is now a time to acknowledge your own power to create, to sustain; to know that you are sufficient unto the self, to know that you could survive on a basic level. That is the learning experience here, do you understand?

It would be wise to reserve your resources now, for resources are being wasted by governments and people. Many feel that governments are controlling resources and artificially manipulating prices and the economics of goods. They feel that there is an abundance, enough for all; but this is not so. Governments are not withholding from people, but the trust of governments and political leaders is no longer there. In other countries where the people have not been told the truth for a long time, the distrust is becoming powerful. There is much dissension.

Oil is a natural resource that is being used carelessly. There is oil at this time, but if it is not conserved and used in a more deliberate manner, it will be used up. There are many working now to find alternative resources and a different resource will be available for automobiles and heating. This will not come about for a few years when it will be available to the many.

Greed at this time of global change will destroy all. The changes will happen as enlightenment of mind comes to some leaders and the people of the world force change.

What is the most important message you have for us on Earth?

It is a simple message: It is important that each being on the earth learn to take responsibility for what he or she creates. The cycle we have spoken about, both its destruc-

tive and learning aspects, has a greater magnitude than your conscious mind can perceive. We have no pictures for it presently. The earth plane is a plane of balance, positive and negative energy. There has been an imbalance, conflict, because of immersion of humans in the physical, in their own self-centered existence. There is a unification of your planet that will come about from people changing their destructive, negative patterns. But there must be a common effort, a joining together. If each being on your planet takes responsibility for what he or she creates, you will have the peace and balance that you seek.

WORLD CHANGES

Theo, with all these dramatic changes occurring now, what will our world, our society, be like after 1990?

The major upheavals have already started. They will occur in all areas: economically, personally, physically with people and with the planet, with governments, politics. In the decade between 1990 and 2000, the shift will occur. But there is more unification coming about, a harmonious coming together. This must be, for humankind can no longer work with the divisions; for the world, in an ecological sense, is annihilating itself. The coming together must come about to save the planet.

Unification will come from this destruction, for the people and countries most affected by the ecological disasters will stand up and say "No more!" As the disasters multiply you will see the beginning of unification to fight against the political structures. Those beings in countries less restricted by their governments will speak first; the north countries in Europe, do you understand?

There will be much upheaval about this and more interaction with those people in Russia, yes. That is important. You will see a coming together, not only of political personalities, but individuals such as yourselves coming together in like thought for healing the planet. It

*is time, for all people, in every nation, have the same
needs. All need the planet to survive.*

Theo, you have suggested that there will be major
structural changes in the political systems of the world.
What kind of restructuring of governments and political systems will take place in the 5th Dimension?

*What comes about is a unification, a combining of forces
who share a vision, a combination of thought. No one
personality will lead, but there will be a restructuring, so
that, as you think, a committee will be governing. Do you
see? Much input will come from other groups who do not
now have access to political power, from the artistic and
scientific communities; for it is these beings of sensitivity
who will first acknowledge the needs of the planet and its
healing.*

Are you saying these groups will set up committees?
And how would artists and scientists gain the power
to influence governments?

*They would have committees that respond to government
agencies, yes. Know that politicians have much ego involved in their work, and they do not have the proper
education or sensibilities to make wise decisions for this
world at this time. Scientists and artists, and other groups
will now step forward to speak out about the ecological
destruction.*

Is there a timetable for these political structural
changes?

*It is in process now and will be more completely evolved
within a twenty-year period. Groups are now becoming
unified, and it will soon be evident.*

What kind of political changes, specifically, will occur
in our government?

The United States government will change the nature of the presidency. There will be more than one personality making decisions. What you call the "Cabinet" will have more power. There will be a group making decisions.

If the Cabinet has more power, will they be chosen as elected officials rather than appointed?

Elected. People will insist on changes, for they are very dissatisfied with the government as it is now organized.

When do you see this happening, Theo?

It is in the process of happening now. You will see the greater changes in the year 2000. The changes will be in place by that time.

Do you see as dramatic a change in the Soviet government as the American?

Yes. There will be much dramatic change within their government—on all levels. There is much changing presently. The Soviets are seeking a better standard of living, better environments on all levels. At this point there is much competition in the government, which is the catalyst to bring forth change. There is a greater desire from the people for change.

Will the Soviet Union become more democratic?

It will, yes. Within a ten-year period. It has begun now, for there is much upheaval throughout the country. The people are changing within, which is reflected in the outer world experience.

Will the Soviets have more genuinely elected officials? When will the democratic changes occur?

The elections are not as yet. This will come about, but it is not yet accepted. There will be people coming from different factions within the country who will speak of the needs of the people, yes. So there will be more communication beginning now. The government will become more sensitive to the people's needs.

Specifically, when will all these changes be in place?

The changes are currently happening; they are already within the thoughts of humankind. You will see these changes coming about the year 2000; but the fuller government changing, with elections of cabinet officials, by the year 2015.

Will these changes weaken the presidency?

The president will not be as powerful, no. He will be more of a head of state.

If we elect our Cabinet officials, will there be changes in the election format?

Yes. There will be an election for president, but also the election of Cabinet officials.

Will there be major wars involving the United States in the near future?

There will be conflict, fighting, but not, as you call it, a major war. Many fear world conflict, but there will be decisions to avoid the larger conflict before it occurs. There will be more local conflicts, many smaller wars, but they will not go into a major world war.

I think one organization counted over 150 wars going on at the same time around the world recently. Will these many smaller wars continue to expand in number, or will they decrease?

The number will expand for a time, then retract. There will be growing dissatisfaction among the peoples of the world, and the wars will not be supported. There will come an easing and more global identification.

And when will this global identification come about?

It will be more evident after the year 2000, after the completion of this century.

Which other countries will be in the forefront of the political changes?

In the countries you call Europe; those that have been affected ecologically by the Chernobyl nuclear accident, for there has been much contamination that will become more evident.

Will these changes be brought about by even more traumatic experiences than Chernobyl?

Yes, there will be more. They will occur throughout the world, wherever industrial development has occurred. They will also be in what you call the Third World, where the land will be affected and starvation and disease will come forth. Again, the political structures in many of these countries are holding back solutions; they are holding back information, education, food, for the sake of self-righteous activity. The people will group together in protest and will rebel.

So the changes will happen not only within the major powers like Russia and the U.S., but globally?

Yes. But the major industrial nations are beginning to awaken to the growing disaster and are initiating changes. Russia and the United States will be in the forefront of those nations trying to make constructive changes, but pressures from the Third World countries will accelerate this, see? Economic forces will bear heavily upon these changes as well.

Will individual states in the U.S. suffer any major up-heavals from these changes?

Yes. It will begin on the coastal regions, but it will also be in your midcountry. The major upheaval will be in farming; foodstuffs and the like will be affected. It has already started.

Theo, you speak about the world economy being af-fected. How will these changes affect the economic life of the nations?

Because there has been much abuse in every nation, there will be upheavals globally, see? It is taking form now. In the United States, it will affect the southwest, south, and westerly regions . . . and the midcountry. Everything that is influenced by agriculture will be affected. You will also see great effect in Europe, with everything that has to do with food and food production, and also in the East, in Japan and China. China particularly will become greatly involved economically. One person, one nation, cannot change this, see. It is coming about by influences from many sources, do you understand?

All of these changes, in politics, governments, eco-nomics, seem to imply a movement away from the nation-state structure that we now have in place, and to be moving toward a unified world-government. Is that the trend?

Yes, that is the form, like the United Nations. It will not be a new world structure, but work within the United Nations concept. There will be some changes within, but overall a greater strengthening of the community of na-tions.

There has been much ego—leaders forever arguing.

The new structure will seem to be what you would call corporate, but it will not be. It will be more cooperative, with the combining of cooperation and action and the acknowledgment that one is equal to the other, do you understand? These changes will become more fully expressive by the years 2012 to 2015, but the energy for the change has already begun.

You will see the changes beginning now, in your experience. You will see it happening globally. All beings are sensing the shift now. Unrest is rising. Emotions are coming to the forefront. Much anger is being expressed because of the vibrational changes.

What form will these changes take in the art world?

There are many forms of art. In painting, the major changes will be in the use of color. There will be the coming from dark into the bright; there will be more joy expressed through color. In films, you will see a change in the kind of films made; a change of attitudes and emphasis will occur. Films and other art forms will generally be more expressive of the 5th Dimensional reality. There will be less acceptance of violence, for example, and more emphasis on themes of enlightenment and learning. Themes of unity, yes?

Theo, you have said that the arts and sciences will have more control, more influence, in the 5th Dimension world. Which arts will be most effective during this time?

The major effect will come from the entertainment world, especially the music arts. In terms of influence, it would be followed by painting, the use of color. Also, more will come from the written word. There are many limitations now in literature, and there will be more sharing. Specifically, we speak of the Soviet Union. But the activity in the arts will not be limited; the influences of the arts will be felt in other areas with physical expression—in sports, for example, see?

Will the arts, especially music, dance, painting, and writing, move away from what now seems a trendiness and obsession with merchandising, into something with more substance?

There will be more substance, as you call it, yes. But, understand, there is a necessary involvement in what you call "trendiness" to open doors.

How will these changes occur in music, dance, and theater?

It's already begun in dance. The dance has been in a traditional, accepted form, yes? But that is changing, broadening out. There will be more involvement with music in film and theater, which will, in turn, encourage writing. A sharing of life-styles through the arts, life experiences from one country to another, will begin to take place.

Theo, you said that there will be a greater sharing of the arts "outside" the art world. You mentioned sports as an example. Will the arts have an impact in any other areas?

Yes. You will see rapid and dramatic changes in the medical establishment. There will be greater use of the arts, healing tones and music, healing colors—a utilizing of the arts to create a healthy wholeness for the prevention of diseases rather than healing after the fact.

When will the medical establishment begin using colors and music in that way?

You will see this within a five-year period. It is beginning now and will become more widely accepted within five years. There will be resistance by some in the medical profession, but that will not last long, for the results will be of great interest. The combining of arts and medicine will bring quick and dramatic results in healing.

Will the use of the arts in healing be helpful for major diseases like cancer?

Yes, and other diseases. It is a way of balancing the whole body. Utilizing all the tools of sound, color vibration, meditation, will allow a greater balance within the body and facilitate healing. There are many diseases that will be affected immediately through the release of stress.

Which of the arts will be most effective in treating major diseases? Can you correlate the arts with diseases?

You may correlate color for most diseases. Color is very important for calming. The use of quiet colors, soft colors, in the healing environment will be nurturing and loving. This will facilitate healing. Music may be used in the same way for a similar effect. It will also facilitate healing of many diseases.

SCIENCES

Theo, could you give us some guidance on which areas of science will experience the most dramatic changes as we move into the 5th Dimension?

Most dramatic will be new discoveries involving the space program. New developments in communications will link up the world more closely. A sharing of satellites, and more advanced computers, will allow this. There will be more international cooperation in the sciences.

Which countries will be in the forefront of this new cooperation?

The more affluent nations—the United States, Japan, and the Soviet Union. European countries will have an interest, but these three will dominate.

Will there be major breakthroughs in physics?

Yes, in physics new discoveries will come in the area of brain physiology—dealing with mind, consciousness, thought. The power of thought will be seen more as being the creator, you see?

Will the new discoveries give us more objective scientific understanding of how thought occurs and just what is the "energy of thought"?

Yes, there will be discoveries in understanding the power of thought and its creative energy and the impact thought has on the material world. This will take time, however, for the research will not show why this is true. It will show more the result of this power than how it works.

In other areas of science—for example, astronomy— will there be major breakthroughs?

Yes, there will be the discovery of life on other planets, and there will be further space exploration by man before the year 2000. These discoveries will have a great impact. Through these discoveries there will be greater interaction with other nearby planets—especially Mars. But the discovery of intelligent life in other systems will wait until humankind is prepared in their consciousness to accept it. It could have happened long before now, but humankind was not prepared. They are preparing now, do you see?

So the scientific revolution during the 5th Dimension is not only going to be in technology, but in the individual scientist's mental attitude as well?

That is correct. There are Dimensional energy exchanges here that facilitate advancement in thinking. 5th Dimensional energy will assist in this, see? But the individual scientist must stand firm in commitment to this exploration, to this advancement in knowledge. Many become disheartened when confronted by adversaries, so a strong commitment to the work will be necessary. Many have come forth in this time; many have embodied a commitment to pursuing enlightenment. It is now time, and scientists will find support for this path from the masses. For all humankind wishes for this enlightenment and will sustain the arts and sciences in the pursuit. There are many scientists interested in expansion of consciousness. As they achieve this in themselves the outer world will support it.

But will scientists find financial support for this kind of research?

There is support already in the private sector, but more support from the government will come. There will be more funding for research, for the expansion of knowledge, for there will be breakthroughs not only in the sciences, but dramatic healing in health-care and preventive medicine will create much support throughout the community.

Theo, I was wondering if science and technology will soon be moving toward alternative power sources, beyond relying on our nearly exhausted fossil fuels?

Yes, it will be a necessity soon. What you call the fossil fuels will be depleted so quickly that usage will be affected. They are already almost depleted in the eastern portion of your country. And they are also being used up very rapidly in the West.
    There will be a turning to alternative sources soon—the sun, the wind, the sea; these are all good. But there is

*also the use of the energy in your atmosphere, gathering
and using the electricity in your atmosphere. There is already knowledge of this, but its use has been limited for
economic and business reasons.*

**How will this come about, how will electricity from the
atmosphere be used as an energy source?**

*A receptor will be used to draw the energy, to channel it,
so to speak.*

Will this technology be developed in the near future?

*Yes, it will come about near the year 2000. It has already
begun now, but it must wait upon other discoveries. Electricity in the universe will be used as an energy source,
but it is a continuum, you see. Other discoveries must
come first.*

**Theo, recent discoveries in the science of genetic engi-
neering, in the creation of new life-forms and allowing
private companies to patent the animals, presents our
world with disturbing ethical and moral considera-
tions. Could you give us some insight into what is happening in this area of science?**

*Genetic engineering is here to assist and advance the heal-
ing of humankind. There will be moral issues, most coming from greed and uncaring manipulation of life-forms,
but as consciousness of these issues is raised in your
world, there will be changes of thought and behavior. It
is an opportunity for your world to make choices between
the material and the spiritual, see?*

*In the 5th Dimension energy, and the consciousness
shift that is occurring now, an awareness will arise in
humankind regarding responsibility toward what it is creating.*

In the time of Atlantis there was an expansion of

science without heart. But there are many Atlanteans upon the planet now who participated in those destructive attitudes, and they have greater wisdom in the present.

Many Atlanteans are coming back into existence now because of the similarities between our civilization and theirs?

That is correct, for the technology now is at the same destructive point, and there is a great awareness of this within those beings. And it is in this consciousness, and the evolution of thought, that a balance between body, mind, and spirit will come about. There is a desire for wholeness now that has not been on your planet before.

You say that many Atlanteans are coming into existence now, but you've also spoken about the Pleiadeans and that many of these entities are now on Earth. What is the reason for this?

The Pleiadean energy aids the balance, the bringing forth of the wisdom of the 5th Dimension energy. They are the peacekeepers; they are teachers and more highly evolved in the sense that they understand the power of thought and its creative energy.

You have said that they exist in a 6th Dimension energy, yet they come into human bodies and function. Do they retain 6th Dimension consciousness? And why are they coming here?

That is correct. There are many Pleiadeans that have experienced earth-plane lifetimes before. Know that the earth is but one choice of experience, and that the soul can choose other dimensions, other planets, other solar systems, to participate in.

So the Pleiades is another level or dimension that human beings can move to when they wish to enhance their own soul's evolution?

That is correct.

SPACE EXPLORATION AND UFOs

Will new discoveries coming from our space program happen in the near future?

There will be new discoveries, for explorers will interact not only with other planets, such as Mars and the moon, but will interact with galactic energy. They will experience input from other dimensions that they will not be able to discount.

What kind of discoveries are you speaking about?

There will be interaction with other dimensionary beings, as you call "UFOs." That is your terminology, but it is interaction with other galactic beings. So it is not that scientists will simply gather their data, but that there will be contact with other beings as well.

Do you mean that it will be happening here on Earth or in space, or on another planet?

It will be both in space and on Earth.

We already have reports of UFOs and beings from other planets visiting Earth, but the contacts always seem to be with ordinary people who are not necessarily believed. Will scientists or people from the government experience these contacts in the future so the experiences will be more accepted?

The planet as a whole is being prepared for this interaction so there will be more acceptance from scientists and the government. There will be those in higher positions who will experience interaction with the galactic beings. These will not be discounted. You will see more interaction in the immediate future. As we have stated, the completion of the twenty-six-thousand-year cycle has aligned the planets and allowed the highways of the universe to be more open, so the interaction will be greater now than in the past. Your planet is now prepared for it.

When will this direct contact occur between our leaders and other dimensional beings?

The interaction will occur more fully in the year 1990. Within a five-year period contacts will be documented; communication in the governments of the world will come forth and involve the scientists.

What information from the galactic beings will be most helpful to us?

What will help the ecology of your planet, for there has been much destruction.

Will these contacts with galactic beings be secret within the government, or will the public know about them?

In the beginning there will be some secrecy. Then the information will be made public.

Theo, could you comment on the reports that some contacts with extraterrestrial beings have been very unpleasant. People have reported being experimented on. Are these kinds of contacts happening; and are there certain groups of galactic beings that we should be wary of?

Yes, there has been some experimentation here. But there is not a desire to harm or frighten. Much of the discomfort comes from fear. When there is more communication and understanding, there will not be as much fear or misunderstanding.

Theo, do you see us forming a colony on another planet anytime in the near future?

That will come about, yes. Preparations are now being made for that. Much of your information from these galactic beings will assist in this evolution of your space program. It will not be initiated until early in the next century, after the year 2000. The first colony will be on Mars.

Will we also have manned space exploration outside our solar system in the near future?

That will not come about in your lifetime.

When we make contact with UFOs, will there actually be humans traveling on their spaceships? Will scientists actually bring back firm eveidence of what is really happening? Will the media be involved and report on these contacts? Will it be that open?

It will, yes. The media will be involved and serve to reduce fear.

So the media will be traveling on spaceships and sending back reports on what it's like?

Yes, they will have that experience.

When will these contacts between the media and UFOs occur?

They will come about at the end of your century.

In what other ways will the media help bring about 5th Dimensional changes?

They are information disseminators. They will communicate information not only about space, but about individual growth. They will take note of these galactic beings using their personal power for the benefit of this planet. It will be an experience, an enlightenment, do you see?

CRYSTALS

Theo, many people are now interested in crystals and other forms of natural energy on Earth. Will these forms of energy be more commonly used by people living in the age of the 5th Dimension?

They will, yes. It will also be acknowledged that crystals are facilitators; they are organic activators for humans and act as conductors.

Are there any specific types of crystals that would help us move to higher vibrational states?

There are many crystals, but the most widely beneficial would be your quartz crystal. It is best for raising you to a higher consciousness.

What does quartz do specifically for consciousness and changing our vibrational levels?

It clarifies, energizes, and activates the body and mind. You may hold it or have the crystal on your body. But recognize that the power comes from within you and the crystal itself is only a conduit or conductor to enhance it. You can use the quartz to draw energy to you directly or direct energy from you. It depends on your intention, you see?

Which type of quartz would be best overall?

The clear quartz would be best overall. There are other crystal structures that facilitate healing. They are conduc-

*tors of specific energies. But overall the clear quartz is
most advantageous.*

**Then the clear quartz relates to higher consciousness?
Are there any crystals that would help you to a higher
physical vibration and allow you to move through
space?**

*There is the larger quartz. What you call terminated twice,
or double-terminated quartz, would facilitate this physical
transformation.*

**Some have said that fluorite is a type of crystal that was
brought here from another planet to help facilitate the
5th Dimension change. Is that true?**

*The crystalline structures facilitate change, yes. All of
them! Fluorite is also a facilitator. But understand that it
is the consciousness of humankind that uses the energy
within, that allows the change. Brought from another
planet? We find that of interest, but we see it not. Know
that the crystalline forms are a part of your Earth, and
they give balance, even give grounding sometimes. They
are part of the physical universe in which humans exist,
and it is advantageous to use these forms, to be a part of
them.*

**How do you become a part of the crystal? You speak of
consciousness being within yourself and going out to
the crystal. Should one specifically program thoughts
into crystals?**

*This can be done, yes. If you wish to clear a particular
part of the self, you may program a crystal for this clearing. You ask for its assistance in this vibrational shift, do
you see?*

*To program the crystal you hold it, send energy
through your body into the crystal to activate it. If you
visualize it as being activated, the crystal will become a*

magnifier of change. If you hold it in your hand and energize it, you can see the light encompass it.

How long does the crystal hold the program?

Until it would be cleared. If you wish to clear it, cleanse it with sunlight for a period of time so that it can continue releasing energy as it clears from you.

Theo, what is the best way to use a crystal? By that I mean, if I wanted to facilitate higher consciousness, would I hold it against the third eye area, the crown chakra, or just hold it in my hand?

If you want a stronger activation, you would hold it against the third eye area. But you could hold it in your hand on the right side when you're activating, and on the left side for balance, you see?

If you want to deactivate something, say, the left side —how do you do that? Could you change the physical vibration and rid yourself of something?

Yes, you could. Hold the crystal on the left side and visualize the energy coming out through the left. It is a visualization of light, you see?

Theo, are there other materials on Earth, or specific places that have special materials, that are helpful to people? I understand many people feel that certain areas of the earth have electrical powers?

There are many energy vortexes on Earth. You would find them in the mountainous regions of the southwest. But there are many different energy areas throughout the world.

Many call these places "power spots." Are there any you would specifically recommend as being best for people?

That is individualistic. But to determine which location may be best for you, you should stand on the land and feel it resonate within your being. See if you are drawn to that place; if so, you must learn to trust the areas you are drawn to. Places such as Tibet have areas of great power. And South America. Some would feel it most strongly in the southwest of the United States, some in the northwest, others the northeast. It is what registers well within the individual, you see? Human beings are drawn to the power areas that are best for them. Learning to be open to the place, and to trust your feelings, is what is important.

Are there any specific locations that would be helpful for us?

As just given, it is individualistic. But Arizona, New Mexico, Colorado, Washington, areas in the California mountains. Areas in Maine in coastal regions. There is power with water in Virginia. These are all particularly strong areas. There are others that are strong, but not as powerful as these at this time.

DEATH AND SURVIVAL

Theo, you have said that each being is a part of the global change and that those who do not wish to be part of the 5th Dimension transformation will leave the planet. Will these people actually choose to be in a place where death will occur? What happens to those who have opted to die . . . and to those who opt to stay?

Yes. There are many choosing to depart the planet at this time. Those who have chosen to participate in the change will stay; those who may find the shift too intense will depart, will go to other places to learn. Those who are not attuned to this experience will depart.

Then those who are caught in an area of destruction have chosen to be there?

Yes. The choice of whether to come or go is yours. Many fear death because they think of it as a negative, but it is a positive expression of being. Know that the earth plane is but one expression. Do not limit your thinking that this world is all there is. There are billions of choices in the universe in which an energy or spirit essence can participate. That's a relief, is it not? For those who do not like it on this planet, there is an option.

Theo, is there anything you can tell us about AIDS?

Many beings will seek release from the planet with this disease. It is not a judgment but a choice, a way to go forward into another expression, do you see? Each being is a part of the 5th Dimension shift, and those who do not wish to be a part of the transformation will leave the planet.

This virus has been brought forth in this time in support of the cleansing of the planet. It is as with cancer and other diseases during this time. All beings are coming into balance with themselves, are becoming more energized with the 5th Dimension vibration. But there are those who wish to depart and choose different ways of doing this—and the AIDS virus is one way.

If someone chooses to leave the planet, this is not to fear. Honor the choice with unconditional love and acceptance. The expression of love and communication at the time of death is extremely important—not the separation. Encourage understanding and communication, for this is part of the lesson of such transformation. It is now that the consciousness of humankind raises. Through sickness and death there arises a greater understanding of the physical structure—and the honoring of them comes about. Such experiences bring forth an attunement of individuals to one another—they bring forth unconditional love.

Know that death is not an end. This virus is a vehicle for many to depart, not unlike other diseases. It is just more fearful, but there is a clearing, or healing, of this within a three-year period. There will be a known cure by 1990.

You have said before that we will find a cure for AIDS within the next few years. Could you tell us more about that?

As with many of the diseases on your planet, you will see a vaccination come forth that will be a deterrent. Those who have contracted this particular virus, or activated it within their systems, have chosen this way in which to depart the earth. In this way they seek a higher learning and are a lesson for this world.

What will come into play here is the balancing of the body's strength; a part of the vaccine will be a part of the virus. It will help in building the body's immune system.

But once someone has the disease, you are saying that the vaccine can also cure it? When will this take place?

There will be an arresting of the disease by the vaccine. Know that this virus stays within the body and can be activated again if care is not taken of the body. People should become more cognizant of the wholeness of being —of body, mind, and spirit in proper balance.

The vaccine will come into use within a three-year period of this knowledge. But its general use will not take place for five years. There must first be an acceptance by the government, you see?

Theo, it is said there are over two hundred different kinds of cancers. Will the cure for cancer come about overall, or for different kinds of cancer selectively? Will there be a chemical, or a medicine, that will cure *most* cancers?

There will be combinations, medicines that will build into an overall cure. There will be one medicine that will affect several different kinds of cancer, and another that will be a mutant of the first, you see? But environment plays a large role here. Yes, and all the stress affecting the body. There has been much destruction to the environment, which becomes destructive for the human form—for it is also a part of the planet's ecology, you see? As stated before, these things are not disconnected; they are part of the whole and will be cured as a wholeness of being comes about.

Theo, what happens when somebody dies?

There is a separation of energy, the electromagnetic field, which can be measured now with instruments. This energy that is the soul separates from the physical structure —which is no longer needed. And what is the purest form of energy, the soul, as you call it, then proceeds into a dimension where it assesses its own experience. In this dimension there is an overview, an awareness of unlimited expression, do you understand? All is known to the soul: there are not the limitations as in the physical dimension. Depending on the individual souls' choice, some incarnate again, some remain present with those they are closely tied with vibrationally, some do not. Understand? Some go to other dimensions, other planets, for their expression; you see?

You have said that death, like other experiences such as out-of-the-body experiences, is always a form of enlightenment. Why is this so?

Experiences out-of-the-body, as you call them, are a confirmation of power for some. They are a form of enlightenment because it is a change, a moving forward, a completion of one form of learning and going forward into another. Each step is an enlightenment, do you see? The enlightenment of death comes from becoming more finely attuned to the experience. There is a moving within, an acknowledgment and expression of the experience. This is enlightening, especially for those too immersed in the physical.

For some the enlightenment comes from being free of fear. Many fear death because they have feared life; they fear their mortality because they fear pain. What happens with the transformation of death is the release of fear and a greater understanding of life. This is enlightenment, do you see?

Theo, you said that some souls go to other planets when they depart. How does this happen?

At the point of death you change energy forms; you go into a higher elevation of vibration in the molecules of your being. You go into the universe, so to speak, in an electric expression. That is magic to most conscious minds, is it not? It is then that you choose another expression, whether it is the earth plane or another planet; or some may even stay in the electric mode, if you would. It is all choice, do you see? Human beings have limited themselves into thinking that the earth plane is the only choice of expression. But it is only one . . . there are billions of choices. The conscious mind cannot perceive all the choice there is, for it does not have pictures or symbols for it.

Know that there are an infinite number of energies that have been created by the God-source. Know that the earth is only one choice of experience or expression. There are other planets, other solar systems; there are galactic experiences; there are dimensional experiences not limited to physical forms. Many of the beings upon your planet come from other solar systems and other experiences besides the earth, do you understand? This is what you call "reincarnation."

There are billions of dimensions to choose from— energy dimensions, planets, solar systems. Your planet is but one experience, understand?

REINCARNATION

Theo, you mentioned reincarnation. Once you go into another dimension, to other planets, do you ever come back to Earth to reincarnate?

It is the choice of the individual. It is the energy, the vibration, the soul, if you will, that chooses the dimension to join.

So you can travel back and forth between dimensions if you wish to?

You may, yes. Each personality chooses perfectly what dimension is best for its life.

Will we, at some point, be able to exist on other planets than this one? In the same form that we are in now?

Yes, there will be the learning of how to control the vibrations of the physical structure so that one can move more freely, understand?

Why is this knowledge so hidden?

That is what is changing now. It is men's minds that have closed, and they are now being opened.

Do we choose what our next life is going to be?

Yes, you choose what all your lives are going to be. Know that you are in a limited time frame and are breaking yourself free of those limitations. But there is always an assessment, an evaluation, of what you want to experience. This brings you to a choice. Do you understand?

What is the purpose of all this if you can look ahead and see what is happening? Are we just acting out some divine plan, or do we have actual choices to make?

You have choices to make. We could speak to you of the future, but we give only what is the truth of the moment because the willpower of humankind is great. By will and the power of thought things can change; what is the form can take different shapes, understand? You are the creator of your experience.

In other words, when you choose a dimension, a life, you choose a certain existence, but the actual details of that existence change during the experience because of your individual power of will and thought?

They do, for you create everything in your experience. Know that the purpose here is to achieve your learning, in whatever form or experience necessary.

Know that willpower is of the utmost importance in the physical being. Power comes from joining will with the inner self, with the God-source within. Many ignore this, and do not seek their soul's purpose. Growth is affected, and the soul would feel the need to incarnate again to achieve this purpose.

Many who incarnate into the physical body wish to forget the soul's experiences, and by this they undermine their spiritual growth. They do not go upon the path they have chosen. It is very important for human beings to understand this, for then they would not have the tendency to blame others for their failures. To be sure, it is very hard to accept in the conscious mind that you are entirely responsible for your own personality, for your own destiny. If beings on the earth could look within the self by meditation and grasp the inner self, or God-source, there would not be so much pain.

The decision to incarnate is the soul's, but it is a gift from God that you are free to choose. You decide which family to incarnate with, which life-style to live within, which people to associate with, which works to perform.

In every personality there is a striving for perfection, an effort to fulfill the soul's purpose. God's gift to you is life; what you do with it is your choice. You may waste the power within or use it to learn. This beautiful power is within everyone, as well as the possibility of expansion to a limitless existence. With the power within, you are limitless.

Theo, you said that sometimes groups of souls incarnate together. Why is this? And is this what we would call meeting soul mates?

Many times there is a gathering of like-minded individuals to share knowledge and be supportive of one another's growth. This is to aid the group as well as the individual. In a sense this is a soul mate, as you use the word. In your terminology a soul mate is what is compatible soul that you can interact with, a companion soul that creates a balance and a learning, is it not? There are many such groupings, yes. The mate of your soul, if you will, is the equal in energy and balance. Know that the soul is energy. Think of your soul mate as a vibrational energy input that creates a balance, a wholeness within. These energies are called upon at all times, whether within the limited physical or in other dimensions. Your soul mate, as you call it, need not be present in the moment-to-moment experience of your earth life, do you understand? It is a continuum of vibration and balance.

So it's possible to meet someone briefly, be deeply moved by him or her, and never see the person again, and yet have the feeling that he or she could have been a soul mate?

Yes, there are compatible souls that enrich and enhance the experience of life. There is the creation of that sense of connectedness, of balance and harmony, but not necessarily the need to spend your present life with them.

So the meaning of a soul mate is not a single entity that you are absolutely drawn to for every lifetime, over and over?

No, not in that sense. Many seek that out, romantically, yes. But know that in this time of the 5th Dimension you will be drawn into many circumstances and relationships in order to advance your soul's purpose rapidly. In this time you will be clearing old patterns, understanding new visions, and accepting the power within you, faster than at any time ever known in your past . . . during what you call your history. So there is much interaction between incarnating souls, yes; but it can be momentary, or it can be years or days. Whatever is necessary for the individual souls' learning, do you understand?

What about strong friendships, or people you work with closely? Do they have karmic connections, or previous lives together?

Yes, sometimes you will feel a strong bond. It is possible to have worked together, side by side, in many lifetimes. There is then a great support for one another, very telepathic, great harmony. Together you can advance both of your knowingness, utilizing your power together because of the past harmonies. There is a wholeness or a completeness that aids both.

This is an expression of identical energies, two parts creating balanced energies, much as you think of male and female as becoming a balanced whole. They are identical when balanced in energy and whole, see?

You must understand that the soul has an unlimited view of all that has been learned previously and an unlimited opportunity for expression. It has an understanding, a knowing, of all that is needed to learn or experience. The soul, from this higher viewpoint, then chooses a time frame in which it wishes to incorporate that learning. And know that there is a combination of souls that gather to

one another to assist, to support the growth mutually, do
you understand?

Does that mean that groups incarnate together, or may
part of the group stay in a higher dimension instead of
incarnating? And is one ever encouraged to incarnate
when one doesn't want to?

The answer is both. Groups incarnate together, yes, as has
been given. But groups also stay in higher dimensions,
unlimited, together, where they continue to support and
assist one another along the way.
   Sometimes, yes, a soul is encouraged by the group to
incarnate; but the decision is always independent.

Does anyone ever die on the earth plane by accident?
Like an infant who dies before having lived at all?

There are no accidents. Just because the body is small
does not mean the spirit is. For some souls there only
needs to be a short time upon the planet. When one has
completed one's purpose, even if that purpose is to aid or
support another by an early death, then dying is still the
choice of the soul—even within an infant body. There are
even those who enter the body for a short period of time
simply as teachers for those about them; do you under-
stand?

Theo, why can't we remember our past lives? And if
the sum total of our experience is within us, in our
souls, in our physical bodies, is everything I've ever
thought, dreamed, or done present within me as I
speak?

You do not often remember past lives because you wish
to get on with the problems of this one. Some memories
do come through, though, don't they? You can, if you
wish, call upon those memories of higher learning, of
wisdom, that you've gained to aid you in the present life.

How is this done?

In calling upon what is the higher self, you release the conscious mind of its control. This allows your subconscious, or the higher self, to become involved. You can do this in a meditative state, by altering what is the conscious state; do you understand? You may use vibrations, such as the OM sound. Speak the sound as in the word "home," not clipped, as a word but as a vibrating sound that is universal.

Using the breath, in and out slowly, relax the musculature of the body, feeling all parts of the physical self become relaxed, dropping away as if it's not there any longer.

If the mind wanders from this, gently draw it back to the sound and the rhythm of breathing. Allow this to become a floating feeling within the body, yes? This facilitates an altered state of consciousness, as many call it. It releases the control of the conscious mind so that the all-knowing higher self manifests. It is letting go of the limitations of the physical mode, yes? Memories of your higher learning will then come into your consciousness.

But do our cells, our physical cells, have memories?

The cells are a hologram of knowing, yes. It is all that you are and have become. Not only are your memories, your talents, and learning contained in these cells, but there is a generational impact where actions from a family, or group, are carried over from family to family. It is the keeping of your soul's record, do you understand?

So while karma exists as a law, the individual and the generational thing we have with our parents and grandparents is also part of the karmic link and our own choice?

Yes, there is also a generational expression or involvement within the soul's action. But the generational, and

*the societal patterning, has been effective within all, do
you understand? Each thing affects every other thing. The
universe, after all, is a unity, yes?*

**Theo, if we all keep coming back through reincarna-
tion, and the number of beings is constant as they cir-
culate between dimensions, how can you explain that
there are more beings on Earth than ever before?**

*Many question why there are more souls or entities in
your physical world at this time. Know that there are
infinite numbers of energies that have been created in the
universe. Know that the earth is only one expression out
of billions. There are many souls that have been incarnate
on other planets, in other civilizations, that have chosen
not to incarnate into the earth plane until this time of the
5th Dimension. Many have waited years because it has
now become time for them to be of help. Others have
come at this time of 5th Dimension change to learn and
further their own spiritual growth.*

*All entities will incarnate into many different worlds,
to experience all that is necessary for their growth. To
become perfection they must experience all that is offered
by the God-source, so it is possible, even necessary, to live
many lifetimes in many dimensions. The God-source offers an infinite number of choices to souls. It is very complex, much more than the conscious mind of man can
comprehend.*

*As the 5th Dimension continues many will come to
remember their learning from other lifetimes, from other
civilizations. The soul retains these many lessons and talents. The knowledge of each soul is vast—as is the mind
of man. The soul—and mind of man—is limitless. Comprehension of this is going to come about gradually. Mind
expansion will come to all, and all will be understood by
entities on the physical plane.*

*The unity of all souls, the coming together in en-
lightenment, is necessary. It is important to the God-
source for all souls to unify in perfection. During times of*

change, as with the 5th Dimension, human beings must learn to work together, for by working together, by coming together in unity, you will all endure. This is why it is important for those on the physical plane to understand the message of the 5th Dimension, for without this enlightenment they will be sorely troubled and confused.

Theo, if there is such movement between different planets by incarnating souls, are there beings on other planets that are aware of us on Earth? And if so, do they use our Earth to channel information?

Yes, there are others aware of the earth and communicating. But much energy between these places and the earth is recent, because of the coming energy shift of the 5th Dimension. It has allowed, so to speak, highways to the universe to be opened up. There is much energy present now as the changes come forth.

There will be an acknowledgment of what you term extraterrestrials. There are some that are presently in physical form on the earth. Highly evolved beings have come here to help in the evolutionary process as the vibrations of the shift occur. The opening to the universe allows entities from other dimensions, from other solar systems, an entrance onto the earth. These galactic beings, shall we say, are in the physical as well as other dimensions. They are not to be feared, as has happened in the past. For enlightenment can come through acceptance of them, do you understand? There is much galactic energy about now. There will be in your present experience the coming of spaceships, or UFOs, as you call them. But this is not to be feared but welcomed as a learning experience.

And what's important now is that we connect with this galactic energy? What are we to learn from that?

You are a part of the universe, are you not? And it is now time, during the 5th Dimension energies, to become attuned to the universal knowledge and not to be so self-centered, yes?

Know that there have always been visitations from other planets, other solar systems. Especially from what is called Pleiades and Orius. There is much Pleiades energy present now.

There is a knowing within humankind, a memory brought forth from the past. The information will be imparted unto the world and shared. The information is eternal, and humankind is being prepared now for this knowledge. The opening to the universe is part of this.

The Theo tapes take us into a new world, create a new vision of tomorrow. Humankind and the earth, two vast fields of energy, will finally merge into a unified whole as the 5th Dimension energy takes effect. This is not just a message channeled by a single "higher consciousness" group entity called Theo, it has the power of an echo resonating around the world.

I believe there is a reason for the growing number of channelers, a reason that millions of people are awakening now to spiritual and psychic realities. To be frank, I don't believe it really matters whether the interest is expressed as a simple fascination with the strange or occult, or whether it is expressed as an identification with a subtle spiritual reality that opens one's soul to a personal "divine" purpose in one's life. This may seem harsh, but I believe each individual will eventually have to travel the bridge between matter and spirit into the 5th Dimensional world; each person will have to open the spiritual doorways into his or her own spiritual center. So while it is important that each of us help our brothers and sisters to achieve spiritual wholeness, the powers at work here are universal. What matters is that there is a giant, magnetic, powerful wave of people opening to a larger, more spiritual, reality. This is the reason that opening the self and learning to live with the power of the 5th Dimension are so important. Nothing less than the spiritual evolution of the planet Earth is taking place.

5

Relationships: Man and Woman

TWO ASPECTS OF LIFE IN THE 5TH Dimension have enormous significance: children and male/female relationships. The reason for their importance is that human relations will be the personal arena where most people will learn about themselves and their role in the 5th Dimension. Most people will not be celebrities, or major political, scientific, or artistic figures. In fact, most of us will learn about ourselves through personal experience, through learning how to cope with the problems of love and marriage, childbearing, and child-rearing. These are the areas the majority of people will deal with on a day-to-day basis and where the greatest lessons will be learned.

Time and again Theo has emphasized the importance of this.

There are great changes of male and female energy coming forth in this new 5th Dimension energy. The changes will be most dramatic in male/female relating—such as has not been known in the past. Now you will come forth as independent individuals to share your heart, to share the fullest expression of your being. You will reject the rigidities of the past. Communication will be better, and relating will be a preference, not a need: for each being will be recognized as independent; you will acknowledge and know that each being is responsible for the self on all levels.

Only then can you make agreements and share in truth.

Mistrust and misunderstanding between people has existed for centuries. And it has been ingrained in your society for hundreds of years. Know that you are breaking these barriers, changing your thoughts and changing the form of relationships. It is an intense undertaking.

And know that the beings present on this planet during the 5th Dimension transition are strong entities. You have chosen to participate in this dramatic transformation of humankind; so you should honor the self in this movement forward.

Theo, men and women have had anger between them that goes back for millennia. It's old karma, and it seems like such an overwhelming problem that I don't see how much we can expect to accomplish.

First of all, realize that you are not going to change the billions of people on the planet . . . then it is not so overwhelming, yes? Where this transformation begins . . . and where it takes place, is within the individual. The responsibility lies with each and every personality. The answer is not found in being addicted to changing another. It is found in changing the self. This is important. It is also important to allow the fullest expression of being, to trust the fullest expression of the self, the totality of the self. This allows for change to occur, yes? When you focus upon changing the self, it is not as overwhelming as when you are addicted to changing everyone else, yes?

But in order to have relationships, in order to be intimate, we have to be vulnerable, isn't that true? And I just wonder how vulnerable human beings can be? How totally trusting, totally open, and innocent can we be?

Depends on the circumstances, does it not? When you are closely involved in a relationship, if you trust the self and remain open to that trust, vulnerability does not feel as frightening. That is why when you stay in the present, in moment-to-moment experience . . . then enlightenment comes.

Fear comes from being too far into the future, or too far into the past. To live life fully is to be in the moment. And so you become vulnerable, you are open, receptive, and sharing, for that moment does not seem as overwhelming then. Do you understand?

Are there any wounds deeper, or more fundamental, than the ones men and women inflict on one another. Scratch the surface of almost any personality, be it man or woman, and you will find a deep wellspring of yearnings intermixed with the disillusionment created by a culture that pits its men and women against one another. The very idea of competition between men and women is symptomatic of a misplaced, almost sick, perspective.

This is changing now. The protection many have set about themselves is for survival, yes? But that is what is changing now in the time of the 5th Dimension.

All beings do this . . . male and female. You do not trust one another, for the patterns have been set time and time again in mistrust. The barriers of this mistrust are also breaking down now. They can no longer serve as survival ways.

In our society competitiveness and aggression are both considered virtues: therefore it's no surprise that these traits—especially when highly developed—would spill over from the dog-eat-dog world of survival into one's personal relationships. What has

happened in our society, unfortunately, is that the virtues of the
marketplace, of the job environment, of the competition and "success syndrome," have caused men and women to be confused
about their roles with the opposite sex. The result of this role
confusion has been that men tend to deny the feminine aspect
within themselves, and women tend to reject the male part of
their temperaments.

But this is not to argue in favor of traditional roles. On the
contrary, rigid roles create a confused conformity that is not natural to human nature. "Playing" at a socially accepted role twists
male/female relations terribly out of shape.

*These roles are no longer needed with the coming of the
5th Dimension. Understand that there will be a change of
roles for both sexes—a greater combining and sharing
will occur. Humans all want the same basic thing—unconditional love. That is the radiance, that is what is coming forth now in the 5th Dimension . . . not to use one
another manipulatively. This love is to be given openly.
Then it is easier for you to get along with one another.
Not to say that there will not still be disagreement, and
not to say that you will not have differing points of view
from the male and female perspective. That will be! But
you will have a basis of trust and completeness within
yourselves so you will not destroy one another as you
have in the past.*

As the 5th Dimensional energy influences our civilization,
change is clearly taking place. Some real progress has been made
in the recent past. Many examples exist of men and women learning to work harmoniously together. For all the negative judgments
expended on American women as too aggressive, and American
men as too juvenile and weak, at their best, individual men and
women have risen above stereotypes and rejected the confusing
roles thrust upon them by our culture.

The idea that women do the feeling and that men do the
thinking is painful in its stupidity. At its cartoonlike worst, anyone
should wonder how reason and feeling can ever stay isolated from

each other. But the stupid fiction continues. Thus, the continuing frustration, anger, and misunderstandings between male and female. It is an ugly thing to watch. It goes against every good in humanity and destroys the capacity for self-improvement.

Men and women are meant to work together. They complete one another. Each brings a balancing wholeness, a complementary energy.

I have always been fascinated by the differences between the male and female energy and how this balance of energy affects our personalities and capacity to grow. The basic differences in physical form are obvious—they are an expression of nature's purpose. But the male energy, it seems to me, has more to do with extending out, reaching out to the world, while the female energy gathers in, has more to do with taking in and nourishing.

In Theo's description of the 5th Dimensional life-style between men and women, the necessity of balancing their respective energies is constantly emphasized. The balancing of these "sex" energies will play a vital part in finding one's true higher self.

The energy within each of you is both male and female, and it is a balancing on all levels that is being achieved now with the coming of the 5th Dimension. We have spoken of energy being changed, the electromagnetic field altering, and the energy coming forth throughout the body as the 5th Dimension energy shift is felt. This is to assist in balancing the right and left brain, the male and female energy, for a greater clarity and understanding. But there are many alternatives here.

Do not be addicted to being right. That will help in assisting the balancing of energies. Release the self-righteousness. That is important for both male and female, yes? Males must know that they have as much responsibility for this change as females. To have balance, to have completeness and wholeness in relationships, is the responsibility of both sexes.

Communication is also important. When a woman speaks to a man, she speaks from the heart, from the emotions. The man hears this from his understanding of the world and his own experience. And his experience is of the outer world, hers is of the inner world. So even words can be misconstrued, do you understand? Communication is a most important first step. Check if you are hearing, if you are listening and understanding the other's intention and inner meaning. Learn receptive listening.

In the 5th Dimension, relationships must be created wherein the trust of one's self blossoms forth. As you develop this trust in the totality of your being, you allow yourself to become vulnerable and to accept one another. Do you see? For in this comes strength—taking on the responsibility for your personal learning and also openly supporting the experience of others. Then the release of judgment comes, yes?

But first the anger has to come out, and many are angry now. You will see this come to the forefront. There will be upsets, and communication will be angry at times. It is part of the release of the 5th Dimension energies that are at hand.

Then do we need to accept the anger and support the release of it?

You need to embrace it, to acknowledge it, to love it. All must be done. All of the emotions should be brought to the forefront, not put aside or put away and subconsciously made untrue. It is the embracing of the emotions that brings release and freedom, yes? It is part of loving the self, is it not?

Be clear in your own being, for being fully present with your self creates a peacefulness, a balance within, a nonattachment, a nonjudgment, in which you can interact in an unconditionally loving way. Do you see?

Theo, what can we do to help our emotional release . . . to help us deal with our anger, frustrations, and anxieties? How can we create an emotional release in ourselves when we experience anger and resentment with the opposite sex?

Using the breath is extremely important. This helps to center the self, to calm the emotions, to cleanse the self. Drinking clear water is important as well.

During the energy changing of the 5th Dimension it is important to do what grounds the self—for there will be much feeling out of balance, many releases in minor illnesses such as the common cold. These are forms of expression within the physical structure that are being released.

Diet is important, especially for balancing the physical structure of the being. Soaking in water is also important. Swimming is an expression that shifts and clears the polarities. Stretching, such as yoga practice, is also good.

Using the breath also clears the energy field of the body. Water is extremely important, yes. It helps calm you, helps the being avoid short-circuiting. It is a cushion for the cells, and it calms the body and mind.

Theo, you have spoken about what women have to share with men in carrying their inner vision, their intuition, into the world. What is it that men have to share with women in the 5th Dimension?

Men have their vision, but in a different way. The men have grounding in the world. They have a knowingness of the earth, a knowing of nature and survival. They are the protectors, the hunters, the providers—that has been their way. In essence, women have done the same thing, but it has been taught them by men. It is a natural gift of strength, of balancing and understanding, that each individual has within. Both men and women have all the components necessary already. Women have known this truth, and the men are now coming into the awareness that all is within them as well. Greater sharing is the important result of this knowledge. The 5th Dimension will bring this awareness on more quickly.

You have mentioned the female and male anger, and the differences concerning the male and female energy and their developing roles at this time. What started

the anger of the female toward the male? At what point
did it begin?

*It began in what is now designated as the 3rd Dimension,
when the male power and ego set aside the female energy.
It was the time of the Essenes, a time in which the women
were leaders; but they were set aside as the men took
control in a political way. The anger began in this period
of time.*

*Today you will find many females incarnate who
have experienced the Essene times, so these vibrations
have been carried forward. It is here that millennia of
karma, the generational patterns of many, are being
changed now. It is in this time that women see the men
as weak and ineffectual. This is not the first time in your
civilization that this has happened. Early on in Egypt, as
well, this occurred when females were discounted.*

*But this is being resolved in the 5th Dimension pe-
riod, for there is no longer time for such competitiveness.
It is a time of coming together and balance, of unification
of all humankind.*

*In this time of change, the independent individual
utilizing personal power in the world will promote
growth between male and female. It is also important in
this 5th Dimensional time to understand that you should:*

Share the knowing as it comes about,
Not be fearful of personal power,
Not sit in judgment of one another,
Not withhold information,
Not manipulate with your knowing—or power.

*It is a time for all beings to live in truth, for each has
much to share with the other.*

One of my clients had many questions about male/female
relationships because she was going through a divorce, and it
affected, she thought, her ability to love.

**Theo, I wonder how the emotion of love—especially if
you have loved someone enough to marry him or her—**

can turn to nonfeeling or even hate? I already have
enough fear of rejection in relationships, and fear falling in love, so seeing this happen in a divorce has made
it a hundred times worse.

*Understand that relationships are transformational. Each
person has a different, independent reason for committing
to another. One cannot judge another's experience, but
know that each person draws unto him- or herself exactly
what is needed for his or her own growth. Just because
one personality does not complete a marriage—as you
think of it in your mind—for the entirety of a lifetime,
does not reflect your life. This type of relationship may
not be for you, may not be your type of experience, and
you would have nothing to fear.*

Theo, you speak of unconditional love of oneself, that
this love is not *selfish*, but *selfless*. But when one acts on
this belief and tries to actualize the truth of one's self,
one often runs into people who misunderstand and
misinterpret the action. This is difficult, especially
when it happens in more intimate relationships. How
can you communicate to people that such actions take
place out of a love for the universe, rather than denial
or rejection of them personally? How can that communication be lovingly expressed so that it meets with a
positive reaction?

*Not being addicted to being right is important. It is also
important to acknowledge what is true for the self—and
to allow an unconditional love of self to come forth. But
you are all individuals and will not always agree with one
another's viewpoint. If you all thought the same, you
would be bored.*

*But when you cannot convince another, then you
must radiate what is your true being. Share that, your
true self, for it is a gift to the world. If there are those close
to you who are threatened, then they are responsible for
their own feelings.*

Each being is totally responsible for what he or she creates in his or her experience and feelings.

You must look carefully when you wish to protect another and ask: Whom are you protecting? It is usually the self, is it not? Trust that if you stay in the truth of yourself, you will speak out and communicate the truth. It may not be liked at first, but it will be respected if it is given from the heart.

Other questioners were concerned about relationships and marriage. Some even asked whether they had been in a relationship in a previous life. And, as with most of the other questions dealing with relationships, Theo emphasized several key points:

- Living in the present moment
- Trusting the self
- Balance within the self
- Acceptance and openness
- Nonjudgmental, nonmanipulative love
- Individualism and responsibility for all one's actions

Theo, what will marriage, or being together, in the 5th Dimension be like?

The form of marriage, and the legalities of your society, will continue much the same, but the commitment within relationships will change. The commitment will be of the heart, of sharing, of common experience and lifework. Independent individuals will come forth and share their strengths in their relationships. There is no longer only the passive and the dominant roles. That is where manipulation occurs. Relationships in the 5th Dimension will involve the coming together of peers, of those who are equal in strength and certainty within their selves. This is important, not only for individuals, but for the planet. The planet is in need of this balancing created by humans existing in love. Do you see?

SOUL MATES

Theo, you have said that there are people who are soul mates, and that when they get together in a relationship it is a real kind of "electrical" bonding. Was there a single energy in the beginning that split into two parts? Were they literally one?

Yes, it begins as that.

Are these two parts identical energies, or are they balanced energies, much as you think of male and female as being opposite energies?

They are part of the whole, are they not? Complete, yes . . . a wholeness. It is identical when one is balance to the wholeness, do you understand? And there is positive-negative energy produced . . . then the coming together completes the wholeness, yes?

You have also said that soul mates do not necessarily choose to stay together, one of the reasons being that the relationship would not work within this world. Why is this?

There are times that it would work, and times that it would not, for the intensity is so great that there can be friction. Know that there is a continuum of balance, and that when the energy is embodied in a human being, there are other issues that the individual must work on— or he or she would not be embodied on the earth. Do you understand? Many have thought of soul mates as being a perfect union, and in truth it is, yes. But in acting out their roles in this life, there will be imperfections. Remember that you are humans.

Soul mates do not necessarily have the same life work, then?

That is correct. It is not necessary. Some do, however, for it is individual.

So the term "soul mate" has more to do with the attraction, and finding of each other, than it does with finding your perfect other half to spend your life with?

That is the romantic view, is it not? But it is not romance that we speak of here. Not that it could not be romantic, but that is not the purpose of the soul's embodiment: the purpose is the balance of energy, do you see?

The balance of energy does not mean that there is a balance of intellect, and other human qualities. For each individual has particular leanings that he or she chooses when embodying. At times these choices are not compatible with the balanced energy of the mate; at times they are, do you understand? This cannot be discussed in general terms, for there is too much that depends on individual choice, too much individual experience here. Remember, the experience is important, not the judgment of it.

Theo, you have talked about how relationships are changing with the coming 5th Dimension energy transformations. How can people use these energies to deepen and strengthen their relationships?

Communication is most important. There must also be an acceptance of one another's thought and beliefs—and not a sitting in judgment of one another. Also, a release of judgment and the allowing of full discussion of each person's expectations will help. Expectations cannot be met unless they are voiced and understood, yes?

This time of the 5th Dimension will be a release of manipulation in relationships: This can no longer work in the new energy that comes forth in this time. Manipulation is a part of what is fear . . . and a lack of identification of the self. The new energy now brings forth an attune-

*ment to the self, an acknowledgment of the outer world,
and an allowing of vulnerability.*

*Old forms cannot work anymore in the 5th Dimen-
sion. Old patterns of interchanging male/female energy
that have existed for centuries must change. Equality and
the sense of individual energy is what will bring people
together. There will be a coming together to share, to
empower one another. Do you understand?*

SEX: THE POWER BEHIND THE PROBLEM

Theo, you talk of male and female energy: how will
these changing energy patterns in the 5th Dimension
affect a couple's sexual relationship?

*A finer attunement within the structure of the individual,
within the balancing of the male and female energy, will
come about. There will be a sharing of that energy, a
movement toward completeness within the sexual relationship. There has been manipulation, has there not? An
expression of this manipulation has been within the sexual act. This has occurred for centuries, but it is now about
to change.*

How will the change occur?

*As individuals become more finely attuned to what is
whole within them, become more sensitive to their partner, a oneness in the relationship will occur.*

*Sex is an expression of the spirit. As the being be-
comes attuned to the 5th Dimension energies, a finer understanding and sensitivity will come about, do you
understand?*

As this attunement to the 5th Dimension energies becomes more acute, how can individuals use these energies more effectively? Especially in their sexual
relationships?

Communication on all levels is necessary, not only verbal, but even in meditation where there is an energy exchange, do you see?

You speak of attuning one's energy to one's partner. How can couples fine-tune their energies when they come together in a sexual union?

Intention, attitude, it is best found in the meditational process of attunement.

A change of intention and attitude? That is what is required to enhance sexual union?

Yes, it is to look within the heart at the intention and attitude that one brings to the sexual act.

Then couples in the 5th Dimension will be using sex as part of their personal evolution toward enlightenment? How can couples facilitate this evolution in their sexual life? Are there any special methods you would recommend?

To meditate together. To clear the consciousness. To focus upon the awareness of the body during meditation and sex. To experience the moment fully, yes?

In your civilization the sexual act has been a way of controlling personalities, has it not? It has been restrictive. Control and manipulation, often of the self, have been common—expressive of emotional blockage and feelings of fear. This is one personality controlling another.

But the sexual act is of love, the essence of love; it acknowledges humanness and enhances those in love. Many use the sexual act to express their anger and fear as well as their love, yes?

But in this time of change many are drawn into relationships in order to advance more rapidly. You will understand and accept the power within faster during the 5th Dimension.

*Sex does not hinder you; properly used, it enhances
you. Sexual energy is sometimes called kundalini energy;
it is energy that allows balance within the physical structure and enhances the flow of energy within the chakra
system. The kundalini energy, sexual energy, enhances
meditation and brings forth enlightenment—especially
when done with a loving partner.*

5TH DIMENSIONAL SEX

In the western religious tradition the body has often been viewed
as something evil, or, at best, as something that should be con-
quered and then denied. But if the body is simply an aspect of
spirit, and the sexual energies an expression of that spiritual force,
then bodily sensation and sexual energy become a unified power
that can move the self toward fulfillment. This is the goal that
Theo describes as coming forth now in the time of the 5th Dimension.

You cannot feel another's body if you cannot feel your own;
you cannot love another unless you first accept and love yourself.
Once such acceptance of yourself comes, then an openness and
acceptance of others follows. This is the path to destroying the
strange and exhausting subject-object sexual games most people
play.

Everyone engages in sex for different reasons—some for sensation, others for power, still others for security or emotional reasons. Most people experience sex on the sensation level, for
consciousness during sex is usually focused on the physical feelings you are having—especially during orgasm. Your partner's
consciousness is probably also focused on these feeling states.

Sex, even when sought out as an act of love and affection,
finds each person using the other—to one degree or another—as
an object, even if only an object that is creating sensation. There
is a subject-object separateness, the power of ego and personality,
that keeps lovers apart. Sex is experienced as something happening to yourself, and at the best of times as something done in
combination with a partner. The drama of the physical union is
therefore as limited as your own personality and capacity for enjoyment.

But there are other forms of sexual union, other ways of join-ing with another in love. Theo often speaks of oneness, of union, of moving beyond the limits of one's personality into an experi-ence of wholeness. This advice applies to sex as well as psycholog-ical growth—in fact, it is all part of the single continuum of an individual's self-fulfillment.

Sex is possible without the subject-object separateness, where it is perceived as something happening to you, but where *you* are the happening itself. In such a sexual moment the sense of self is not lost but enhanced by the experience of true union, by a con-sciousness of total identification with things outside of yourself.

But how does one begin to break down these barriers between lovers? How does one change one's attitude, open oneself to being vulnerable and totally giving? These seem difficult challenges in their own right, and then to add the dynamics of sex, and the love relationship between male and female to them, makes the whole task seem impossibly complex. But it isn't. As Theo has mentioned many times, these changes are all part of God's purpose and are being aided by the energy shift of the world into the 5th Dimen-sion. And there are definite steps we can take to help ourselves make these 5th Dimension transitions. *This is 5th Dimension sexual union.*

Sex, as described by Theo and as it will be transformed in the 5th Dimensional world of tomorrow, exists as a form of human consciousness that reflects a kind of open attention or "contem-plation." A meditation! In short, sex is experienced during a mind-body unification within meditation with a loving partner.

The sexual act is an expression of enlightenment and bal-ance. It becomes a meditation, for during sex the purpose is to be aware of the spirit. The sexual union is an act of being in the moment, which is an act of meditation. . . .

When Theo talks about balance and sexual equality, it does not mean a "pure" male or a "pure" female energy. These are social and religious classifications. Sexual fulfillment is rather achieved through the woman realizing her masculinity through the man and the man realizing his femininity through the woman.

A finer attunement of the balancing between the male and female energy will come about, a sharing of that energy, a movement toward completeness within the sexual relationship.

BEING FULLY IN THE SEXUAL MOMENT

Oddly, desire for the intense sensations of sex—or even love— often deprive one of the opportunity to become totally involved in the *immediacy* of the experience, in the "here and now" of each moment. For example, if a couple is dining together, and the man, even while he seems attentive and involved, is thinking of going to bed with the woman later, he is not really there—his consciousness is in the future, picturing the moment when they will make love. This anticipation destroys his capacity to enjoy the moment together and denies him the pleasure of experiencing the other person completely.

And even if his anticipations become true, he will not be satisfied, because he will continually be caught up in the future. Let's say the couple get along and end up together in bed. If the man has not learned to stop anticipating and cannot control his consciousness from moving into the future, he will continually miss the full enjoyment of the moment. Suppose he is kissing the woman, but his consciousness is on the next step, perhaps touching her neck or breasts. He will not be able to fully enjoy the sensuality of the kiss himself or become completely involved in the sharing of the kiss with his partner.

His anticipation drives him on, and he succeeds in caressing her breasts; but again he is not completely involved in the act but anticipating the next stage. He moves on to caress her genitals, but again he cannot take complete pleasure in that moment because he is anticipating entering her. And even then he cannot enjoy the moment because his consciousness is partially in the future: He will be anticipating orgasm. And only then, if the orgasm is powerful enough, may he forget himself and focus on the here and now. Yet that is not because the man has learned to live in the moment, but because an orgasm is such an overwhelming feeling that his consciousness probably wouldn't be strong enough to be anywhere else. He becomes dominated by the sensations of orgasm. It is probably one of the few times when he is capable of being totally in the present moment. Time and again this sequence of incomplete feelings could happen to the man and he would not learn to enjoy every moment of sex as a complete, fulfilling whole in itself. Obviously, the same insensitivity can be true of women.

Then, of course, there is the traditional "bodice-ripper novel" description of sex. These peculiar and warped descriptions are not hard to find, for they are drowning in clichés and excesses. In one popular book on the sexual experience of women, the author describes the excitement of intercourse and the approach of a climax with such excessive language that the value of the whole experience is diminished.

This is it. This is the moment of ecstasy when a woman soars along a Milky Way among stars all her own. This is the high mountaintop of love, of which poets sing. Her whole being is a full orchestra playing the fortissimo of a glorious symphony.

This is supposedly a description of the highest sexual experience a virginal bride can attain. Is it any wonder that sex in our society is a confusing experience for both men and women? Or that disappointment is common?

The point of all this is that, unfortunately, many common misconceptions and downright silliness are being sold to the public as a *true* description of the ideal sexual union. And sadly, this kind of confusion is not limited to romance novels and popular books on sex posing as "expert" descriptions of human sexuality. The tradition of confusion goes back as far as human history itself.

"This woman whom thou gavest me, she tempted me and I did eat," complains Adam when talking with God about his wife's behavior—this is perhaps history's first domestic argument. But at the same time Adam is accusing his wife of seducing him; he is projecting his seed, his passion into her. How many times have we seen this particular piece of male confusion: Woman as seducer, and at the same time, woman as object of desire. Rarely is she seen as a partner in sexuality, as a sharer of the other's passion and involvement in the beauty of the senses.

And for the woman an equally confused role exists. Females

are forced into paradoxical role-playing. She is supposed to remain open and receptive to the male initiative, yet also remain demure and virginal—an inexperienced creature who yet, mysteriously, can appreciate with abandon all the male's loving lust. How's that for confusing?

Role-playing! For centuries men and women have been forced into confusing roles, so it is no wonder that manipulation in relationships is as common as sex itself.

Human beings are not objects to be manipulated, but are part of a *process*, a living, dynamic process of life. No role or manipulation of one's partner can ever satisfy the sexual energy within the human spirit. Yes, sexual energy within the spirit. It is a spiritual force, a power that can move an individual to an explosion of enlightenment.

On its simplest level, if we think of spirituality as being an awareness of the inner identity of all things, then sexuality would become a major part of the spiritual experience.

Yet, as Theo has said many times during channeling sessions, sexual energy *is* spiritual—not simply a part of the spiritual experience. It is enlightenment!

Theo, in our society the traditional purpose of the sexual union has been to procreate. Will the energy shift in the 5th Dimension change the purpose of sex from the traditional procreation and pleasure to an expression of enlightenment?

Yes, it is an expression of enlightenment and balance; and that will be effective globally, for it is energy, do you understand?

Then the fine-tuning of sexual energy during lovemaking is truly an act of enlightenment?

It is, yes. The sexual act becomes a meditation, for during sex the purpose is to be aware of the spirit, yes? And aware of other, of the partner, yes? So it will not be that one is in the past and the other is in the future. Both are in the moment of the experience. So the sexual union is

an act of being in the moment, which is an act of medi-
tation leading to enlightenment, see?

It is a continuum. It is an altered state of conscious-
ness that is achieved within the sexual act.

When sex is set apart as a means of control, a good or evil thing, a black-and-white issue, then it can't work in relation to the rest of our life. It becomes a duty, a role-playing part of one's sexuality rather than an expression of the whole person. Sex as only a compartment of one's life means that it can be labeled: The compartment can be labeled anything an individual, or a group, or society, wants it to be. It is an unspiritual force, separate from the universal principles that move life on to its highest evolved state.

Sex will remain a problem in our society as long as it remains isolated, divorced from the total feeling of love and sensuality.

To avoid this, we must first allow ourselves to be spontaneous, to react openly and joyfully to our own sexuality. This also means involving the whole play of inner feeling in our sensual response to the world. Only as we can learn to accept without grasping, to be free in mind (consciousness) as well as in body, can the fullest play of sensuality be open. When this state of spiritual involvement, openness, and spontaneity is reached, we are freed from sex being merely now good and now bad, now guiltily inhibited and now lustful, now controlling and now surrendering.

In fact, it is spiritual involvement and spontaneity in sex that will eliminate the exaggerated expectations so many of us indulge in.

As long as sex is played out as an object-subject game, the aftermath of intercourse will be anxiety, guilt, or disappointment. The reason is that we grasp for sensation, for an isolated, compartmentalized moment of intense orgasm, which makes sex a burden rather than a gift. For if orgasm is a goal, then assessing whether you've reached the goal or not, whether the effort to reach the goal was good or bad, will dominate your consciousness —and influence your sensual involvement—and you will not be fully in the sexual moment.

On the other hand, if your involvement in sex transcends the isolated goals and/or "effects" of sensation, and is not grasped at but accepted as a total and immediate experience, then a full and spontaneous immersion of your "self" in the "other" occurs. Sex becomes a transcendent involvement in something larger and more powerful than the self. In this kind of sexual involvement, the orgasm is not a sudden ending, but rather a fulfilling expansion of your total being; it moves you into a transcendent and satisfying peace that lingers on and on.

I must make clear that the kind of spontaneity Theo recommends as necessary to move sex toward an exalted state of consciousness is not the same thing as a promiscuous breaking loose from all self-discipline or sense of restraint. And also, it is not the so-called "healthy" sexuality of an animal or biological "release." Sexual spontaneity in the sense Theo describes it within 5th Dimensional experience is rather an open immersion of the self in love, which incorporates the total being—sensuality, sexuality, and consciousness.

In effect, Theo is telling us that life is a mystery that is meant to be simply experienced, and not a mystery that needs to be solved like a problem.

Western science, unfortunately, will not help us understand our very natural human sexuality—at least not so long as most things in life are defined as an expression of oral or anal eroticism, of infantile incestuousness. I, for one, cannot imagine that all human beings are reduced to an anal or oral fixation of one sort or another. It seems to me that such theories lead to rigid and harsh judgments about human behavior. In such a scheme of things there is little room for change or personal evolution. You are free to alter your destiny in precisely the degree you realize your inner self as the author of your life—and this goes especially for your sex life. Once these truths are understood, then you will be able to experience "being fully in the sexual moment."

Sexual Exercises

Let's get rid of one of the worst misconceptions right away. A question too frequently asked is: Are there any special positions one should practice?

Positions are irrelevant. As Theo has repeated time and again, the important thing is *attitude*. Consciousness is crucial—where the point of awareness is at any given moment. Be concerned first about the position of your mind, not your body. This is why Theo recommends a form of mutual meditation/sexual union; it is the thought that is important, and thought is directed by learning meditation in combination with your sexual partner.

At first this may seem strange because most books dealing with meditation avoid sex—and any physical pleasure—as strictly off-limits. Why? Because most of the early religious groups who practiced meditation saw sex as a distraction from their spiritual pursuit. The ultimate aim of meditation has traditionally been attaining enlightenment, a kind of cosmic consciousness.

Some modern teachers, such as Gopi Krishna, aren't afraid to speak out about the "higher sexual energy" that can be attained with spiritual sex. Gopi Krishna feels that sexual energy is the power fueling creative genius and religious ecstasy. When individuals attempt to deny or alter the sexual energies, which they do when they play the subject-object game or manipulate their partners, then the very biological and spiritual basis of our lives is subverted. Psychological and physical problems are then inevitable.

In the early stages of meditation there are sometimes erotic sensations in the pubic region, and the male organ experiences powerful involuntary erections.

Gopi Krishna and other modern teachers are finally beginning to recognize that the energy released in meditation is the same energy fueling the sex drive. Theo emphasizes this continually—energy is energy and powers the life force whether it be biological or spiritual.

In the *early stages* of sexual meditations, partners see each other not as objects but on a broader, nonsexual level. When your consciousness is freed from seeing your partner as an object for your sexual enjoyment, you will experience him or her on a deeper level of being. Then the sexual act takes on a deeper meaning, and your whole person becomes involved in the lovemaking, not simply your genitals . . . or your self-image . . . or your ego . . . or whatever kind of role you've created for yourself.

The way to begin this process of sexual evolution is to create a sense of intimacy, to explore each other's bodies sensually without thinking of the sex act itself. And even in the later stages, when penetration may occur, the direction should be toward experiencing the "wholeness" of the moment, not toward reaching a climax. The end result of this effort will be that you begin to feel your partner more completely . . . and that it is simply enough to *be* with him or her. The moment is complete . . . nothing more is needed, and especially not rushing toward a climax.

The key to being successful in sexual meditation is *not trying* to make something happen—and equally, *not trying* to make something *not* happen! It can be achieved only when your consciousness is focused on the full enjoyment of the now moment in every exquisite detail.

When doing the following sexual meditation exercises, you should not worry about any particular position. In some cases, when a specific position is necessary for greater ease in breath control, it will be made clear. And while positions are not all that important, *where your consciousness is focused is vital.* When these meditations are done properly, sex is experienced on an entirely different level; deep feelings of love are foremost in your awareness, sexual sensations are vibrated throughout the whole body in a continuous rhythm, and the sense of a separate self experiencing pleasure with a partner is completely absent.

EXERCISE ONE (Introduction to Sexual Meditation)

There are many ways to begin sexual meditation, but perhaps the simplest is to sit facing each other, relaxed, and with no expectations. Simply look into each other's eyes without any desire to touch or do anything more. Do not stare or look directly into your partner's eyes. The point is not to degenerate into a staring contest or any ego-personality games.

Let your gaze rest between your partner's eyes. You will obviously still see your partner's face, so be aware of it. This is a person you feel strongly enough about that you want to make love. Let this realization fill you: love the eyes, the nose, the lips, the face, of your partner. Begin to focus on him or her as simply being there—an individual you care deeply for.

After a short while you may begin to see a circle of light at the point between the eyes. When it appears, gently hold on to the image—*don't grasp at it*—and focus on the light. Your partner's face may even begin to alter, to change into exquisitely beautiful, glowing images—or, alternatively, into ugly, deformed images. Don't hold on to any of these perceptions; let them pass away as simply part of the vital energies of life being rapidly exposed to you. Let your love and acceptance of your partner dominate your awareness.

As you succeed in this, a sense of oneness will grow as you just sit and look into the face of your partner.

As this sense of acceptance, love, and oneness grows between you, other things may start to happen. For example, an urge to touch, to simply caress the glowing skin of your beloved may become strong, and your hand may slowly raise and touch. From here allow yourself to progress, following your heart and the loving urges spurring you spontaneously on.

As sexual meditation continues, partners often find themselves caressing in a highly sensual, even nonsexual, way. Let it happen, for this is the path to complete union. But do not rush to intercourse; do not create expectations with any gesture—let things happen slowly and naturally. Feel the urge strongly first, then allow your body to respond, to answer the call to reach out and touch.

Often you may find yourself and your partner in a position lying next to each other, still looking into each other's faces; or in a position where the man is lying on his back and the woman is sitting astride, facing him. In both positions you can continue to gaze into each other's eyes, your hands free to explore and love each other's bodies.

This position is helpful to the rhythm of sexual meditation because the woman is able to moderate the degree of direct genital stimulation so that arousal proceeds in a mutually satisfying way. It is not unknown for couples to sit joined together in this way for an hour or more without reaching a climax. This particular phase of the meditation is very important, for it helps free your consciousness from *expecting* something to happen. Expectations are reduced, hopefully completely! Further, this moment of the meditation allows you and your partner to become totally involved in the here-and-now experience. Your bodies are joined together in the most intimate possible way; you are still looking lovingly into each other's eyes and touching every conceivable part of your bodies. The senses are heightened because they are part of the focus of your consciousness.

If the penis becomes soft in this position, it doesn't really matter because it will still be held within the vagina. The full, loving contact will remain. Your involvement in each other will remain. If the male feels uncomfortable because he's lost his erection then he is still too bogged down in performance games. He should reestablish sensory contact with his partner, renew concentration on the face and form of his partner. Forget performance, and focus on contact, on the immediate sensations . . . and feel how perfect the moment is.

When your consciousness is no longer focused on performance or even the sensations of sex, when your consciousness is totally involved in simply *being* with your partner, then you are beginning to learn how to use sexual meditation. You are free from the grasping, from reaching to fulfill expectations, free from the trap of disappointment. You become able to flow with whatever sensation or feeling or impression comes to you. In short, you can fully enjoy the moment.

The most significant lesson this meditation teaches is that your consciousness, your awareness, your *thought,* creates the reality of your world.

This is the message of Theo and the coming of the 5th Dimension. Thought is reality; it is the creative power of your life, and how you use thought determines each moment of your experience. Sexual meditation is invaluable precisely because it reinforces this truth—your directed consciousness can even be used to enhance and liberate your sexual life. In effect, sexual meditation becomes simply one more way to accelerate your journey into higher consciousness.

Couples in the 5th Dimensional world, in their sexual unions, will be using sex as part of their personal evolution toward enlightenment. . . . Sexual energy is purple, and it is used for enlightenment. . . . Sex is an expression of spirit, do you understand? As the being becomes at-

tuned to the 5th Dimension energies, finer understanding
and sensitivity will come about, yes?
  Sex is an expression of enlightenment and balance.
. . . The sexual union is an act of being in the moment,
which is an act of meditation leading to enlightenment,
see?

Meditation during sexual union is deceptively simple on the
face of it. The man is lying on his back with the woman on top—
as just described in Exercise One. You can just as easily lie side by
side, meditating and gazing into each other's eyes. The difference
between sexual meditation and normal sexual activity is in the
use of your mind. Most people use the sex act for some form of
relief—relief from the tensions of the day, from anxiety, from
deep-seated personal problems, to enhance self-image—from any
number of socially generated ills.

Sexual meditation is directly opposite from this externally directed energy. It is not to relieve or direct your energy outward, to
get rid of the pressure of the day: Sexual meditation is meant to
contain energy, to recycle energy within yourself and your partner.

Ordinary orgasms seem like a mad explosion of energy, so
afterward, relieved, you can roll over and go to sleep. Orgasm as
tranquilizer.

Orgasms achieved during a sexual meditation are regenerat-
ing. You feel revitalized; you have both become generators of
positive energy. Nothing is lost or expended; you feel radiant with
new energy. This is why during a sexual meditation the male can
maintain an erection for hours, allowing the two of you to be in a
deep embrace for as long as you wish without ejaculation. If, by
chance, the beginning meditator feels his erection beginning to
leave, only a small movement for a short time—a loving renewal
of contact—can reestablish the erection. Then relaxation and re-
focus on oneness dominates again.

Ordinary sex, precisely because it is goal-oriented, is hurried,
frantic, full of wild rushing. Obviously much is missed during this
kind of sex. With sexual meditation you and your partner are
relaxed, generating energy between you so you do not become

tired. Ordinary sex exhausts: Meditation sex vitalizes. With ordinary sex you cannot repeat the act too often—you must rest between. With sexual meditation you can make love as often as you like.

Unlike instant coffee, instant oatmeal, and instant gratification in our society, sex cannot be instant. It cannot be rushed. The more "instant" it becomes the more exhausted and disappointed everyone is. Sex should be unhurried. Not lazy, not uninvolved, but actively participating in a relaxed way. You are simply not rushing because you have nowhere to go, no orgasm to reach for, no self-image to reassert, nothing to prove to yourself or anyone else. You have nowhere to go because you are totally involved in the experience of the moment.

EXERCISE TWO (For More Advanced Sexual Meditators)

Relaxed sexual meditation is, basically, combining forms of sensory-focused meditation with the sex act. But it is important as you move into the more complicated sexual meditations to remember there is no hurry, nothing to prove, nowhere to go. *Involve yourself in the experience of the moment.* That is the key!

After meditating together as described earlier, join the genitals together and continue the meditation. Focus on the genital contact. For the woman, she can become conscious of the male penis within her—focus on that; try to experience your partner's sensation; become one with his sensation of being inside you. Feel the moment as he is feeling it. Try to become one with his feelings. What is it like to be erect?

For the male, the same focus will be helpful. Imagine what your partner is feeling. What is it like to have a penis within you? Focus on that reality as you gaze into your loved one's face. Feel her reality, the warmth, the texture, the pulsing life all around you.

When you feel deeply involved in your partner's sensations, move your awareness to other parts of the body. Feel your partner's legs, back, shoulders, arms and hands, neck and head. Feel your partner's skin where it touches yours and then live his or her experience. Feel your awareness roam over your own body, joining the sensations of your body and your partner's body. Allow your body sensing to flow *into* your partner's body, sensing the whole of your partner's body as part of your own. You are joined; you are two parts made into a single unit. Accept the feelings and sensations you intuit about your partner's body as your own. Let your awareness flow through both your bodies at once. Touching your partner's eyes is touching your eyes; touching your partner's heart with your awareness is touching your own heart. See yourself as having one body with four arms, two hearts, two heads. You are a unique single unit.

If your position allows it, touch your foreheads together with gentle pressure; feel your foreheads merge, and see yourself as bodies merging together, melting into one unique form. As your foreheads melt together let your minds join as well. Let your inner worlds meld together, your mental and emotional viewpoints become one.

Believe it or not, after a time the distinctions between you and your partner's consciousness begin to fade, and a kind of mutual awareness develops: "Is this your idea or mine?" Eventually even that question becomes irrelevant. A peculiar kind of mutual body awareness develops, and you can *feel* the sensual energies of your partner—or, at this stage, you yourself begin to feel them as if they were your own.

As your senses meld and your consciousness seems to expand to include your partner's, a vibration begins to build. Sometimes it becomes so strong, it seems that the single unit of you and your partner might explode with the intensity. Accept what is happening; let the vibration take you; let it build, and do not pull back fearful of its power. By pulling back, you recede into separateness again—the defensive individual protecting the self!

Allow the intermingling to continue; let whatever occurs continue; acknowledge without judgment all sensation. Do not even think How interesting, or Boy, this is great. No judgment, no critical thinking—simply accept it all.

At this point your separate identities are so intermingled that the quality of communication alters once again. Everything becomes a kind of self-communicating, all within the singleness of being of your united selves. The recognition comes that love is everywhere, love is everything. You and your partner are simply a point of consciousness in a universe of consciousness sustained by love. Love is really self-love; it is the self loving everything and being loved in return, all the same, ultimately.

In this state there is a quality of endless waiting and a feeling of overwhelming well-being. It is not orgasm as such, but rather a euphoric state of union with all things.

The vibration ceases and is overtaken by a thrilling stillness, a silence encompassing the universe. In this form you are a cosmic couple, a single living electric reality. The mind is not diminished as in normal orgasm, but enhanced, expanded to incorporate everything. The magnetic world around you is no longer separate but part of you, and you are it.

As mystical and obscure as this may sound, it is as close to a description of the experience as can be offered. How does one explain a candle flame dissolved in the sun yet retaining its ultimate soul, or the sudden, explosive exaltation of a raindrop falling into an ocean and becoming an integral, significant part of a great universal whole. It is, after all, indescribable.

Eventually the cosmic couple will separate into two entities again. Your bodies should remain very still. No abrupt ending. Allow yourself to remain motionless until your minds individualize again, until your sense of body becomes completely your own again. Wait . . . wait . . . and wait some more before you try to separate your bodies. When it is comfortable, move your bodies slowly as you disengage. The sensation is like being reborn again into the world. But once you have experienced this dissolution of self into another, once you have experienced your consciousness become one with the universe, you will never be the same again. You will have experienced the 5th Dimension.

6

Children:
A View from the
5th Dimension

Theo, I wonder why it takes a child about a second to learn what it takes most of us a lifetime to learn—how to be in tune with ourselves spiritually.

It is society that has told you that you do not know . . . (that blocks greater awareness of the spirit within). The child is well aware of it . . . the child within you is aware of it . . . and can learn immediately.

Jesus saw children who were being suckled, and he said to his disciples: "These children who are being suckled are like those who enter the Kingdom."

His disciples then asked Jesus: "Shall we then, being children, enter the Kingdom?"

Jesus, like every other master-teacher, taught that children offer a unique vision of the world. In fact, rather than "we," the adults, being their teachers, we can learn from children if we but open our vision. Children can be the vehicle for great teachings on our journey to higher consciousness. A child lives in the here and now, in the stream of consciousness as yet unaffected by the rational mind and by the limiting restrictions of our society. A child responds, fully and spontaneously, to each new situation as life unfolds.

A child reflects the level of consciousness—and awareness— that surrounds him or her. The thoughts and actions of adults in their world create a response that forms children's reality as adults. This makes the responsibility of parents toward their child's development enormous. And not only parents' actions but thoughts as well can create a warm, loving environment for the child to reflect in his or her own character. When you are full of anxiety and tension, the child obviously picks up on it. Children are like highly sensitive barometers of the atmosphere emanating from the adults around them. The child takes in all sense-percep- tible vibrations, is fed by them, grows from them; he or she is directly affected by adults' state of being.

It may be a frightening thought—and clearly an awesome responsibility—but your perceptions and attitudes toward your child directly influence how that child develops. If you see your child as a nuisance or a pain in the neck, he or she will become just that. No matter how well masked you think your inner feel- ings may be, images and classifications you attach to a child will be sensed and determine his or her reaction to you.

The child's response to circumstances in the environment come out of his or her own particular unique nature. Each child is a being receiving the world in specific ways determined by their unique abilities for reacting to it. Taint this pure reaction with an adult's anxieties or neuroses, and the child immediately reflects these colorings.

As adults, we can help the child not because he or she is weak or vulnerable, but because of the great creative energies with which each child has been gifted. It is this pure, highly sensitive and responsive energy that needs protection from external inter- ference. If the adult can allow the child a clear path for develop- ment, if as many obstacles to the child's own purity of response as possible can be eliminated, then the child may have a chance to attain full fruition of talent and potential. Otherwise the problems and needs of the child resonate on into adulthood . . . and even affect our adult relationships.

> *It is possible to have a balance in adult relationships when one recognizes that need. When there are difficulties in adult relationships, they are coming from expectations that were unmet as children, and they carry forward into relationships as adults. For, understand, there is a continuum in all relationships; whether it is parent and child, whether it is a man and a woman, whether it is between the self and work, there come into play the patterns of thought that have been set in the mother-father-child triad, do you understand?*
>
> *So there is a continual playing out of the patterns that have been set and the expectations that have been desired. As these are fulfilled or understood, then there can be a completeness. Do you understand?*

But the pattern continues, from generation to generation, until the child is given the freedom to develop without the burdens of its parents and culture being passed on to it. Adults suffer from unanswered needs of childhood, often without recognizing what is required. To suggest that they have a child within who has unmet needs is often considered downright insulting.

The child learns early how to survive and is well aware of the parents' level of emotional maturity and adapts to it. I think that, because we live in such an addictive society, at least 95 percent, if not more, of our families are dysfunctional. These are patterns passed down from generation to generation. The old patterns can no longer work in the 5th Dimension energy shift, and we all now have the opportunity to break out of these molds and have a healthier relationship with our children.

Theo, is it important for us to experience our grief or childhood deprivation and then to let it go?

Experience it, yes. It is a release, is it not? It is also a form of growth, of rebirth, of rejuvenation. There is a choice—

*you can resist it so the pain stays longer, or you can em-
brace the experience and it becomes easier.*

But, of course, the point of all this is that if the child is allowed
fuller expression of emotion, then these repressed feelings need
not become a problem for the adult. Childhood needs resonate on
into adulthood and, according to Theo, affect our adult relationships.

**Theo, if in our childhoods our primary needs are not
met, and in some way as adults we are still needy in
that regard, is it even possible to have healthy adult
relationships without those needs being recognized
and resolved? And how do we go about resolving those
needs?**

*You are all parts of "being," child and adult, male and
female, do you understand? If a child has been deprived,
that child still feels the deprivation as an adult. It must be
acknowledged, do you understand?*

*How is this accomplished? When one has an under-
standing that there exists a child within, a child that still
needs nurturing, there will be a greater listening to the
child. One begins by accepting the child's needs and acknowledging them, as you would a child of your own
who is in need.*

*Many still have the needy child within—abandoned,
discounted, ignored. It is step-by-step that one learns to
nurture the self, to look within; to do that for the inner
child, to listen to it, yes? It is important not to shove the
inner child aside and say that he or she does not count.*

*The intellect of the adult is very strong; it is the one
who sits in judgment, yes? The child is the feelings, is it
not? You would parent your own child; you would nurture it, acknowledge it, love it. That is how this is accomplished.*

With this issue, as with so many others, Theo stresses the
importance of personal responsibility and self-reliance. For even if

there is a nurturing adult relationship, one must still learn to open the self to the inner child and answer his or her needs.

Theo, when we are in a relationship and these feelings from the child come up and are not met, is it then our own responsibility to take care of that child in ourselves rather than depend on help from the relationship?

It is your responsibility, yes. Ultimately you come into the world alone and must learn to nurture your whole being. You will also leave the world alone, will you not? Realize that in a relationship the other personality has his or her own needs. They may or may not be capable of nurturing you in the ways that you wish—so the main nurturing must come from the self. One cannot expect another to fulfill all needs that are within you, do you understand?

The obvious question now arises: If we accept the idea that a needful child exists within each of us, and that we pass the problems of childhood on from generation to generation, then how can we break the pattern? How can we nurture the child within us, answer his or her needs, and, equally important, how can we allow our own children to live free of these problems?

These are large and complex problems, but Theo has touched on some answers that make sense—at least to me. One basic approach is, interestingly enough: "play" . . . an experience we all are familiar with but few actually understand—especially in relation to children and their need to have an outlet for their complex feelings as they grow and mature.

I know that for myself I have always been the adult constantly taking responsibility for everyone else. It is a continuous effort to remain aware of, and to acknowledge, my own child within and not abandon her as I have done so many times in the past. To be more aware of my feelings is difficult because it is easier to care for others than to take care of myself. Does that sound familiar?

Now, as we become more aware of abandoning our own child within, we hopefully will learn not to expect our children to "grow up too soon," and will allow children the freedom to fully express the qualities of playfulness.

Theo has recommended one meditation involving the child within that I have found very helpful. If it is used regularly, you will become much more sensitive to your child within.

Theo, you frequently talk about visualizations and using the imagination. Can you give us an example of using the imagination creatively and how it can help us achieve 5th Dimension consciousness?

Imagination, and using it in visualization, is a creative force. But you must learn to trust it, to allow it to flow freely, allow it to draw the self back to the childlike quality within. The young do not limit their imaginations or their thoughts. It is the adult who has the limitations, yes? So allow the child within to rise; see the self as a child and embrace it, become it. And then the imagination can flow.

Do you do this during a meditation?

Yes, when you are relaxed and in a meditative state. As you are proceeding into the meditation, see the self in the mind as a child, and ask the self at what age the child is. Embrace this child; become him or her. You can even envision yourself in the child's body sitting in meditation. Breathe slowly; feel the open, uncomplicated energy of the child. There will be a lightness about it. This is a meditation that should be continued periodically. Some will have an instantaneous knowing and sensitivity; others will need to experience the child several times. There is no wrong way to this meditation. The process is what is important.

PLAY AND THE CHILD WITHIN

At one of my seminars I remember that during a discussion on children and play, one man said, "I still don't know what play is, but whatever it is, I like it." Indeed, the child in us all also still likes play even if we've traveled too far from the purity of our responses to understand what is happening. Play, or a joyful response to life, is essential for proper growth and spiritual wholeness.

Believe it or not, there are still many parents and teachers who do not consider children's play important. Far more common is an eagerness to give preschool children an academic head start. Multiple programs across the nation are now selling the idea that children can start the hard work of academic learning almost from birth. These people fail to understand why play is so necessary for a child's development, how it provides fantastic opportunities for learning and the building of self-confidence. Fortunately, some psychologists recognize that play is healing, that to "play it out" is a natural self-healing process that childhood allows.

I now realize that I had children so I could have an excuse to play. I could play with them, be silly, have fun. Obviously, it is a sad state of affairs when we feel we need permission to have fun and play.

In fact, Theo has said that the capacity to be as joyful and spontaneous as a child can deeply affect our adult relationships.

When you are in relationship with another, and one child is present and the other may want to come out and play, then there is joy, yes? For each can nurture the other within the playfulness and spontaneity. The joy of the child is important for life, yes?

Play for the child is essential in many areas, for during play skills our ability to have social, emotional, physical, and mental well-being is learned. Play sharpens and deepens the imagination and is even a survival tool for children. It helps children to express and come to terms with many of *their* fears and hurts—for which *they* may not yet have words available for clarifying *their* feelings. Play becomes a vital form of expression—especially without the word-concepts that human beings use to defuse so many tensions.

Through the natural healing power of play, children have the opportunity to cope with—and master—their emotional wounds. Such coping techniques are obviously necessary whenever children encounter traumatic events in their lives—for example, separation from parents, death, etc. The greater the trauma, the greater the need for an effective outlet: Play offers a ready release for these powerful feelings.

Theo often stresses how important it is for us to allow grief or any childhood deprivation full rein by favoring openness to childhood experiences. Allowing these feelings to surface is equivalent to a rebirth.

Remember Theo's answer to an earlier question:

Experience, yes? It is the release, is it not? It is a form of growth, of rebirth, of rejuvenation.

Play begins at birth. Infants immediately begin relating to the world in "play" terms, and their power to teach and nurture is initiated by it. Infants begin to explore—and discover—their mother's and their own body as being the first "toys." And one of the first and most important lessons infants learn is that they are entities *separate* from their mothers. Trauma! How do infants adjust to this early and harsh reality?

First, they begin to discover this sense of separateness at about eight weeks of age. Through physical sensations—for instance, nursing and sucking their fist, they start to learn that their body encloses the limits of "self." As Theo said earlier:

You ultimately come into the world alone, in essence, and must leave the world alone. Do you not?

But here is where play can help, where Theo's ideas from the 5th Dimension of consciousness begin to offer guidance.

"Playful" cuddling and caressing at this point can initiate the development of trust over fear and mistrust. One psychoanalyst, Erik Erikson, believes that the predominance of trust over mistrust is the primary goal—and achievement—of these earliest stages of life. He suggests that this "basic trust" is crucial to—if not the keystone of—the infant's identity.

I also believe that we must show infants how much they are loved and how divine they are even while they are still in the womb. Research by some psychologists indicates that infants are aware of our thoughts, attitudes, and intentions even in the womb. Theo would agree, for trust is the building block of self-confidence and self-reliance: These are the pathways Theo often mentions.

For it is child that has the trust, is it not?

Evolvement through a trusting response to life lends children the basic support they need, otherwise individuals will have trouble meeting life's challenges and developing an optimistic outlook.

It is vitally important that playful interactions between parent and child take place. Such play helps babies develop a good feeling about their body and sense of self. Acceptance at an early age of one's body as pleasurable, and a deeply valued part of oneself, is the basis for the adult's healthy sex life, for an open and spontaneous, trusting and sensual outlook. In short, play becomes a foundation for self-respect and acceptance of one's total body and all its sensual reactions.

As any parent can tell you, children want to explore their own bodies and become upset if they are reprimanded or prevented from doing so. But if parents have a relaxed approach to sex and to children's exploration of their own body, then many misconceptions and unnecessary guilt can be avoided later in life.

Clearly, play is as essential to a child as breathing, eating, or sleeping. As strange as it may appear to those who do not recognize the value of play, children could not live long without play. And even stranger is the idea that it is as impossible for a child to survive without play as it is to survive without air or food.

I am deeply in tune with these feelings, and firmly believe in the value of play, but even I was surprised when I came across research that shows what happens through failure to make provisions for playtime.

One research group, working with the noted psychologist Rene Spitz, found that although sufficient nutrition and hygiene were present in "well-run" hospitals and institutions, there were still unusually high mortality rates among infants and toddlers in orphanages. The group's study led them to one hospital, which they referred to as the "Nursery." This institution was distinguished by the use of play in their program. Unlike the other institutions studied, the children in the "Nursery" were thriving. Their development was normal, and by the time they were two years of age, they exhibited all the achievements and skills of children raised at home.

The children nurtured at the other orphanages in the study had been denied extensive play, and by the age of two they were still at the level of ten-month-old infants—unable to walk or talk. In addition, they were psychologically disturbed and very susceptible to fears and illnesses. Touching is important as well.

It is clear that we all, child and adult, male and female partners, are interrelated in an overwhelming intimacy. Even as we struggle to find ourselves, we affect those around us. And when it is the child, the open, trusting, susceptible child, our responsibility to make ourselves whole becomes paramount.

As Theo says, even as we change, we alter the reality of those around us.

> *As you change, your children change. As one personality alters, he or she changes for all around. Know that all thought, all expression, all energy, affects everyone. Do you understand?*
>
> *You are aware of the rays of light from your sun. It touches all, does it not? It enhances healing, the growth of all, does it not? Think of the self like the sun, and like the energy of the sun, radiating out to touch all. It is the energy of one being.*

People who are in day-to-day contact with children have a powerful influence on the formation of these children's behavior. If the children are surrounded by people who are power-oriented, then the children will assimilate this, and more than likely, when they are grown, will consider power to be the main ingredient for happiness and a successful life.

If a child is hurt by an uncaring, manipulative person, he or she may grow up to seek gain through personal power and prestige, equating domination and control with the formula for winning in the game of life.

What, then, do loving parents do to avoid harming their

child's development? Love! Play! Words that seem simple and even a cliché are powerful realities to the child.

Parents also need to take responsibility to heal themselves. They need to acknowledge their own addictions, their own destructive patterns. They need to love themselves unconditionally.

If children grow up around people who are not rigid or controlled by power addictions but who interact with the children in a loving manner, who easily and naturally respond to the children's sensibilities, then the children will develop an organic sense of harmony. They will feel connected to the flow of life and will reflect it in their behavior as adults. Children with a loving and caring environment will radiate a higher awareness and be full of regard for all other life-forms. Such children will have an inner understanding—and belief—that love and an increased awareness leads to self-fulfillment and happiness.

This point of view is vitally important to us. If we are to begin breaking through the habits and social entrapments in our lives, then it will be done through self-awareness and sensitivity to the life surrounding us—and especially to the spirit and well-being of our children. It is our responsibility to disentangle ourselves from the habits and cycles that not only trap us but in turn trap our children.

When we are open to change and growth in ourselves, then we clear the path, in a sense, for our children not to be ensnared by the same seductive cycles we have suffered from.

One way we can do this is to avoid quick and critical judgments of a child's actions. And while it is difficult, we must strive not to become upset when a child's needs or actions interrupt our own plans or life-style. Too often parents try to dominate children, using a power trip: "You'd better listen or else . . ." Another power manipulation (which, by the way, children quickly learn to use themselves) is to put a child in his or her place: "You're just a child . . ."

Do you accuse, inflict guilt or punishment, threaten or bribe your child? Do you ridicule or belittle him or her? The old golden rule applies here: How would you feel if you were treated in these ways?

We could start with the simple rule of substituting alienating criticisms and reproach by using the word "I" more often, speaking of our feelings in the immediate, in the here and now, not in the future, as with threats.

Instead of saying "You are bad; you lie and can't be trusted," we can modify our language. How about: "I don't like what you did, Johnny, and it is hard for us to do things together when I can't rely on what you say."

It isn't wise to bring up past mistakes, or threaten with future punishments. In fact, if you can identify all your derogatory labeling and spurious analyzing of your child's character, you can go far in improving your handling of your child.

The judgments we make of our children or others usually are projections of our own sense of self-worth. I know that much of what I thought my children needed from me and their father were clearly my own expectations that were unmet as a child. When I finally figured that out, it changed my relationship with my children immensely.

It is helpful for children to be around adults who communicate openly and honestly, as it assists them in dealing with life's challenges. If you open yourself, and are willing to communicate your true feelings, your children will learn to honor these feelings and respect your honesty. This is especially wise, for children's ability to tune in to your feelings is keen and accurate. In short, expressing your own true feelings is training children to be honest and open with you.

Children must learn to recognize the great power of honesty. Honesty should not be treated simply as a virtue but an ideal children discover for themselves. It is this kind of interaction with children that can be a tremendous aid in their development toward higher consciousness.

Theo, many of us have been dealing with nurturing the child within. Is this particularly necessary now with the 5th Dimension energy present?

It is, yes. It is necessary now to honor the fullest spectrum of being, the child, the mother, the father, the triad within. You are all coming into balance with that spectrum within the self; for as one does this, as one is in complete balance with oneself, then the unconditional love radiates out to the world. Does it not?

And it is the child who has been abandoned. The childlike quality, the spontaneity, the humor, the playfulness, has been abandoned in your world—yet is necessary for your salvation. There has been too much seriousness. Joy and laughter bring forth the healing for your planet and people, do you see?

The child is the continuance of life, and the old cliché remains as true today as when it was first uttered: Children are the future of the world.

Children come to Earth not only with their genetic code intact but with ideas that will guide and manifest during their lifetime. It is this potential within the 5th Dimension child that will aid in the next step of the planet's evolution.

Anyone who has been present at a birth, or watched children grow from their open, unengineered response to the world is aware there is a greatness to the human personality that begins at birth. With an almost mystical affirmation of life children seem endowed with unknown powers that can guide us to our own future. Children become our teachers—if we open ourselves to the experience. This is why honesty is so important, for not only do we delude ourselves when we are dishonest, but we communicate the lie to our children.

Children may not understand the words they hear their parents speaking, but they understand the feelings underlying them. As children grow they learn that the words and feelings do not match, that somewhere something is wrong. The children begin to realize the adults are lying—and have been lying for years. They say one thing and mean another. And in order to get along in the world you have to play the same games. If Uncle Jack is terribly fat, and sensitive about this, you don't mention it. You learn to pretend that the reality doesn't exist. If a cousin has a wretched case of acne, everyone lies about its severity.

As these lessons in social and personal lying multiply, children soon realize that life is not as simple as it once seemed, and they are forced into a pattern of lying by the adults, who scold, cajole, and punish them if the little lies are not accepted as reality.

The children's lying takes on the same qualities as the parents', and the children soon learn to cover up their true feelings. Along with this comes the tragedy that the children learn to cover up how they feel about their own inner life. They even have to deny their own power, which, of course, affects their potential. They learn to deny the divine within. And, according to Theo, this pattern of denial lowers their vibrational level to that of the basic physical being. Thought has created a reality, which it may take a lifetime to unravel.

THE PSYCHIC CHILD

The child clearly knows how to play, is openly curious about the world, and is not yet closed to any possibility. As yet there are no *shoulds* or *should nots*. And this includes the psychic world.

Children are the most responsive of all to psychic energy. And, I believe, adults have a clear responsibility to respond openly, noncritically, when a child suddenly begins "talking" to an invisible friend, or has impressions that seem bizarre or strange to the rational, logical adult.

Many adults are aware of the psychic world, yet even today most are more likely to squelch a child who talks about it, with "Oh, you're making that up," or simply, "Stop that nonsense; there's nothing there." At this point many children stop "seeing" anything; more likely they simply stop talking about their experiences with adults. But sooner or later the suppression of the child's sensitivity to the psychic world will occur. A child cannot long resist the harsh disapproval of parents.

Since children are gifted with a psychic nature peculiar to them, it is the adults' task to respect that characteristic of childhood. In fact, children's true creative energy may be intimately tied to this psychic world, and, if it is, adults can do irreparable harm through stifling it. There is immense wealth hidden in the depths of our psychic world, and children must be encouraged to explore their fantasies and psychic impressions during imaginative play, dreamtime, or simply talking with an invisible playmate.

When children say "This is my friend" and there is no one visible, it is easy to simply respond normally: "Oh, good. Tell me what your friend's name is," or "What does your friend look like?"

Don't discount the child's vision with responses like "I can't see him. You're making him up." How much more sensitive to the child's vision to respond with "I can't see him as clearly as you do; would you tell me more about him?"

Theo has said, *Just because the body is small, doesn't mean the spirit is.* And I believe this deeply. We must let children talk about their inner life, just by letting them be open and expressive about what they feel and see.

Many children even have a lively interest in past-life experiences, although they obviously don't put it in terms of "reincarnation." All of these traditionally no-no subjects are open playing fields for the curious expanding mind of the child.

I feel that if we remain open to children's experiences, their wisdom, we adults could learn things of great value.

In one question-and-answer session during a seminar a parent asked how he should use this 5th Dimension reality when dealing with his child. To me the obvious answer is not to talk down to them, to acknowledge their equality in spirit. Our responsibility as parents is to guard them, to keep them strong and healthy in mind and body, yet to allow them free rein in learning the ways of the earth. Yes, we must guide them, but any changes we wish to make in children's behavior will not come from forcing them to be what *we* think they *should* be but by allowing them to discover for themselves, by allowing them to blossom into their own unique personality.

In the past child-rearing has been one of control and manipulation, but now is the time for releasing control and giving unconditional, nonjudgmental love. It is not adequate to say "You are going to college and becoming a doctor; I don't care if you want to be an artist." If parents will not learn to give up the control games when dealing with children, then a shock is in store for them.

Theo often makes a point of mentioning just *how special the 5th Dimensional child will be.*

Theo, I would like to ask about children in the New Age, and specifically about babies that will be born in this time. Can you give us some insight into how these babies will be different?

Many of the young ones born during this time of the 5th Dimension will be very mature souls. They will be very bright, much more active and enthusiastic. Much wisdom will be imparted by these young ones. It is important to acknowledge their childlike quality, for they will be very serious and directed in their actions.

They will be more sensitive to the wholeness of being, more accepting of the personal powers that they have. They will know from early on about past-life experiences. Their insights should be encouraged. Do not discount this knowledge but support it.

So they will have greater ability than our generation? Will they be intellectually superior?

There will be a greater awareness, yes. There will be a greater balance between the right and left brain functions, between the linear and creative aspects of the brain.

It is thought that we use about 10 percent of our brain's capacity right now; will the babies of the 5th Dimension use more of their mental ability?

Even in the present there is a greater use of your mental capacity—we would say 12 to 15 percent is being utilized now. Expansion is already happening. When supported in their knowing, the young ones will utilize 20 to 25 percent of their consciousness. But they will also be able to accept—and assess—the knowledge from the subconscious.

In what other ways will the 5th Dimension children be different?

They will be educated at a very rapid pace. Their retention of knowledge will be greater. They will be physically more healthy, stronger and bigger. Their bodies will be more physically able to combat disease. And their consciousness, because of their greater acceptance of their subconscious powers, will allow them to release the stresses inherent in living in your civilization.

Will children born during this period of the 5th Dimensional shift have a special purpose in choosing this time to come into the world?

They do, yes. Many wise beings are coming forth into this transformational time to assist humankind to a higher expression. They are teachers, if you will.

If children born during this period are coming to the earth with a special purpose, a teaching role, should they be given special care or training in preparation for their role? And should their parents have special preparation for the task?

That, too, is changing already. There is now an acceptance of being, the honoring of what is the wholeness of the human spirit. The perfection, the divinity, of this being must be communicated. Speak to the children of this divinity and its acceptance within themselves. It is important to nurture these beings in this attitude, to develop a nurturing sense of acceptance and love. These beings will demand it, do you understand?

They will teach their parents more than the parents will teach them. There will be an exchange, yes. But these beings coming forth now have great wisdom that will be remembered. It will be well for the adult to listen to the child, will it not?

Are there any special meditations that would benefit these children?

Communicating with the young is very important. Meditation with them would be good, for it would allow the adults to release their own restrictions of mind and become more fully attuned to the children. They would gain insight telepathically, a sharing, do you understand?

Then it is a form of mutual meditation, or group meditation, between child and parents?

There is that, yes. It is important as well that each parent —father and mother—have such experience equally with the child. It is not the same role that has been for centuries, where the mother has the total responsibility for the child's nurturing. During the 5th Dimension it is necessary that the father shares these responsibilities.

Men, fathers, are very conditioned in patterns that reject such a role. How can they be helped in making this transition of roles?

The transition is coming forth now. One way will be because of the changing of your economic structures, with both parents having a life path expressive of work. Do you see?

You mean that the economic and social changes being brought about by the 5th Dimensional shift will force the male into a more active parenting role?

That is correct. It is a major trauma for people now. For it is happening in the present time. The defining of masculine and feminine roles is changing, coming more into balance. This will not be dictating that "this is masculine" and "this is feminine"; it is more a realignment of a fuller human role. Do you understand? It is a sharing, is it not?

Communication helps bring this about—speaking about the expectations of the male and female. Those in their middle years will have the most difficulty now, for this age group has experienced the old patterns that have been around for centuries. The young ones to come along will not have this struggle. Do you understand?

This situation implies an even greater chasm of misunderstanding between the 5th Dimensional child that is coming and the traditional parent?

That is the assistance the child will give to the parent, is it not?

But from the parents' standpoint, if the parents wish to contribute to this transition and to help the 5th Dimension child into a fuller expression of his or her power, what specific recommendations can these people have to help them fulfill their role?

It is important for the entities of this experience to acknowledge the growth within self, for as the parent changes the child is affected. Do you understand? The shift and change of attitude and thought patterns within the adult assist the child. The spoken word is not as important as action. Enlightened behavior, see?

   This involves a commitment to analyzing the patterns of the past, individually, and releasing what is inefficient, releasing what is no longer of service, and sharing those changes with the child. Communicating! Do you see?

If there is going to be a changing of the sexual roles during the 5th Dimension, would it be helpful to start with the children now, to teach and show them that they are not restricted to specific kinds of roles or behavior, that they have a freedom to experience life? Do you have any advice on how parents can guide children so that they understand they are not bounded by the traditional roles that have been laid on them?

Allow children choice, respect that choice, and give guid-
ance that will protect them against harm. Give guidance
from the heart, from personal experience, but not to dic-
tate a path. Do you understand?

II

DOORWAYS

INTO

THE

5TH

DIMENSION

*There needs to be a balancing
of the body, mind, and spirit.
That is the opening into the
5th Dimension.*

7

Channeling: Using Guides to Enter the Doorway

It is time to become aware of —and acknowledge—the uniqueness and beauty of your human spirit upon this planet. Many seek the sensational rather than the truth. But it is a gift for many to become attuned to the spirit, the soul, the essence of their being. It is the asking of your heart to become a part of this 5th Dimension transformation, to become a part of the process of the spirit. For many who open themselves to this process become a gift unto the planet. And the 5th Dimension reality becomes a part of your being.

Life has changed for me in many ways since I started channeling. Most importantly, I have learned that there are spiritual forces helping to shape our lives. Yet, above everything, I have learned that there is the reality of our own "untouched spiritual selves." The major tragedy of our age is not those things so often commented on—poverty, war, disease—but the unsolicited self, the untapped spiritual dynamics within. Touch these powerful centers of consciousness, utilize their resources, and a renaissance emerges in your life.

Channeling has drawn me into these bright, clear states of consciousness. I call them the sunlit moments of my awareness, for they illuminate what has been previously shrouded or obscured. With the opening of my spiritual awareness came a shocking but not unsurprising insight into those opaque envelopes surrounding living objects. That I could see this aura, or more accurately "feel" the inner individuality of people (and even animals) impelled me further into the beauty of the forces underlying life.

Opening myself to channeling, to the subtle voices of the spirit, also thrust me into a broader and more pervasive sensitivity.

While I believe everyone has an innate ability to reach these higher realms, to open oneself to this form of inner guidance and inspiration is not as simple as many of the New Age gurus make out. Yes, channeling is indeed an innate ability, opportunity, a natural way of knowing that awaits any individual willing to prepare. But it takes honesty, willpower, perseverance, and an uncompromising commitment. Without these characteristics it becomes too easy to fool oneself.

Channeling can happen in many forms, such as art, music, healing, writing, listening to an inner voice, and direct voice. To honor your own personal form of channeling is most important. I believe that the form most emotionally and psychologically acceptable to you is the correct form for you to follow.

Those who channel come from every profession and personality type. There are no stereotypes even though the media makes us out to be empty-heads encased in turbans. While frauds and the greedy do exist in channeling, as in all walks of life, I have found that most channelers are kind, sensitive people open to new ideas; people who enjoy the new and positive; people who are sensitive to others and sincere in their desire to do good. Practically without exception, all those whom I have met want to help heal the planet.

Anyone interested in developing his or her psychic abilities or who wants to work in channeling must realize that these abilities will not solve all your problems. Psychic abilities will not help you find love, fame, or financial success. Channeling is not a panacea for today's complex problems. What it will do is change the way in which you see the world. It will change your attitude, your sense of responsibility, your openness to change and the opportunity to grow. Lessons offered you in this life will become an integral part of your day-to-day existence, and it is these changes of the self that will ultimately bring you more joy in life and a greater sense of power and accomplishment.

A channeler, as any seeker, comes face-to-face with the self— with the inner patterns of will, with the surprising shifting energies of the internal life, which can often be confusing and destabilizing. And even though improperly used inner energies can, and do, sometimes destabilize a beginning psychic, it should be remembered that above all these experiences create new opportunities and build new strengths.

Once the opening to the inner world has been blazed, one sees life with a clearer vision. I know I am very fortunate to have had access to these realms of the spirit, to watch the interplay of energy between the world of spirit and the world of matter.

For me, the essence of the channeling experience is captured in one line by Theo.

To bring a new voice into the world: that is the function of both the channeler and the guide. And as in music the voice must be clear.

Once you learn to trust your inner voices, to follow the guidance of your higher self and your guides, great changes will naturally occur . . . and great rewards will follow. The rewards may not be in the form you hoped for, however. But that is part of the excitement—allowing small changes to surprise and awaken you even further. It is an acknowledgment of the little miracles or magic every day.

Channeling will help you clarify your destiny, and help show you the way your soul wishes to travel.

Theo, many people are puzzled about just what a channel is. Can you give us some insight on this?

Channeling is the use of energy by beings with a greater universal understanding. These beings use the energy of the channel's higher self by aligning it to a higher universal energy. This facilitates the transfer of information through the channel. There are different levels of energy, different levels of refinement. Some beings are closer to your physical energy on Earth, and these beings cross the barriers between energy forms quite easily. Those of more refined energy exist on a higher plane and use the channel as a form of communication. But the channel's physical energy must be refined to do this. It is a combination of many things, do you see?

What happens to the channel, to the physical and psychological aspects of the channel, when entities from other dimensions come through?

The energies between the two dimensions are hooked up so that there can be a resonance, a harmony between the entity and the channel. There is a closer bond, a wholeness of being. The vibrational energy of the channel is raised so that it may harmonize with the energy of other dimensions, see?

Do all guides change the vibrational level of the physical bodies of their channels? And do individual guides have different vibrations of their own, or are all of you similar?

There are different energy levels, for all entities resonate according to their own spiritual evolution. They are on different planes of consciousness. There must be a blending between the mind and body of the channel and those of the guide.

Can you give us a description of what it means to raise the vibrations?

Raising the vibrations is done by using the electromagnetic field of the body, there is also a resonance within the soul of the channel, with the evolutionary spiritual facets of the channel. There is a blending as the channel becomes more finely attuned to the wholeness of his or her being.

Understand that there is much confusion on the astral level, and the guide must raise the channel's energy through that. This is done by touching the electromagnetic field, the aura of the being, the cellular structure of the physical body—the entirety of the being. It affects the mind, the consciousness predominantly, but the whole being is involved. The thought of the guide, the energy of thought, reaches out and touches the electrical field of the cells, the energy, the soul of the channel, see?

Many people are puzzled about where the personality, or self, of the channel is when the guide takes over.

As we have stated, there is blending of the guide's energy with the consciousness of the channel. The consciousness shifts frequency, steps aside, alters, and moves over to allow the new energy of the guide to participate, do you understand?

So the guide and the channeler exist simultaneously in the same body?

That is correct; there is a harmony of energy, a blending, do you see?

How would you define what a guide is for the people of Earth?

A guide is support from the universe; it is the soul, the essence of the being, that is to assist the path of another. Many guides protect; they are finely attuned to the souls of others and are often called guardian angels, do you see? This compassion exists because there is a greater un-

derstanding, for many guides have been embodied on this planet and have compassion for its beings.

Are all guides positive in their thought and action, or are there what we might call evil or destructive entities?

There are many different levels of being—yes, different levels of expression of consciousness. We do not speak of "evil"; we speak of confusion of spirit; we speak of what is not highly evolved or finely attuned. Yes, there are those who are in that condition.

If people wanted to open themselves to becoming channels, how could they protect themselves from these less positive, less life-affirming, entities?

Begin by asking that the highest good be brought forth through you, that Divine love do its work in and through you. Also encircle the self with white light, a cloak of love through which only the highest vibration may penetrate. These are affirmations that should be made during meditation when preparing to channel.

What is the relationship between the higher self of a human and the energy of a guide?

The higher self is the purest essence of being; it is the soul. In relationship to the guides, it is equal to one in a pure state, in the guide's purest essence. Each draws unto itself an equal energy, do you see?

What are the different forms of channeling?

There are several forms. There is the written word, direct voice; there is art, painting, sculpture, music. There is the clairaudient, or inner mind hearing; there is clairvoyant vision; there is healing. There is psychokinesis, or utilizing the vibrations of objects to receive knowing. These are all different ways that a channel may open the self to higher levels of knowing.

Theo, there are many who reject the spiritual. Why are these people so negative and rejecting?

Fear, fear of change, fear of the unknown. Many lack self-esteem and reject the acknowledgment of their own power.

They reject their own power? Why would they do that?

Because of the limitations that they have placed on themselves, because of the patterns within the structures of their lives. It is also fear of losing control, fear of abandonment, fear that they will not be accepted—it is fear on many levels.

LEARNING ABOUT CHANNELING

To channel, the first requirement is to learn to set aside your own thoughts and become receptive to a higher guidance. It is important to affirm that you are ready and willing to accept a guide. In this highly receptive condition you will become a channel for the higher energies who are waiting to build a bridge to this world.

We are ever present in thought form. We are ever present to those in the physical plane, even to those who do not accept these phenomena. (All of you) are guided by mentors and guides who are only able to act or help you when asked to do so.

In the Eastern teachings there is a long tradition of power transmission from teacher to pupil, or from guide to channeler. Hindus called this *darshan,* an unspoken influence that flows between an elevated or saintly teacher and the pupil. Thousands of devout seekers would travel many days to simply be near great personalities like Buddha, Muhammad, and Jesus. The same influence happens with teachers like Gandhi.

We are ever present in energy form. We are not visible to the ordinary eye as we are to the vision of sensitives or channelers.

Christ and Buddha, too, are teachers of high energy and vibration who have come forth into your world to teach. Also Muhammad. There have been many teachers. Understand that you are all teachers and students. One is not greater than the other.

Great teachers are clearly powerful transmitters of energy and wisdom. In fact, the power is so overwhelming sometimes that they evoke fanatical devotion and loyalty. An irony for the great teachers is that even if they do not accept their followers' unquestioning faith and strive to create self-reliance in their followers, their power is too infectious. A kind of contagion of energy often takes place that overwhelms the emotion of the followers even though the teachers' message may not be fully understood.

For this reason it is not always the message that is important to the followers as much as the feelings—the transmission of positive emotions, the feelings of love and acceptance—that are the magnet attracting the faithful. And this is, I think, a danger, for without learning to trust the self more fully the pupil loses one of the most valuable assets he or she possesses—*self-reliance.*

Theo always emphasizes personal responsibility and self-reliance, especially for those who would teach—but also for those who seek to learn.

What you teach is transformation, and what comes forth will be the sharing of experience—the sharing of the heart is the gift. What is received by others, by the pupils, is their responsibility. Keep your heart open and stand firmly in the truth of the self, do you understand?

To become attuned to the spirit, the soul, the essence of what you are is the gift that is given unto the world— the truth of your being. It is the asking of your heart that this energy be channeled into you, is it not?

It is the pupil's own spirit that must accept the responsibility for decisions—not the teacher's.

Even if skeptics reject the idea of telepathy, or mind-to-mind communication, few can deny that a magnetism communicates itself in the presence of exceptional personalities. What is this "presence" except a kind of nonverbal communication. Surely it cannot be examined under a microscope, but it is there nevertheless. It is a "perceived" reality; it is convincing because we *feel* its power. In a way it's like love, or any strong emotion. Powerful emotions cannot be seen or even proved to exist by scientific measurement; but they carry their own proof by their very power. You cannot *prove* love to someone who has never felt it, but no one can convince you otherwise once you've experienced its power.

Experience is the only validation that love exists. The same is true with experiencing the psychic or one's guides. Those who have not experienced it, and are not open to sensing the psychic world intuitively, will never be convinced.

But that's acceptable; each one must choose one's own reality, each interpret the world in one's own terms for one's own reasons. In that way the individual determines his or her own future. It cannot be any other way. It is the attitude, the intention, of consciousness that creates our own reality. And once we create an attitude of acceptance, of opening ourselves to the possibilities of other worlds influencing our own, we begin to bridge the chasm between the physical and spiritual dimensions.

As Theo has said time and again, thought is the energy of creation; and consciousness is potentially capable of transcending all the limits of physical form. Consciousness is capable of opening to immensely wider fields of activity than the normal patterns it follows when trapped in physical form.

> Thought is the creative force of your universe. It is the energy about you—as you think of an aura about you. It is electric. It comes into the thinking processes of the conscious mind of the being—but it is an energy form. Do you understand?
>
> There are many dimensions in which we interact. We are drawn now into the 6th dimension so that this communication can be channeled forth. But we are from a dimension that is much higher. The conscious mind does

not have pictures for that. It is vibrational; it is light; it can be made manifest or not. There is no limitation to knowing as there is in the physical form of the earth.

Not only is channeling possible for anyone who wishes to walk that path, but many are being moved in that direction by the energies of the 5th Dimension shifting.

The channel through which we speak, and others like her, enables us to help bring enlightenment to the world. But much work needs to be done; much opening to the spiritual realms must be accomplished. During the opening to the 5th Dimension reality many people in the physical plane will become more sensitive to psychic phenomena. Many will be in contact with our vibratory level through meditation and prayer. This will bring profound changes to the world, and it will be not as divided as it is at this time.

With the greater number of people meditating and praying, and becoming more open to the spiritual and psychic realms, a new enlightenment of mind will result, which will be followed by a unifying force.

True growth has to take place within one's *whole* life. A synthesis between the outer and inner worlds is obviously necessary —and this is the point that Theo makes constantly. As we experience the 5th Dimension energies we are confronted with the constant challenge of adjustment, of balancing and accommodating opposing but complementary forces and alternate realities.

The sense of separateness we all feel as we attempt to create this balance between the two worlds in our lives is, in fact, artificial. It is an illusion of form, of thought images and physical impressions. We call these worlds "separate" because we feel ourselves physically distant from the spirit world, because we allow ourselves to *believe* we exist separately.

But these impressions are not complete; they are only partially true on a purely physical, material scale. They are not the complete "true self." There are, in fact, many other worlds where separateness is dissolved because consciousness has evolved. We all recognize the reality of the physical world, many of us also accept the reality of the world of ideas, and still others see the reality of a transcendent world where minds join in a joyous communion. These are the psychic realms, worlds where we can experience a fuller reality.

There is a greater wisdom within individuals, a wisdom that accepts stepping beyond. That is what the 5th Dimension is about. Stepping beyond what are one's limited views. There is an expanded awareness, an expanded consciousness, that is coming about. The entities of this planet not only have experienced the earth, but in other dimensions they are carrying forward their wisdom and knowledge to this time.

AN INTRODUCTION TO DEVELOPING YOUR CHANNELING ABILITY

Overcoming the barriers of ego and self-centeredness is one of the necessities of channeling. "Forgetting of the self" is how Theo has described it. There are many ways to accomplish this, some simple, others complex. But the most important is to learn to "open" yourself spiritually. To learn to do this is one of the main purposes for the coming of Theo and other higher entities. In other words, our "psychic" abilities do not exist in a vacuum; they are part of a greater plan—a plan involving the movement of the heavens into new vibratory levels, a plan creating new arrangements of reality called Dimensional shifts. The end result of this universal activity is human enlightenment.

What happens during spiritually "open" moments, I believe, is that we unify our two selves (matter and spirit) and our consciousness becomes a channel for higher "thoughts." Consciousness exists simultaneously in both vibratory realities: the physical reality of our bodies and the spiritual dimensions. At these moments we become open channels for higher thoughts and perceive the world in a new, broader perspective. In effect, we become more enlightened. This, as Theo has said, is the vital purpose of the 5th Dimensional energy shift.

*Now is the time to speak of a new light, or a new en-
lightenment coming forth. There are many entities, and
channelers, who will bring forth words from God and a
new enlightenment of the mind. There will be a new light
coming forth for the physical world, a new involvement
in religion and new thought forms.*

*You see, the time for this enlightenment or new light
or New Age will be very soon, not a lifetime. There is
much to be brought forth to the world.*

*We speak of it now to explain our purpose—to alle-
viate the tensions in the world and to open the minds of
those who have powers in this phenomenon of the sixth
sense—and to bring forth a new voice into the world.*

*Many working in this endeavor, such as the channel
from whom I speak, will be coming in contact with others
in the field. There will be much knowledge coming, a
generating of energy toward enlightenment with others
of like attitude. The people of the world are becoming
more aware, and the enlightenment of many is coming
forth in this period.*

Scientists are now theorizing that psychic ability is probably
an inborn quality and common to all people. Theo has repeatedly
said that all people will become more sensitive, and even *psychic,*
as the 5th Dimension progresses. But, as I said earlier, the first
step is to become open to the idea. To relax the obsessive self-
concern that so dominates our everyday lives, to relax the controls
of the conscious mind.

*All in the physical plane have this ability (to channel) if
they wish to open themselves. Opening the self means to
relax the conscious mind and let the subconscious mind
come forth. . . . It is the purpose of psychic phenomena—
expansion is a good word—that all people will try to
expand themselves in this manner and become "psychic."
The 5th Dimension energy will aid in this transformation.*

Preparing Yourself to Channel

Many scientists today describe the universe and all things in it as "vibration" or an electrical charge. Einstein based his theories partially on this belief. Channelers make use of these vibrations to interpret and deduce facts about a person (telepathy or clairvoyance), or an object (psychometry). But most channelers often find it easier—and I am one of them—to pick up and feel these vibrations as emotions or experiences that are difficult to describe in words. So it is important to be open and nonjudgmental, to simply accept uncritically whatever comes. To be this open is difficult, but for anyone curious about his or her psychic ability, and who is open to experimenting, there are some easy ways of developing and putting these talents to use.

First, it is important to relax, which can be done in a relatively short time. Lie comfortably on a bed or sofa in a darkened room. Relax and imagine yourself lying on a green lawn, or floating on water. Try to feel tension leaving your feet and ankles . . . your knees and thighs . . . your abdomen . . . back . . . chest and neck . . . eyes . . . ears . . . scalp . . . until every part of you is limp. This may take practice, but you must free your mind from focusing on your physical self. I've found that using slow breathing, done by inhaling to a rhythmic count of 8, holding and exhaling to a count of 8, is very helpful. Use the breath to become aware of where the tension is in the body and to release it.

> *Use the breath, in and out slowly, to relax the muscles of the body, feeling the body dropping away, relaxed, as if it's not there.*
>
> *If the mind wanders, gently draw it back to the breath. Allow this, the floating feeling of the body, yes. This facilitates the release of the conscious mind so that it is receptive to the higher self. It is letting go of the limitations, yes?*

It is important to learn to concentrate on one thing with undivided attention. Just concentrate on *one* object or *one* sound.

When you have mastered this, concentrate on visualizing a blank screen instead of a physical object. Practice as much as you

can. After a time you will be able to do this automatically whenever you wish, wherever you are. Soon you will be able to simply
project an object, or an individual from whom you wish to receive
thoughts, onto the screen to obtain a message. If you can't visualize it, feel it, because the object of this exercise is to learn to
focus and it doesn't really matter *how* you teach your mind to
focus.

Theo specifically will describe a questioner as *visual*, or *non-
visual*, and give suggestions based on the person's natural incli-
nations.

> *You are not a visionary, so don't look for pictures so
> much. The manifestation of your power, of your knowing,
> of your sensory power, is in feeling. Your solar plexus is a
> barometer of knowing. But you get a feeling, a knowing
> of another, and the conscious mind wants to assess it, to
> control it. Trust that knowing. Ask for confirmations to
> come forth in your outer experiences.*

Begin experimenting with a card in a sealed envelope. Ask
mentally "What is on this card?" Then relax and wait, quietly,
expectantly, but peacefully. When a vision appears, accept it. It
may appear in segments. After you have identified it, make your
mind blank again and ask whether this is indeed the right symbol.
Ask for this confirmation several times. If the same vision keeps
reappearing, you have the answer.

Record the message you receive quickly. It may be fleeting—
like a dream—and you might not remember it long, particularly
when you are a novice.

Remember to guard against allowing any of your five physical
senses to impose themselves on your consciousness while trying
to receive psychic impressions. If there is interference, you will
perceive a blurred "double exposure" image whose meaning you
won't be able to make out.

Another technique involves concentrating on "feelings." It is
a short meditation that helps relax you and open your subconscious to your guides. This meditation brings complete relaxation
of the body and opens the subconscious to the soul.

To empty the mind and body, so to speak, concentrate on a certain point of the body and feel the flow of God throughout that area. Expand the area to include the whole body. Focus on the feeling of God's love; make a central point in the body or the head. The middle of the abdomen is a good place to feel this flow, this love of God flowing. Concentrate on this feeling, releasing all parts of the mind and body. This will open up the subconscious mind, and the guides can then be helpful to the entity.

HOW TO PROTECT YOURSELF IN THE PSYCHIC REALM

Energy is the way higher guides communicate with this world, and energy is also the way we adjust our minds and bodies to improve ourselves. And that same energy, often in the symbolic form of visible "mind-light," can be used to protect yourself from destructive forces.

Dion Fortune, a renowned psychic and teacher who lived in the early part of this century, even wrote a book about psychic self-defense where light and energy are used as a defensive shield against evil or destructive forces. Using only the basic meditation and mind-control techniques taught by Theo, you can learn to defend yourself using this shield of light. In fact, they can be used whenever you feel threatened or fearful . . . or even anxious.

USING A CIRCLE OF LIGHT

A simple way to create a circle of light around you is to see yourself sitting or lying in its glow as you meditate. Begin by envisioning a flow of energy radiating out from your head—or your heart; either is good.

First, picture the energy pulsing and growing stronger, brighter, and fuller. When you feel ready, let the glow begin to move down your throat and neck, expanding to encompass your shoulders and upper chest. Continue to picture the glow moving down your body, section by section. Don't rush it, and pause as often as you need to in order to strengthen the light.

Remember that the light is created from *your* energy, which is the same universal energy that makes up your mind, body, and spirit. It is energy there for your use. If the light seems to dim, it is within your power to strengthen it.

When you can see, or even feel, the light surrounding you, begin to play with it. Expand it; let the circle around you grow until it's as large as a house. Make it dense, a richer light full of sparkling energy and power. Point your hand and extend the energy in a line toward something farther away from you. Try to infuse the object with your electric power; feel it surge down your arm and out of your hand, the energy immediately being replenished from the fiery core of you, which is in touch with a universal source.

Some psychics call this our "source self," others our multidimensional self.

Energize the room you are sitting in with the power of this higher source self; send it to other people so it may link up with their own positive *source* power.

Not only does the creation of this circle of light, some call it a "bubble of light," create a *safe space* from within which your channeling can take place, but it creates a strong and open connection to your source, or higher, self.

The same circle of light meditation can be used in healing sessions by directing the light as a healing power toward a specific part of the body that is wounded or in need of a healing or rebalancing of its energy. Use the circle of light to send loving energy to those in need—even if they are not present in the room. The energy from your source self is not limited by physical boundaries and can be sent to distant places if your concentration is strong enough.

If, for some reason, you could only learn a single meditation that would help you in developing your channeling ability, this might well be your choice. It is such a valuable technique, and serves so many positive aspects of your development, that it should be one of the first meditations you work on.

GREETING YOUR GUIDES

To be able to use your channeling powers you must try not to think about your fears or worries and to eliminate destructive emotions like anger and self-pity. "Wrong" mental pictures attract poor future experiences: like attracts like where the mind is concerned. If your thoughts are negative, your mind will draw you to more negative experiences. Theo often speaks of the power of the mind and the danger of allowing fear to influence us.

You must also *want* to use your channeling powers. If you do not truly believe you can—or doubt their existence—your ability to develop them will be impaired.

Entities in the physical plane use only a small percentage of their mental capacity. They should be using more. It is coming forward now through this knowledge, and through entities such as this channel who are sensitive to what is called the "sixth sense." But it is not unusual. Everyone has this ability to open oneself but needs to learn how to use it. It will be accomplished through the acceptance of one's own mental powers—of thought. This is very important, for when people in the physical world understand how much power they have in their own thought, they will gain control of their lives and not be so harmful—either to themselves or others.

The important point is not that I am channeling Theo and, through them, find myself in touch with universal consciousness, but that anyone can open him- or herself and experience the same reality. That's what the transformations brought on by the 5th Dimension energy shifts are all about—a rebirth of awareness, a new awakening to a great reality. The universe has always been there . . . waiting . . . open to anyone who prepares properly. Yet traditionally only a few psychics and mystics, only a few isolated individuals, have worked to open themselves to this greater reality. But Theo's message is simple: The 5th Dimension energy influencing our world at this time is changing everything, and many individuals, millions of people, will be awakening to the challenge.

Human beings are noticing the difference. That is part of the 5th Dimension. A finer attunement, a growing aware-

*ness of change. Today there is a rebirth and an under-
standing of the spirit taking place in your world.*

One of the purposes for my channeling is to allow the Theo
group to speak directly with people. They have not been incarnate
on the earth before, but they are teachers and mentors. They say
that they are from angelic forces—if that is the way we want to
perceive them. The Theo group's purpose is to help elevate the
consciousness of humankind on this planet, to help others get in
touch with their own form of channeling—whether it is "direct
voice," as I do, or healing, art, clairvoyance—whatever form that
is psychologically and emotionally acceptable. They say that when
the time is right, the way will be open for anyone who wishes to
channel.

*Students will be drawn unto the teacher, do you under-
stand? The teacher does not rush about creating students.
Many times a seeker has rushed about the world seeking
this teacher or that, only to find that when arriving home
the correct teacher has been waiting. It is well to keep this
in mind, for there are many teachers, wise beings from
other worlds, within the world at this time.*
    *Simply to have the heart open, to be a seeker and to
allow its evolution, is the right action.*

Sometimes beginning channelers may have difficulty actually
reaching their guides. One way to get over this problem is to use
the following meditation as a doorway.

MEDITATION TO OPEN TO YOUR GUIDES

After your normal relaxation exercise period (where you tense
and relax muscle groups and breathe deeply and regularly) begin
your meditation by picturing your neck and the back of your head
opening to an energy flow. Let the energy flow move over and
around the area. Picture the energy opening electric pathways into
your mind, and accept that your guide will initiate contact along
these fields of energy.

If you experience tingling, or slight "electrical" feelings

around your scalp and head, just let it happen—go with it. Begin verbally asking your guide to come closer; ask for help in opening yourself to the higher states of consciousness where your guide exists. As the impulse comes to you, and as you feel ready, again ask your guide to come closer. Keep repeating this idea over and over again. Repeat this whole sequence until you begin getting clear impressions of words, images, ideas, or a sense of the presence of another personality.

But most importantly, maintain a relaxed, open, and accepting attitude.

Theo says that major changes in our energy patterns occur during these meditations, or "centering" exercises, as they sometimes call them. By changing your body's energy patterns you can raise the frequency level of your body's vibrations.

Centering within is the most important exercise of the limited human experience. To do this, one must meditate and align the body so that the energy flows may be corrected. It is important that the energy flows be in correct correlation to the electrical flows in and around the being. To channel these electrical impulses, they must combine and flow together. Taking into consideration that all energy affects us, when you are trying to reach the highest frequency, it is essential to maintain the highest vibration possible. You may maintain a clear vehicle in which channeling of the highest vibratory essence may come by keeping the physical body in alignment and attuned through diet, exercise, and meditation.

If this is done, the attitude will be elevated as well, which will keep you attuned to the highest possible frequency. Keeping within this centering process will manifest positive action/reaction in your life.

If your guide has still not manifested to you, begin to pretend you are channeling from your own unconscious mind, that a greater wisdom will come to you directly from the deeper aspects of your higher self. To "pretend" is *not* the same thing as fooling yourself into believing that your fantasies or delusions are real. To pretend that you are channeling is a form of guided use of your imagination; it is using the power of imagination to open the channels of your mind. Once you feel you are open, begin to respond as if your guide were actually with you. Ask yourself questions that are important—and that you genuinely want the answers to—and wait quietly for a response.

Sometimes it's helpful to write down the impressions you are getting at this time. But remember—as with all such techniques —do not grasp or reach for connections to your guide. If your guide is not appearing, it is probably for a good reason: Accept that thought and continue to work to open yourself up. Remember, also, that all of these techniques help you to expand your consciousness and prepare you for further, more spiritual, experiences. They raise the physical vibratory level of your cells and eventually will move you closer to your guide.

Occasionally a guide comes in by using a surprising or unexpected form. For example, the guide may begin the connection with a channel by transmitting images or colors, or powerful emotional feelings that clearly and wisely answer the questions that have been asked. All of these are ways of contact used by guides. Frequently what is happening is that the guide is answering the beginning channler's call for help and is adjusting the body's energy system to accommodate a fuller and more powerful transmission of energy.

One of the things that can inhibit opening yourself to your guide is to critically question every thought and impression that comes to you during meditation. Thoughts such as That's just me, just my unconscious mind talking, or This is too simple. It's only normal ideas . . . nothing spiritual, nothing from a higher consciousness . . . This type of questioning and critical analysis can only slow down your development.

Many of the ideas and thoughts you will get during channeling may seem simple to you, or to be communicating information you already are familiar with may seem to be from your unconscious. But if you begin a critical, intellectual analysis this early in the training sessions, all you will succeed in doing is blocking further opening to your guide or delaying development of your psychic abilities.

Do not let your mind get in the way.

Your overall purpose in these exercises is to relax and accept the idea that you can channel and that your guide will answer at the proper time. To doubt is human, and a common problem, but it should be put aside whenever it happens. To doubt, along with learning to trust, are the two most frequent problems mentioned by beginning channelers.

> *Trust your inner voices. You are to affirm the recognition of yourself for a start. Know that you are good; know that you can achieve all that you want to achieve. See it as happening now. If there are blocks in your way, see them as gifts for you to look again with fresh eyes at the commitment you have made to yourself. Trust yourself; stand firm in your commitment, and you will achieve what you want.*

Another major problem you may confront is the fear of losing control. This was, in fact, one of my greatest early fears. I was haunted by the idea that I was losing control of myself. And mixed in with this fear was a powerful fascination: What's going to happen next? I asked myself. Why am I allowing this to happen to me?

You see, I had a lesson to learn when I started channeling: my task was to learn to accept, to trust, to open myself to the higher realms and forget my everyday problems and fears. Later I learned that these problems are quite common for many beginning channelers. It is part of the process we must go through. All of these tasks and problems help prepare us for the coming of our guides, for opening ourselves and allowing our guides to assist us.

> *You all have guides about you. You may not feel attuned, but your guides are here and assist you along your way. It has been your asking that brings it to you. But you must help. Meditate more. Raise your vibrations through meditation, even if it is only a five-minute meditation each day. This will allow you to release, and allow the love in, allow the assistance about you to come in.*

Sometimes guides will transmit to a channel according to the channel's personality and talents. For example, a guide may use colors and images for those people with a natural sense of color and design. This may continue for months. But be aware, this is natural: The guides are using what is most accessible to them— the channel's own talents and abilities.

If you continue to receive pictures and images rather than words, perhaps you might start channeling by describing, or writing down for your own use, the symbols you see during meditation.

Remember, guides transmit by using energy, and often a symbol is closer to their true intention than words—which, as we all know, can be ambiguous. And don't forget, as you describe the images you see, that you are building a stronger link with your guide because you are creating a transmission of trust.

Do not get discouraged if weeks go by and you don't feel that you have made contact with a higher intelligence. Some people take up to several months before they can clearly feel their guide's presence. In addition, some guides connect so gently with their channels that you may not be aware of their presence. But remember, your guide is always present when you call—even if you can't be sure of the connection. One way to recognize when you are beginning to channel is a sense of heightened awareness and a feeling of well-being.

As you begin to communicate what you see and hear, and as you become more practiced at channeling, you will learn to recognize the presence of your guide and learn to distinguish between what your guide is communicating and what may be coming from your own unconscious.

Don't forget that the two biggest problems during the early training period are: (1) to put aside your doubts and trust the information coming through; to communicate what you are seeing and hearing without critical analysis; and (2) not to let your fear of losing control put you off. Your guide will not "blank" out your personality or in some mysterious way take away your identity. On the contrary, most guides emphasize self-reliance. The fear of losing control is generated by your conscious mind, which needs to control everything in your daily life. But moving from the control of the conscious mind is exactly what happens in channeling.

*In calling upon the higher self you are releasing the con-
scious mind of its control—and allowing what you call
the subconscious, or the higher self, to become engaged.
You can do this in a meditative state, in trance channeling.*

If you persevere and avoid letting these two concerns divert
you, then you will surely become connected to your guide. At that
point you will find that channeling is a broad and exhilarating
path to a higher understanding, to a life moved by dimensions of
thought and experience you never dreamed existed.

CHANNELING FOR OTHERS

As you progress in your experiments in channeling, you will probably be asked to help others—to answer personal questions about
people's purpose in life, about health problems, love, marriage,
finances. The list is as endless as the complications of living life. If
you decide to channel for friends, or even strangers sent to you by
friends, there are several ways to guide yourself that will make it
easier.

First, do not anticipate what your guide will answer to people's questions. In other words, get out of the way and trust the
information coming through. Sound familiar? Trusting is not only
a problem when developing your own powers as a channel but
continues on into the more regular connections with your guide.

Second, do not judge the information that is being channeled.
There is often no right or wrong answer to most questions—especially for questions dealing with human problems. There are
many ways to solve problems, and if the answers from your guide
seem overly simple, or just plain "commonsense" advice, don't
judge them. Often people are looking for confirmation of decisions
they have already reached and your guide is aware of this and
giving support in terms the questioner will identify with.

Third, don't take people's problems personally. You are not
responsible for making other's lives work. You cannot solve the
world's problems. Remember, as Theo says, people are responsible
for their own reality. Only they can change their situation. Some

people may use the advice your guide offers, while others will ignore it and go on as before. There is nothing you can do about this; your task is to offer an open, clear channel for your guide to communicate through. This is done by taking the same advice you will often be giving others: Stop judging; be an open and loving channel for the positive universal force to express itself.

Trust the divinity within yourself, and share that. Acknowledge the feelings, acknowledge the truth of your higher self. Affirm that Divine love is doing its work in and through you now. It is easy, is it not? Call upon that energy to assist you, and know that each person is unique, perfect, beautiful, and a gift unto the world.

8

The Thought Bridge: Doorway of the Mind Affirmations and Visualizations

It is the immediate that is important. Thought creates reality, and energy follows thought.

As Theo teaches us, "thought is reality"; it is the energy that fuels the universe. The implications of this are staggering—especially considering how set in our ways most of us are.

Theo has taught me that nothing exists *before* "thought." What we think about, what we give attention to, becomes reality. Thought is like the spark that ignites the willpower and creates action in our lives.

Thought is the creator; it is electric. It is what is made manifest in the material world. One does not have any

material object unless it is thought about first . . . and
then created. Do you understand?

Thought, as Theo has described it, is a subtle form of pure
energy ("electric" is their word in order to make it more under-
standable in our world) and can be used in any way you want—
for good or ill, for positive or negative goals.

Thought is that power that creates all things, so when you
think in positive and loving ways, it creates that essence,
that vibration. When you think in negative patterns, that
vibration is sent out into the world.

Your thoughts also affect your whole belief system; if you set
up negative thoughts in your mind, then your overall belief system
will be influenced by those destructive images. Negative ideas feed
your belief system, which then sends those negative "thought
energies" back to your conscious mind as *beliefs* or *attitudes*. It
becomes a vicious cycle. It is this cycle of negative thought patterns that Theo advises changing, which we will go into in more
detail shortly.

We should ask ourselves why we usually accept so quickly
every negative thought that pops into our heads; why don't we
give equal weight and value to more positive thoughts? Belief in
the destructive powers of the mind implies belief in its curative,
positive abilities as well. Take the issue of health, for example.
That the body and mind acting together can heal is becoming
more accepted as scientific investigation continues. Each mental
or physical symptom is beginning to look more like a clue to a
conflict inside the body and mind, which carry their own healing
powers.

This does not mean that there are no diseases afflicting the
human body but rather that mind/body conflicts help set up an
environment in which a disease can take hold and flourish. The
more science explores the mind/body relationship the more evidence is accumulated to show the presence of a conflict within the
mind/body system that has disrupted the whole.

This is where belief is so important. If a person is committed
to a worldview that accepts the idea of having no control over the

internal, autonomic bodily functions, the positive thought of healing—say, one's blood pressure—will be impossible. Such a person
will reject any possibility of the mind healing the body; in effect,
he or she will succumb to a negative thought pattern and deny a
more positive belief system that may well cure the problem. The
release of rigid belief systems allows you to feel empowered over
your own life. You begin to feel the exhilaration of being the
"cause" of your life experience instead of simply the "effect."

Those who automatically accept negative and destructive
ideas about the inner mind's abilities slow their own growth. In
effect, they resist the flow of their own inner lives toward spiritual
completion. To be frightened of emotions, or to reject your own
internal power to create reality—which most people do constantly
—means burying even deeper certain thoughts and ideas that
have the power to help you grow. This psychic armor against your
inner life only reinforces negative belief systems and sets up additional barriers between the conscious, analytical self and the self-
healing capacity of your inner being.

*Change, upheaval in personal experience, holding on to
the past—all bring forth fear. For when old forms no
longer work, fear develops. Many do not want the responsibility that comes with change, do you understand?*

If you are frightened of change, or reject the inner powers of
your psyche, your ability to communicate with the subtle universe
surrounding you is diminished. If we think of the inner mind as
an elaborate computer—which, unfortunately, most people in our
culture still do—capable of only mechanical functions, then that
is all the mind will be capable of doing.

Part of the mind, of course, does work like a computer. But
the problem is that many assume this logical, rational functioning
of the mind is its total ability. The sad part is that this particular
negative thought pattern, or negative belief system, will prevent
any greater use of your inner self. For once you accept that the
logical, rational mind is all there is, you have denied a major part
of your mental capacity. In fact, all such cultural biases have crippled the full use of our bodies and emotions and have prevented
any fuller use of our minds as well.

The important point to remember here is that those who see
their normal world in a new way will also see *themselves* in a new
light.

Accept the idea that your own thought is the creator of
your life and every moment becomes an opportunity for
making a positive choice.

What if certain experiences occurred that showed us our
biases and preconceptions about the world were mistaken? How
would most of us react? Some, no doubt, would panic. Still others
would respond with disbelief, derision, and rejection. And perhaps
a small group would respond by accepting the new experience for
what it is and readjusting their worldview to incorporate it.

For example, what would happen if a man lived in a world
that had, say, only two colors—blue and gray—and suddenly as
he was sitting under a tree he saw a bright yellow light in the sky?
If he was an educated man, his first reaction might be to believe
the new color a hallucination. If the experience happened repeatedly, he might eventually realize that his two-color world of blue
and gray was not the complete truth or the whole of reality.

If he did not become terrified that his secure, familiar world
of blue and gray was being shattered, and if he could integrate this
new perception into his view of reality, his understanding of the
world would be considerably greater than before this experience.
He might even reason that if one color beyond his normal world
of blue and gray existed, then there might also be others. This
knowledge could lead him on a pursuit, one might even call it a
spiritual quest, for a fuller and truer picture of his universe. This
is the position in which many psychics and channelers find themselves. They have seen a more complex, subtle universe, full of
color and marvelous mysteries.

As Theo has said, we are all teachers, all seekers of enlightenment, and as the 5th Dimension energies take effect we will all
begin to see a greater reality.

You are seekers of truth and light. As this comes forth,
as one perceives a greater reality, the knowing must

be shared. Each being is therefore a teacher and a student. . . .

What you bring forth in this time of enlightenment, in this period of the 5th Dimension, will have an impact on what you call the New Age, and it will have an impact far beyond anything in ages past. You are but on the threshold.

If our two-dimensional friend in his blue and gray world could open himself to these new dimensions, oh, how his world would change. Rather than just a simple two-dimensional world of blues and grays, his universe would suddenly be opened into an exciting broad spectrum of possibilities. Alternative realities would open up, and his consciousness would broaden into rich new dimensions—which is the reason for the coming of the 5th Dimension.

Such a new vision of the world would change everything—even his relationship to his environment. Everything would suddenly be tinted with yellow and gold; each moment would bring a new perception of his world. Each person who experienced this extra color, this extra dimension, would expand his or her personal vision of the world and ultimately even alter his or her perception of self. How one saw the world would be changed, and how one "thought" about the world would have also changed. Thought alters reality; it is the energy that structures our belief systems, that guides our perception of the world.

Thought is the creative force of your universe. It is the energy about you, similar to what you think of as your aura. It is electric. It comes into the thinking processes of the conscious mind of the being. But it is an energy form, do you understand? It is intention and attitude that is important, for thought is the creative force, is it not? Action is first brought forth from thought and intention, yes? That is why all beings are totally responsible for what they create in their experience.

If new experiences cause a revolution in our view of reality, they also create a new hope, a thirst for change and personal evolution. The outer world of physical experience is melded into your inner growth. Thinking of the world as a living, pulsing, vibrating creation that can be touched by your innermost psychic sensibilities not only helps you to evolve into a new and different person but allows a truer more objective examination of the world to be integrated into the "crystal cabinets" of your mind, to use William Blake's beautiful description of the spiritual aspect of the mind.

This internal, vibrating psychic crystal contains our preferences, our preconceived notions, our beliefs, our delusions and emotionally charged attitudes. But also lying within the "crystal cabinet" is the potential to use its vibrating power, to expand its function beyond its normal psychological conditioning. You can change its structure and thereby change the belief system that guides it. You can do this by changing your attitudes, *changing your thought patterns*, by developing what I call a "thought bridge."

And if you don't do this willingly, if you don't open yourself to greater dimensions of reality, then it is going to happen anyway. It is this psychological, cultural conditioning that 5th Dimension energies are going to shatter—which will force each individual to confront the contents of his or her own "crystal cabinet."

> *There is no longer time for superficialities, for deceptions and trivialities. It is of utmost importance that beings find the truth in themselves. Truth may not be liked, but it is to be accepted, do you understand? Truth is a blessing that the beings on this planet give as a gift unto the world.*
>
> *It is the structure of thought that is changing . . . here and now! This has not happened in your civilization with such magnitude before. It is society that has told you that you are unaware of the truth. But the 5th Dimension will bring a shift of attitude, a shift of thinking, that opens the mind and heart to their fullest expression. This is of great necessity. Truth will out, yes?*

But how is this done? How can we learn to use thought as a creative force in our lives? Two important answers are given by Theo. One, that we must first look within the heart.

One must look in the heart and become clearly aware of one's attitudes, to be aware how one views each experience—and the intention by which one pursues experience, yes? In the attitude one receives the lesson. In the intention one pursues the experience. Each person has that choice, of conflict or peace, yes?

The second way to use thought properly is to create a "thought bridge" that will allow you to experience several dimensions of reality at the same moment. In effect, once you learn to build a thought bridge, you have created a path crossing over into the 5th Dimension reality.

What Is a "Thought Bridge"?

A thought bridge is simply a point of awareness, a place where your consciousness can perceive the broadest possible view of "reality," a point where your mind simultaneously observes the full dimensions of your physical reality and the multiple dimensions of your spiritual reality. But it is a bridge, or a point of view you reach by creating positive thought patterns that allow you to move from being immersed in the problems of the physical world to the higher vibratory energy fields of spiritual consciousness.

To cross over this thought bridge, you must learn first to be alert to negative emotions and negative thought patterns. (As Theo says, look within the heart and become aware of attitudes and intentions.) Second, you must follow the three easy steps for "thought focusing" that I will share with you later in this chapter.

Thought focusing is a simple technique to help you build a thought bridge into 5th Dimensional reality. By using thought focusing you attune the energy of your thoughts to a higher vibrational level that harmonizes with 5th Dimensional energies. In short, the thought bridge is simply a higher point of view, a position from which your consciousness can experience multiple dimensions. A thought bridge is a pathway to higher consciousness, and thought focusing is the method by which you cross over the bridge.

THE POWER TO PREFER

Thought focusing is the most powerful method I have ever come across for creating new and positive pathways of consciousness. The single, simple, unique idea behind thought focusing is realizing that you have the "power to prefer."

When you are calm and peaceful, when your mind is in a "positive frame" you have the ideal opportunity to redirect your thought patterns into more constructive pathways. It is equally important to realize that when you are upset, or in a negative "attitude," you also have a perfect opportunity to create changes in your thought patterns. *You have the power to prefer* one set of thought patterns over another.

> *The fullness of your life can occur only when your consciousness is not dominated by addictions . . . by the demands and delusions you fill yourself with. . . . Only then can you experience life as a stream of preferences flowing before you.*

When used properly thought focusing can wipe out a lifetime of negative thinking. As you learn to use thought focusing, you automatically grow into a higher consciousness. Placing your thought patterns on a positive pathway lets you go forward into life rather than backing away or hiding from it. You can deal more effectively with the *present* no matter how stressful or difficult the situation you are facing may be. If your marriage or love relationship is uncomfortable for you, or if your career seems blocked and is causing you to doubt yourself or your ability, by redirecting your thoughts you can eliminate the pain of everyday problems.

Thought focusing frees your consciousness from "lower-level" involvements with negative emotions; it frees you from addictions, from responding like a robot with your old, negative patterns, and allows you to grow more rapidly because all of your mental energy will no longer be used solely to "handle" such heavy life problems. Theo often says that we have the choice to view a situation and choose to experience it from the point of view of conflict or peace. It is a change of attitude.

The "power to prefer" means simply that *you* are the power

behind your thoughts, that *you* create the negative thoughts, *you* create the emotional upset, and *you* have the power to change it all. You can change any moment, no matter how negative or destructive it may be, simply because you created the moment and it is *your energy* and mind-set that gives anything the power to dominate your attention . . . and, all too often, your whole life.

Know that many have been in conflict because of negative attitudes, yes? Mistrust! Lack of self-worth! So there has been much manipulation—of both the self and others— stemming from these negative choices.

See each emotional upset, each negative thought, as an opportunity to choose your own reality. Each negative attitude gives you the choice to make a decision, to seize a chance to express your preference for a more positive, constructive experience. You have the power to prefer one type of thought pattern over another.

Know that much change can come from thought, which is the creative force, and that the attitudes and intention of the beings on this planet—their consciousness and power of thought—has effect and can cause a universal impact. Also, beings can become more attuned to the 5th Dimension by the power of thought.

Every time you feel fearful, angry, or negative, *remember* that you have been given a golden opportunity to free yourself from such a negative frame of mind, that you have the power to prefer one type of thought pattern over another. Say to yourself: *I have the power to prefer. . . .*

Once the basic idea that you have the power—that it is your energy firing these negative thoughts—is accepted, the next step is easy: Use the following easy method for thought focusing. Once you have learned to use these simple techniques, you will have laid the building blocks for a thought bridge, which will give you an opportunity to see the world from a broad, multi-dimensional perspective—in effect, to cross over into the 5th Dimension!

How to Create a Thought Bridge

The "real world" is only a shadow or reflection of other realities within our universe. I believe that when someone leaves his or her body, he or she moves between the dimensions of matter and spirit . . . and exists simultaneously within two separate dimensions. While the physical body continues to exist in the physical dimension, the energy of thought exists within other, higher vibratory dimensions. The point of crossing over between these different dimensions is the "thought bridge." In other words, we can change our attitudes, alter our thought patterns, and experience 5th Dimensional reality if we choose. The choice, the determination of each moment of our lives, is ours to make. It is how we guide our conscious awareness that creates the change of our thought patterns, which changes the energy fields sustaining our thoughts.

Remember what Theo said:

Thought . . . is the creative force, and . . . the attitudes and intention of the beings . . . has effect—and can cause a universal impact.

Since we do make our own reality, we can obviously make our inner world of thought either an inhospitable hell or a place of peace and beauty. And, following Theo's advice, we can create a "thought bridge" that allows us to stand astride the different dimensions of matter and spirit.

Often what is ugly or destructive is simply what each person creates within his or her own self.

Know that your world is very simple. It is the conscious mind that makes it complicated, for it likes to solve problems. But know that these attitudes, these ways of living, have been in the human mind and action for a long time and that you can choose. It is the intention and attitude that is important, for thought is the creative force, is it not?

When you create new forms of consciousness with your thought patterns, you also create a new way of knowing, a new way of seeing the world. This is why it is vital that you guide your thoughts into positive pathways; in this way the new way of knowing you create will be a positive and constructive one.

Thought is an energy field, an unseen power dominating our lives; we can live more successfully as we learn to guide our thought patterns into positive pathways.

BUILDING A THOUGHT BRIDGE

Every one of us can become a channel for the divine power that vibrates at the core of our beings. What is needed is to focus the attention properly to feel the presence of the divine within. I know this sounds simplistic, but great truths are often simple once realized. The final result of learning to direct your thought into positive pathways, whether it takes a minute or a lifetime, is nothing less than the transfiguration of the self into 5th Dimensional reality, into the highest form of spiritual being. Transforming your thought pattern creates a new vision, because the energy field of your thought patterns changes, which, in turn, creates a higher form of consciousness.

There are three steps in creating a thought bridge.

1. Be alert to negative emotions and thought patterns; learn to recognize them as they occur.

2. When they do occur, immediately use the thought focusing techniques to replace them with positive images and constructive emotions. This is done by visualizing positive alternatives—by using the power of your imagination constructively.

3. Remember to use the thought focusing techniques every day.

Being Aware of Negative Thought Patterns

Most of us protect ourselves from unpleasant situations or ones in which we feel "uptight." But in order to learn how to recognize negative emotions and thought patterns you must never again try to back away from any situation (including those involving people). Welcome the situation; open yourself to it uncritically, nonjudgmentally. Sometimes, as Theo says, we need to feel fear or sadness, anger or elation, or whatever the emotion is, because the earth is a place to experience emotion and learn from it.

> *Embrace the moment; acknowledge it. All of the emotions should be to the forefront, not put aside or put away. It is the embracing of the emotions that creates the clarity, the release, yes? It is part of loving the self, is it not?*

Be aware that most situations, no matter how unpleasant, provide you with impressions from the outside world that help make you aware of your emotional state. If you are to change your negative thought patterns, you must become aware of your response to the outside world. As each situation arises become aware of it, open yourself to it, and accept it noncritically.

But it should be remembered that when changing negative thoughts to positive ones, you should not think of yourself as a "bad" person for having negative feelings or ideas. Accept that you have fears and angers, just as we all do. Accepting that they exist robs them of their power over you, and, alternatively, if you condemn yourself for feeling anger, fear, or other negative emotions, then you continue to give them power. In simple terms, you give power wherever you focus your thoughts, so by condemning yourself for having negative feelings, you are simply feeding another, new negative thought. To avoid this self-defeating trap, simply accept that negative thoughts and feelings do exist and begin working on the positive constructions.

One way to bring yourself to this emotional condition of acceptance is to stop blaming the outside world for your emotional responses. You are the power. You create your own response. You must alter how you see other people and life situations—do not let yourself conclude that anything outside yourself is the cause of your emotional upset or negative thoughts. Whenever you become aware that you are blaming the world around you for your negative thinking, recognize that you are the source of your own unhappiness. Remind yourself that you have the power to prefer positive choices.

One way to do this is to rephrase the negative idea in your mind. If you are thinking "Joe's always late and makes me mad as hell," change the thought to "I have the choice of being angry or accepting of Joe's lateness. I choose to be accepting!"

If your thoughts run to generalizations that are negative: "All men are faithless" or "All women are manipulative," recognize those as negative thoughts that alienate you from the rest of humanity. Change the thought to "Many men are loyal and loving" and "Many women are honest and trustworthy." If you generalize negatively about other "worldly" things (or situations), cars, cities, countries, politicians—whatever the negative thinking might be directed toward—alter the thought pattern to a positive and loving image. In this way you will be altering your thought pattern and creating a more accepting, loving attitude within yourself.

One of the best times to become aware of negative thought patterns—and therefore an ideal time to take corrective action—is when you are angry or emotionally upset. The more emotional you are, the better reflection your desires, attachments, and negative thoughts are showing you about what you think the world "should be like." Identify the cause of the anger or emotion, and create a positive thought to counteract the negative feelings and ideas. I feel it is important to identify where the emotions come from. We are often confused about what the real emotion is. Some people can only feel anger, which may actually be fear, sadness, grief, or some other emotion.

Thought Focusing to Create Positive Thought Patterns

When you are feeling strong negative emotions or thinking clearly negative thoughts, try to identify precisely what is bothering you, and alter the images in your thinking. For example, if you are jealous and angry over your lover talking too long to an attractive person, focus your consciousness on correcting the problem. Say to yourself "I do not want to be jealous anymore. I'm sick and tired of reliving this silly drama every time my lover is enjoying talking to someone. I'm tired of putting myself through all this emotional turmoil when my desires or expectations aren't met." Talk positively about your feelings toward the person making you jealous and angry. Remember all the times in the past you've been mistaken when you became jealous. Rephrase every negative jealous thought that enters your consciousness with a positive phrase. Something like "I trust and love *(use the person's name here)* and will not let these feelings control me" would work fine. But any phrase you choose, as long as it is positive and loving, will do. Repeat the positive phrase over and over again if you have to. It is very important that these moments of high emotion be turned around from negative to positive, so talk to yourself only about the specific problem that is causing the negative emotions. Don't let yourself be sidetracked into a lengthy analysis that only ends up with more negativity.

In this way you are focusing your consciousness on preventing such negative attitudes from dominating your emotions at a later time. And even though you cannot wipe out all the years of negative attitudes and emotional triggers immediately, if you carefully replace every negative attitude with a positive one, and rephrase negative thought patterns with positive ones, it will become easier each time you use the focusing technique.

YOU ARE YOUR OWN POWER SOURCE

Your energy and the power of your emotions creates your own negative thought patterns. *You do it all.* You are not the victim of powers beyond your control. It's all in your own mind. To understand your own power, and to accept that you truly do have the power to create your own reality, keep telling yourself that every negative thought is your power gone astray. Repeat to yourself that you have made these negative thought patterns over the years and you have the power to change them and to stop being the victim of your own negative emotions.

> *You become free when you recognize that you are responsible for everything in your life, when you accept that you make your own choices—either consciously or unconsciously—and therefore create your own present and your own future.*

Each moment of recognition of your own negative thoughts or negative emotions should be followed with the thought that you created the pain you are feeling. You are the power source. Your energy is neutral—it is simply energy—and it will go where you want it to; it will create thoughts that you prefer. To change your attitude, and thereby change your thought patterns, accept the idea that you are the master of your own emotions, of the thoughts that run through your own head.

By rephrasing negative thoughts into positive ones, by consciously seeking positive alternatives to negative feelings, you are refocusing your attitude. With each successful replacing of the negative with a positive alternative, you move closer to the kind of confidence that you are the absolute master of yourself.

Negative ideas ("This isn't working," etc.) will no doubt creep in, but the solution is to use thought focusing to turn the negative around—"Yes, it is working; otherwise I wouldn't be fighting so hard to avoid creating positive thought patterns."

The rephrasing of negative ideas with positive thoughts is not simple word-juggling. If that were the case, it wouldn't work at all. What you are doing is rejecting negative patterns that you've unconsciously allowed to dominate your life for years and replacing them with positive ideas. It is not simple word replacement but replacing negative ideas with positive ones, destructive emotions with constructive ones, angry thoughts with peaceful ones. It is subtly and quietly restructuring your thought patterns.

I believe the mind needs exercise just as the body does. To keep aware and alert is a natural part of our God-given power. Few of us have learned to use our full potential. By replacing negative with positive thought patterns we are beginning a transformation of our life.

Entities in the physical plane use only a small percentage of their mental capacity. . . . This is very important, for when people in the physical world understand how much power they have in their own <u>thought</u>, they will gain control of their lives and will not be so harmful—either to themselves or others.

The most important attitude and intention to radiate out is an unconditional love of self, of the uniqueness, the perfection, of the individual.

It is love that is important, is it not? It is not that one has to like the experience or the circumstances, but to love the experience, for it allows the highest good of all to blossom forth, you see?

To know that you are the center of your own destiny, that through thought you are the creator of your own power, can be frightening. As for myself, this wisdom has helped me to realize that my potential is limitless. I can be anything I want to be: not simply a psychic or a channel but I can be *anything* that moves me closer to my true inner self. I have come to believe, as Theo says, that everything is thought . . . that I create my own peace and good fortune through thought.

I have found, through my own experience, that if I want something enough, it will be there for me. I have found my answers and my peace. All of us have the ability to do this. It is part of our human legacy, a part of the gift of life.

AFFIRMATIONS AND VISUALIZATIONS

Thoughts continually flow through our minds; everything we see, feel, hear—all the awareness of our senses filters through the mind and sooner or later manifests as thoughts. Thoughts make us what we are; they create our environment both internally and externally.

But just what is a *thought* in the fuller sense that Theo uses the word? First, thought is a vibratory wave, a radiation not unlike the energy of light waves. When a thought comes into being, the wave moves outward in all directions equally and continues to flow from the mind of the thinker as long as the thought is held.

But here is the key to understanding the power of using thought in affirmations and visualizations: *Like all other vibrations, thought waves tend to reproduce themselves in objects around them.*

Everyone is familiar with the simple experiment of using a tuning fork to cause a wire to vibrate when the two are held near each other. When a corresponding note is played on the piano, a sympathetic response will be created within the tuning fork, which will begin to vibrate. Glass, especially delicate crystal, will

vibrate in response to a musical note played nearby. Is there anyone who hasn't seen the television commercial where Ella Fitz-
gerald shatters a glass by singing a single note?

The same thing occurs with mental vibrations. A sympathetic
response is aroused within nearby objects that resonate to the
energy waves created by thought. The impact of a thought upon
the minds of others, and objects in the physical world, depends
on the strength and clarity of the original thought.

It is easy to see that if a powerful, energizing, positive image
is created in your mind—and held there—then a clear response
will occur. This is why *positive* thoughts, positive images, are so
important.

Another rule to remember is that *thought creates patterns*, or
distinctive waves within the energy resources of your mind and
body. Just as a sound wave can create ripples on the surface of a
pool of water, so does the energy of a thought create impulses
within your mental and emotional energy pools. With this in
mind, it becomes clear that a negative thought will create negative
responses; negative wave patterns in your mind and emotions will
become part of a destructive cycle.

Positive affirmations and visualizations build energies that radiate out into the universe and reflect back onto their creator.
Think about that for a moment—you receive back what you send
out! When I first realized this, I was stunned. All the negative,
half-baked dissatisfaction and irritations that I let fill my head
were bouncing back at me from the universe? When I picked
myself up from the floor, I began to work on changing my thought
patterns.

This is where learning to use affirmations and visualizations
became vitally important. I discovered that affirmations and visualizations offer you the most powerful tool you could hope for.
When properly used the results can be amazing.

Some General Rules to Be Aware Of

Before getting into specific suggestions on how to create visualizations and affirmations, a couple of principles should be kept in
mind.

1. Avoid aimless negative thoughts. You are yourself a stream of living thought that flows from your mind out into space. It is up to you to direct the power within that streaming energy.

2. Adopt a positive point of view. Your attitude, as Theo constantly reminds us, is your counterbalance to years of negative thinking. Remember that a prayer, a benediction, sent out into the world is a pure form of thought energy. Once you recognize that your attitude influences your thinking, and that your thoughts resonate in the universe around you, then you are on the path into the 5th Dimension.

Creating Visualizations

We have all heard the advice "Concentrate on success; visualize yourself being successful and it will happen." The principle is true, but for the average person struggling to survive under stress it's like telling someone to "think positively" about playing a Chopin concerto and then expecting the person to sit down and play it. This is unrealistic advice because it ignores the necessary preparation and understanding.

The act of visualization is really the "art of mental creation," an act of constructive imagining. Visualization and the action of the mind while imagining accumulates energy within the mind and directs it toward the desired objective. Imagination is the form of thought that opens the mind to other realities. Constructive imagining not only creates new ideas from our "earth reality" but opens us to energy from the universe. So while you are working on creating a visualization, you are also exercising your power to imagine. The energy you consciously accumulate through positive visualization is like food, and it nourishes not only your mind but your entire being.

There is no secret to visualization. Everyone can do it, but first one must be clear about what one desires. Remember that creative visualization is equivalent to a power generator. By visualizing you generate power—*and what you visualize becomes reality.*

To make changes in the material world, energy is first required. The greater the change desired in the material world the greater the energy needed. And creative visualization—along with proper affirmation—is your power generator.

A Simple Guide to Creating Visualizations

First, as always, settle yourself in a comfortable position in a quiet room. The whole point here is to free the senses from as many distractions as possible so that your mind can be free to focus where you wish.

CREATING A MENTAL IMAGE—THREE VISUALIZATION EXERCISES

1. The simplest way to create a visualization is to use your mind as a canvas. Paint in the details; use your imagination to fill in the specific image of whatever it is you desire—a new job, new car, healthy body, etc. Fill in all the details you can think of. Fill the screen of your mind with sounds, with scents, with colors, of your desired reality. *Feel* as much of the picture you are creating as you can. Make it real! This involves your emotions as well.

As the picture becomes clearer, move your mind's eye around the visualization, and as your imagination suggests new details, put them in. The more specific you can be with each object, with each idea, the greater the accumulation of energy. By making the images specific you focus all your mind energy on what you desire. Your thoughts are activated, and the energy of your thoughts is sent out into the universe.

Continue to hold the visualization for as long as you can. If you feel it slipping away, move your mind's eye to another area of the visualization and begin to put in the details of the new image.

2. One of the easiest visualization exercises, and a good one to begin with, is sometimes called "Mental Photography."

Choose a simple image such as a diagram, mathematical formula with only a few numbers or letters, or a simple line drawing and observe it for a short time—say, one minute. Then close your eyes and evoke the image. Give yourself a detailed and complete description of it—either out loud or silently. Try not to open your eyes to check yourself on accuracy—this isn't a test. After you think you have covered all the details, open your eyes and see if you have missed anything. If you have, don't be critical or impatient with yourself. Your primary task here is to evoke the "felt" quality of the thing rather than a complete memorization of it. The completeness of your memory will come with your success at evoking all its qualities and characteristics.

You should do this exercise as often as you can—the more frequent the better. You will quickly see your improvement, and as you are able to describe the simple image fully, choose progressively more complicated images to work on. Begin to add color, dimension, images with a greater number of figures, angles, lines, etc.

Some suggest using a matchbox for this exercise as the beginning object, using the mind to circle around it, observing every detail. Let your mind rise above, circle below and to the sides as you recreate the matchbox in your mind's eye. Get inside the box with your mind, and examine all the minute details of the paper, its texture, dimensions, etc.

This exercise employs an additional element to the simple visual reconstructions—the movement of consciousness from point to point. But the simpler designs, one- or two-dimensional surfaces, are preferable for beginners. You need not stay for long on these simpler images, but they are valuable at first. Paintings are good once you have progressed beyond the simpler constructions.

In the beginning it might be helpful, though not essential, to use a small tape recorder in order to check the list of items you described. If you can write without opening your eyes and without disturbing the vividness of the image you are creating with your mind's eye, try slowly writing down each feature of the image. But this may be too distracting, and if it interferes in any way with your mental picture, don't do it. The purpose of this exercise is to develop your mental "eye," your inner vision, *not* your memory.

3. The third visualization exercise, "The Blossoming of the Rose," is a little harder because it uses a variety of different qualities: form, color, smell, movement, etc. It is similar to color med-

itations, but here the goal is to create the form more than the color or other qualities.

Imagine a small, closed rosebud. Visualize the stem and leaves beneath the bud. It is green at the base, where the leaves enclose the flower, but at the top you can see a small rose-colored point. Visualize this as vividly as you can and hold the image in the forefront of your consciousness. After holding it confidently for a short while, watch as a slow movement begins of the leaves encasing the rosebud. They gradually start to separate, turning their points outward, peeling back to reveal the deep red petals of the rose itself. They continue to open until you can see the whole of the small red flower. The petals now begin to open up slowly until there is a perfect, fully opened rose. Study this perfect creation of yours for a moment or two and then see if you can catch the faint perfume. Try to smell it, to inhale its unmistakable scent. Next, expand your vision to include the whole rosebush, with bright red flowers blossoming all over it. Examine the rosebush; see its base and the stem going into the earth. Picture the earth in its full, rich color. Finally, try to identify with the rose itself, with its strong urge to blossom, to open itself to the sun and sky. Try to feel the vitality in the plant's roots, stem, branches, leaves, and flowers.

End each visualization by turning the picture inward, back into the inner self. Do not simply blank out the picture or turn your attention to something else or let the images fade away. Turn the whole visualization down into the heart of yourself, down into the center of your being. Let the energy flow as if it were colored water rushing down into the dark center of your being where it will remain to energize and nourish you.

Then forget about it until the next period of visualization. Don't let the faint images of the picture you have created filter back into your imagination during the day. This is important, since the energy you have built up will be siphoned off by incomplete images thought about halfheartedly without the proper focus.

Try to repeat the visualization at least twice a day.

Creating Affirmations

The fourth sentence of the Bible reads: "And God said, Let there be light: and there was light." Creation began with the word of God. And throughout religious scriptures the world over time and again the power of the word is emphasized. Religious rituals use music, chanting, and repetitive prayer to evoke the power of the spirit world. These are not new ideas; they are as ancient as humankind's evolving awareness.

What is new during this time of the 5th Dimension is the greater understanding of the why and how of these powers. It is no longer enough simply to say "prayers have power," or "affirmations can change your life." The 5th Dimension is a period of expanding awareness, of greater consciousness—and people during this time *need to understand how to use their power.* For to use one's personal power to change and grow in positive ways is part of the energy activated within all of us by the coming of the 5th Dimension.

There are basically two types of affirmations: the prayer, or reaching out to the universal God-source, and a personal affirmation created by you for specific reasons.

In creating an affirmation that reaches out to the God-source, an excellent phrase is: "I, *(insert your name),* am fully a part of the God-source and the universe around me. I have the power of the universe within me. I am within God, and God is within me."

By repeating this phrase, and visualizing the light of God within you, your spiritual power is activated. The words evoke a positive thought pattern that will resonate throughout your being. Repeat this phrase for at least fifteen or twenty minutes twice a day and the results will be astounding. You will be more at peace and literally feel a greater strength and energy within you.

The personal affirmation usually deals with change—with altering a negative thought pattern, a behavior or attitude that you recognize as unhealthy or undesirable. Theo has offered specific solutions for the problems of dealing with negative emotions and ideas.

Theo, you have talked many times about the importance of thinking properly. Can you advise us about
releasing negative thought patterns?

*Often when one is experiencing negative thought pat-
terns, it is an emotion that has not been released. It is
frequently expressed through anger. When you are experiencing these thoughts, it is best to look for the source,
to go within and see where the negative thought originated.*

How, specifically, do you do that? How do you find
where a negative thought originates?

*Take a quiet moment; breathe deeply to center the self.
Ask the self where that particular thought has originated.
When the question is asked, an impression comes immediately to mind. You can ask at what age this negative
thought process began. The age will come to mind, and
often the reason will be made clear.*

Once we understand the thought's origin, then what
do we do?

*Through this understanding there will be an emotional
release. Do not reject these emotions; allow them to be
felt fully, to be embraced. Do not restrict the feelings, for
emotions that are restricted or repressed will persist.*

So we allow the emotions to exist and the negative
thoughts associated with those emotions will go away?

*Yes, as the emotion is expressed and released into con-
sciousness, the energy upon which it fed is also released.
There are also times when you should speak about these
emotions for a greater release. You will feel as if a weight
has been lifted from your body, for it takes much energy
—physical energy—to repress your emotions. And as you*

release these feelings there will be that much more energy available for your life processes to become stronger.

Is there a specific type of affirmation or visualization that you recommend for releasing these emotions?

Speak in the first person and affirm the positive. For example, you would say, "I, Barbara, bring forth and create unconditional love within myself and within my life now."
This allows the loving of self to be predominant.

So you would always affirm unconditional love; or would you affirm different things depending on what it is you are releasing?

Unconditional love . . . so that Divine love can do its work in and through you. This is also to affirm healing within the self as well.

Do you have a phrase you would recommend for people trying to free themselves from a specific negative habit or problem?

Yes, again use the first person, the "I" form. Say: "I (speak your name) choose to change this process within me now." Repeat this phrase, and also use a visualization where you see yourself in the situation of change. Do you see?

Creating the Right Atmosphere and Using Your Willpower

You are a free agent. You have the choice of working harmoniously with the rhythms and vibratory energies of your nature or against them—like swimming with or against a current. By working with the natural rhythms around you the currents of power lift you up and move you along toward your objectives. This is the way to use your energy efficiently. In short, it is using the energy of the universe to your advantage. You accomplish this by using the various techniques outlined here for affirmations, visualizations, and meditations. But to create affirmations and visualizations most efficiently the techniques should be used in the proper environment.

To open yourself to this "atmosphere of spiritual energy" you begin by creating a feeling of warmth or goodwill in the area of your heart—where your ribs meet at the breastbone. Visualize a glowing aura of light emanating from your heart until it grows and surrounds your whole body. Hold this warm, glowing light for as long as it is comfortable.

This builds up your personal energy and acts as a key to opening the channels of spirit within so the flow coming back into you is unhampered. In effect, you are making yourself more receptive to the spirit dimensions by creating the proper emotional and mental atmosphere.

It is also important to be patient with yourself when you are developing these new skills. Accept and forgive your mistakes and weaknesses. No one achieves perfection overnight. That's an illusion, an expression of distorted thinking. The value of these techniques becomes quickly apparent as you move in the right direction. As you use your thoughts more effectively by sending out the power of your affirmations and visualizations, you will find your life changing for the better. You will become more at peace with yourself, more accepting and less judgmental of others, more loving and better adjusted, more capable of handling sudden or unsettling crises.

In short, you take control of your life. With every affirmation you use, with every visualization you create, with every exercise you perform, you are creating a stronger willpower within yourself. Will is an expression of your energy; it is a commitment to change that rides on the power of your thoughts. By using affirmations and visualizations daily, you are creating new emotional and mental patterns within you. With each exercise performed, your will grows stronger, and the new patterns coming into existence move you closer to your own higher self.

We learn by doing, by taking our understanding and applying it to life. So waste no time; you must *act* in order to achieve.

Growth doesn't exist in a vacuum; it is part of a process that involves mind, body, and spirit . . . and the energy to bring it all together.

Theo has often said that we are only limited by our attitude and by our thought patterns.

On the earth you are limited only in your mental capabilities. When you limit yourself through physical reality, you limit your mind. When you open your mind, you are limitless. You possess no boundaries. There are no people with small minds; they are not of small mind, they have only limited themselves. We wish for them to open this blockage of mind to bring forth all that is possible. The Infinite . . . perfection . . . totality . . . can be experienced by all.

9

Dreams and Dreaming

LEGEND TELLS HOW ALEXANDER the Great dreamed of the root that would heal his friend, Ptolemy, who had been wounded by a poisoned dart. According to Shakespeare, Julius Caesar's wife, Calpurnia, had two precognitive dreams the night before Caesar was assassinated. One was symbolic: Calpurnia "saw" Caesar's statue bleeding. In the second dream Caesar fell under the repeated blows of daggers. Calpurnia tried to warn him but did not succeed.

Marie de Medici, too, dreamed of the assassination of her husband, King Henry IV of France, the night before it happened.

There is also a great deal of religious prophecy and dream interpretation in the Bible. Biblical seers translated God's signs into meaningful directions for the people of Israel. Dreams, the early Hebrews believed, were direct messages from God.

> *We are messengers and teachers from the God-source of the Creator to assist you along the way. . . . There is a wealth of information that is being imparted to your planet now, to the individuals upon it. And in the dream state one gets glimpses of this information. Not at all times will you remember it in a conscious way, but you are receiving, yes?*

The sharing of ideas thus could surely be accomplished by discarnate entities during sleep and through dreams. This is the time when the conscious, critical, rationalizing mind is at rest.

Unlike the time of Freudian dominance when the dogma "all dreams are fundamentally sexual in nature" was uncritically accepted by psychologists, today dreams are seen as highly productive, fertile periods that are complex in structure and scope.

Research over the last two decades has established that many dreams are telepathic. Even though the idea of telepathically communicating information through dreams is quite old, the scientific evidence supporting the idea is recent. One of the most striking, and exciting, experiments done in dreaming telepathically was started in 1962 by Dr. Montague Ullman and Dr. Stanley Krippner at their dream lab in the Department of Psychiatry at Maimonides Hospital in Brooklyn, NY.

Dr. Ullman, a psychiatrist by training, had long been intrigued by people's reporting of telepathic impressions while dreaming. He established the dream lab at Maimonides to investigate, under controlled scientific conditions, the possibility of information being transferred from an agent (sender) to a sleeping subject. Using an EEG (electroencephalograph) to register brain-wave changes, they clearly established after years of experiments that sleeping subjects can indeed receive pictures in their dreams that the agent or sender had been concentrating upon.

The obvious point is: If sleeping subjects receive telepathically transmitted images during the less than ideal "experimental" environment, how much more common might the experience be under more natural conditions. And how convenient for a higher intelligence to send ideas to a sleeping, noncritical mind. Without the benefit of a totally resting mind as in trance states, the dreaming mind would seem a close second choice to channelers for any entity wishing to communicate.

Marconi, the inventor of the radio, is reputed to have once said to his friend, "There is only one thing about radio that I don't understand."

"What is that?" Marconi's friend asked.

"Why it works at all," Marconi answered.

Psychic abilities, such as telepathy, clairvoyance, out-of-the-body experiences, etc., have all been studied for decades. And while no scientists yet seem to understand how or why they work, the experimental evidence is undeniable.

The evidence for telepathy, in particular, is so convincing that those who deny its existence are no longer simply skeptical but blindly rejecting something that disturbs their own limited view of the world.

For me, one of the most intriguing thoughts is that inspired ideas are really the mind of the creator plucking the thought from higher mental realms. This implies that the creator of the idea puts him- or herself in tune with a higher vibrational reality and thereby becomes able to tap its resources.

Just as with telepathy, there is a great amount of growing evidence that higher beings may be influencing human life—especially in the realm of ideas and creativity. New ideas in art, new inventions, original approaches to solving problems in medicine and the sciences, could in part be attributed to teachers communicating from a higher realm. In fact, many of the most original thinkers and creators have admitted that they believe their inspirations come from outside themselves.

There are beings in physical as well as in dimensions such as ours—energy—assisting this vibrational shift of the 5th Dimension. It has begun in the few years past so that there could be an enlightenment of the masses. Highly evolved beings have come here to help in this evolutionary process of vibrational shift on this planet. The highways into the universe have been the opening allowing these galactic beings entrance.

Chester Carlson, the inventor of the photocopier, admitted late in his life that the idea for his billion-dollar invention was due entirely to psychic assistance. He never told the full story during his lifetime because he feared ridicule, but in his later years he spent millions supporting various forms of scientific research into psychic phenomena. And just before his death he related how he was working late one night when a voice suddenly began to instruct him in how to make carbon jump to an electrically charged drum and imprint copies on sheets of paper. The experience convinced Carlson of the existence of the psychic world, and he devoted much time and money repaying what he considered his "debt." It is not surprising after experiences such as these that people begin to see the universe as a more complex, multilayered reality.

Perhaps there is no way of truly knowing how many inventions were aided by higher intelligences, especially since our society is so negative regarding such ideas and rejecting of those who believe in them.

One of the few, besides Carlson late in his life, to admit to such "higher" help, was the inventor of the Singer sewing machine. He was having trouble making the needle of his machine stitch correctly. One night he dreamed of an army of soldiers holding spears up—with every spear having a large hole in its pointed tip. He immediately awoke and realized that he had the solution to his problem. He went to his workshop and put the holes in the top rather than the base of the needle.

The usual scientific explanation for this kind of experience is called "unconscious cerebration." And perhaps the subconscious mind does have the capacity to pull together unconnected facts in novel or original ways, but that theory does not exclude the possibility that, as Dr. Gina Cerminara (author of *Insights for the Age of Aquarius*) says, "On some occasions at least intelligences in other frequency bands send ideas to the minds of sleeping human beings."

I've heard that the Chinese believe dreams are the inspirations of a god or goddess and that they often use a dream book for interpretations. We do the same thing in the West only we don't openly admit our belief in divine inspiration or being influenced by higher intelligences. Many of the dream books I've read refer to the interpretations of Artemodorus, a Greek philosopher. We all know the great emphasis modern psychology placed on dreams —especially Freud and Carl Jung. Modern psychologists now know that the conscious, critical mind generally interferes with the unconscious expressing itself.

It's not surprising, then, that the unconscious has developed other ways of communicating with the outer world. All of the psychic powers we've been talking about are used by the unconscious to let its highly charged, energized thoughts and ideas break through into the conscious world. Dreams are clearly not only one of the most common, but one of the most valuable, ways we can tap into our inner reality.

The dream is a powerful state, for it alters the consciousness. It allows the true self, the true inner being, to be free and unlimited as the body rests. There are times when dreaming is only a release from the activities of the day, of the present experience—and all beings are aware of this release. But on a higher level the energy that you are can leave the body to be taught in other dimensions— and that is happening quite frequently now for beings that seek the light as we move into the 5th Dimension.

PROPHETIC DREAMS

Early in this century an exceptional aeronautical engineer named J. W. Dunne experienced a series of striking precognitive dreams. Being a scientist and having an ordered mind, he began cataloging and checking the facts of his dreams. When he finally wrote a book about his dreams, he developed a complicated theory he called "serial time" to explain precognition and his uncannily accurate dreams.

One of Dunne's most remarkable dreams—"unusually vivid and rather unpleasant," he called it—was about one of the worst volcanic disasters of all time. In 1902 Mount Pelee on the island of Martinique erupted and swept away an entire town and killed thousands.

"In my dream," Dunne wrote, "I recognized the place as an island . . . which was in imminent peril from a volcano. . . . I was seized with a frantic desire to save the forty thousand (I knew the number) unsuspecting inhabitants. . . . All through the dream the number of people in danger obsessed my mind. I repeated it to everyone I met, and, at the moment of waking, I was shouting . . . 'Listen, forty thousand people will be killed unless . . . ' "

News of the disaster followed Dunne's dreams by several days. The reported number of deaths—forty thousand!

Many celebrities over the years have admittted to having precognitive dreams. Mark Twain dreamed of his younger brother, Henry's, death. He loved Henry, and the dream caused him enormous pain.

Twain was staying at his sister, Pamela's, house when he dreamed that he saw Henry's body "lying in a metallic burial case in the sitting room, supported on two chairs. On his breast lay a bouquet of flowers, white, with a single crimson bloom in the center."

The dream was so vivid that Twain was awakened, jumped out of bed, and ran down to the sitting room . . . only to find it empty. His relief was enormous, and he later told his sister about the dream—then he put it quickly out of his mind.

At that time Henry was a clerk on the steamboat *Pennsylvania*. Twain also worked on the boat, but not this trip. The *Pennsylvania* blew up just south of Memphis, and Henry was scalded to death by steam. Twain rushed to the disaster scene. He saw the boy's body being taken away and collapsed from grief.

As Twain relates the events, he later went to view the body. The other *Pennsylvania* victims' coffins were all of plain unpainted wood, but the youth and striking unburned face of young Henry so touched the hearts of people of Memphis that they bought a special metallic casket just for him.

When Mark Twain entered the room, his brother was lying exactly as in Twain's dream. It lacked only the bouquet of flowers. But as Twain stood there—"at that moment an elderly lady came in with a large white bouquet and in the center of it was a single red rose."

Mark Twain had been a skeptic—and a thoroughly rational realist. Yet after this dream and the wake for Henry he became a member of the Society for Psychical Research. He even wrote a book called *Mental Telegraphy* about his experiences.

In our society belief in precognitive dreams has been laughed at; but as we move further into the 5th Dimension, as the energies flooding over our planet begin to take effect, belief systems will change. People will become more open to the psychic. In fact, we need only look around to see it already happening.

One example of how the two worlds are slowly beginning to interact is the Aberfan, Wales, mining disaster twenty years ago in which 116 children and 28 adults were killed when an avalanche of coal slag rolled down a mountainside. It smothered a school in the small Welsh village. When authorities investigated the disaster, they found twenty-two well-documented cases of "dream-warnings" that had been reported *before* the tragedy.

The most striking case was of a ten-year-old child who had dreamed the night before that she had been buried under a suffocating black blanket with two friends. At breakfast she had described the dream to her parents, then reluctantly gone off to school. When the bodies were finally dug out from under the coal slag, the girl's body was found between that of her two best friends.

The *London Evening Standard* was impressed by the reports of "dream-warnings" and established a Disaster Early Warning System to collect and analyze premonitions in the hope of averting other tragedies.

One of the criticisms most often made against cases of precognition is that such phenomena are "psychologically self-ordaining." By this skeptics mean that someone prophesying an event in a dream, vision, or any other means will unconsciously attempt to make the prophecy come true—no matter how ugly or disastrous it may be.

There may be a smidgen of truth in this idea—especially if you accept the idea that the mind can indeed create its own reality. Scientists have, for example, found that when a believer—say, in voodoo—learns he has been "hexed" or "cursed," he may indeed lose all hope and inexplicably die. But the idea that Mark Twain would dream about his brother's death and then do something to bring about the explosion that killed him is too ridiculous to consider. And the theory of self-fulfilling prophecy cannot be applied to events prophesied far in the future or for distant parts of the world—as with Dunne's dream of Mount Pelee exploding.

Theo, can you tell us what a dream is?

A dream is a release of energy that has been imprinted upon the brain, whether it is from the recent past or the distant past. But it is also the mind being informative to the self; it is awareness of the higher self being imparted to consciousness. It is a form of enlightenment.

If the dream is a form of enlightenment, it must be important for people to learn how to receive guidance from their dreams. Can you give us any advice on how to do that?

In order for dreams to be informative they must first be remembered. Before sleeping, ask that you will recall your dreams when you awaken; ask the self to bring forth dreams in a literal sense rather than in symbolic form.

When looking for guidance from dreams, pay attention to the feelings, to the sensations, you experience during the dream. As you become more cognizant, more familiar with the dream state, you become what is called "lucid," that is, aware of dreaming while you are dreaming. In this way you can better decipher the dream and change it. In the changing you also alter the thought patterns reflected by the dream content, you see? That is how you become effective at utilizing the dream state, for you alter the dream as it is happening. This is not so much interpretation, but using dreams to affect your thought patterns, do you understand?

Theo, can you give us any guidance on how we can use our dreams to improve our daily lives?

As already indicated, program the dream state before you sleep; make a request of your higher self, or subconscious, to bring forth the dream literally, to make it more easily understood. Ask also for information to be imparted in the dream state that will clarify your life path.

Understand that some dreams are precognitive, that

is, they assist us in understanding the future; but there are also dreams that indicate the emotional changes happening within. To utilize dreams in this form, to achieve personal change, is most productive, for you receive direct guidance from the higher self regarding your life path.

Can you give us any guidance on how to interpret our dreams?

To interpret your dreams it is best to set the self aside; explain the dream to yourself as if you had never participated on this planet before, as from a purely objective point of view. Do this to explain each thing in the dream. If there is a location, ask what does that mean? This places the conscious self in the dream as a participant, do you understand?

And as far as interpreting dream symbols, can you give us any guidance on how to do that?

That is individualistic. That is why you set yourself aside as if you have come from another place and have never seen these symbols before. It necessitates asking the self for their meaning, do you see? There are many, many books written on the symbols of dreams; their interpretations can be correct for some but not for all. It is necessary to have the symbols resonate within the self, to understand the meaning unto the self. Set yourself aside in the interpretation, and you will feel the meanings. But in the asking, you should also accept the response, be open to the answer, do you see?

    Whenever there is confusion, however, it is best to ask the universe—or the higher self, whichever is more comfortable—to bring forth education and enlightenment in the dream state. Ask and the dream will respond, see?

EXERCISE: A Dream Meditation

A simple yet valuable exercise involves using important recent dreams as the central theme of a meditation.

First, try to recall the dream in as vivid detail as you can. If you don't recall all of it at first, don't worry; much of it will return as you meditate on it.

Second, take each detail of the dream, each major symbol that has clearly presented itself, and meditate on its overall symbolic meaning. Don't analyze it or dissect it intellectually. Deal with it in an intuitive way. Try to reexperience the images of the dream fully. Place each symbol in a pleasant, uncomplicated environment, like the night sky. Or visualize the smooth surface on a tranquil lake, and see the symbol or detail rise up from its depths to reflect fully and vividly in front of your eyes. As it gently floats before your eyes, hold an expectant attitude, quiet but receptive. Listen closely and watch the lake for any other impression that might rise to the surface. Do not press, but learn to wait patiently watching the symbol and waiting for further insight into its meaning.

As each symbol reveals its meaning go on to the next detail you want an explanation for until the central theme and meaning of the dream is clear. Don't be concerned about finding the solution immediately or even during the dream meditation. The desired insight may come later when you're busy doing something else during the day. Or it may appear in another dream. What you are doing with this meditation is setting in motion the deeper forces of the unconscious, and they may not answer you at once.

Repeat the meditation several times if necessary, and if you are not pressing or viewing the symbol or dream in logical terms, deeper insights into its meaning will surely come. Stay in the dream meditation as long as you care to. This is a good basic meditation, for it helps develop concentration and visualization abilities as well as supplying fascinating answers to your dreams.

10

Body Consciousness and the Healing Dimension

Theo on Healing

BODY CONSCIOUSNESS AS A DOORWAY

It has been said many times that the body is the temple of the spirit, and if there is anything that I am sure of it is the truth of this idea. This ancient wisdom is all too often ignored today because it has become so familiar and people do not like to repeat clichés. But a cliché is simply an idea that is familiar—and it still has value if the thought behind it contains truth. The point is simple: There is more to good health than a proper diet and exercise.

What, then, is health? Is it simply the absence of disease? From my vantage point it is a blending of the physical, mental, and emotional facets of life, a balance of the trinity of mind, body, and spirit. In fact, the connections are so intimate that even our attitude toward life and living is crucial in affecting this balance.

Feeling good does not come from a simple formula of better diet and exercise. There are psychological and spiritual factors. On the simplest level the tensions from our jobs, worries over payments due, the well-being of our relatives and friends—all these and more influence us daily. How we adjust to these pressures directly affects our well-being on all three levels of our mental, physical, and emotional life.

Look around the country at the everyday lives of Americans, and it's no wonder that America's combined health is "worse than most other industrialized nations." The reasons are relatively simple to find: the polluted air most of us breathe; the dirty water we drink; the processed, sprayed, chemically adulterated foods we buy and consume; and the stresses of the competitive, insecure, valueless culture we all try to survive in.

Many people say they don't have the time to exercise, prepare the right food, and—more important than all these—to meditate. Yet they will find the time to be sick. Many people seem to take better care of their cars than they do of their own bodies.

If we changed our way of thinking first, then our life-style would shift away from the destructive tendencies we have fallen prey to.

Hopefully, with the coming of the 5th Dimension our consciousness about our bodies—and our health—will be transformed. Even the idea of wholeness, of a body completely integrated and healthy, implies to me an openness between the conscious and unconscious minds.

Theo continually advises people to use the mind as a tool for healing, for truly the body is the temple of the spirit and, properly used, is a doorway into the 5th Dimension.

Your body is still healing. There has been much change in your physical structure as well as your thinking process. See the body as whole and functioning well. Visualize the body as healthy. Breathe health; breathe light into your cells. When you meditate, see energy coming from the earth as a golden light through the balls of your feet up through the body, creating health, creating strength and rejuvenation, and coming out of the crown of your head.

Encircle yourself in this light like a cocoon. The body will
be strong again.

Meditation, visualization, energy, are all keys to a healthier
body and mind. These are all pathways leading to the 5th Dimension.

The modern idea of healing that comes closest to Theo's
recommendations is "holistic" healing. The holistic attitude toward healing is based on the idea that an individual is an integrated whole expressed through the three states of body, mind,
and spirit. These three states are channels for the energy of life,
and this energy must be allowed to flow naturally. If you become
ill, it is because you have fallen out of balance on one plane or
another and are experiencing the disharmony in the form of sickness or disease. The body is influenced by being placed in the right
conditions and has the wisdom and ability to heal itself. We determine our state of health not only by our choice of foods, or by
the way we care for our bodies, but by what we allow ourselves
to think and our interactions with other human beings and other
forms of life.

Health is the fullest expression of all the human faculties and
passions acting together in perfect harmony. It is freedom from
disharmony in the mind; it is a condition where an individual can
express his or her own power most fully. Harmony and unification
of mind and body are Theo's suggestions for healing as we move
into 5th Dimension energies.

Know that the energy is shifting in the physical structure
of the beings on the earth. They are all being affected by
the 5th Dimensional energy shift. The electromagnetic
field is being arced up so that the right/left brain, and the
entirety of the body, can be in a greater attunement and
balance to the new energy.

Everything is affected by, and affects, the flow of our life energy. This energy is called by many names: the Chinese call it chi,
the Egyptians ka, the Hindus prana, the Hawaiians mana; the

names are really unimportant, for it is all one single, universal power.

Your life energy is not only influenced by another person face-to-face, but by someone's voice and thoughts as well. Our life energy is influenced by sounds, light, paintings, advertisements, photography—everything communicating energy affects us. Many cultures whose life-styles have not been corrupted by the pollution and high stress of modern society still believe and practice medicine by recognizing the connection between body and spirit.

Many native American medicine men are doctors as well as religious leaders, and they treat spiritual and physical ailments simultaneously. In many Indian tribes the Medicine Wheel, which uses the circle as the universal symbol of wholeness and perfection, is the basis of tribal health. A great medicine man, Black Elk, once said: "You have noticed everything an Indian does is in a circle, and that is because the Power of the World always works in circles and everything tries to be round. Everything the Power of the World does is done in a circle. The sky is round, and I have heard that the earth is round like a ball, and so are all the stars. The wind, in its greatest power, whirls. Birds make their nests in circles, so theirs is the same religion as ours. The sun comes forth and goes down again in a circle. The moon does the same, and both are round. . . . The life of man is a circle from childhood to childhood, and so it is in everything where power moves. Our tepees were round like the nests of birds, and these were always set in a circle, the nation's hoop, a nest of many nests, where the Great Spirit meant for us to hatch our children."

Wholeness is a complete evolution running the course from beginning to end to beginning again. Black Elk lamented when his people were banished to square reservation houses provided by the U.S. government. For him it was the breaking of his nation's hoop, a break of the sacred circle introducing imperfection and spiritual sickness. He thought it was a loss of wholeness.

Black Elk and many others in the modern world feel deeply the loss of wholeness; it is a sadness accompanying the knowledge that somehow our lives have been splintered, separated, and scattered. Our sense of completeness often seems to have disappeared, and this, I am convinced, is a sickness of our spirit. And it is the reason the 5th Dimension is here.

> *The circle is a good analogy for spirit, is it not? The whole-ness, the balance, the fullest expression, of the God-source. God is all facets of the personality of the being. The wholeness of God is within you; you are a part of it. It works as you work, for you are what God created—a balanced energy, positive and negative, not to be thought of as good or bad. It is what it is. It is a wholeness, a balance. And what each person tries to achieve within the being is this whole. That is what you are doing when you acknowledge and love the self unconditionally. You be-come whole. And that means loving the positive aspects of your personality as well as the negative. If you think a "bad" thought, make a negative judgment, do not hold it to yourself. It is not bad; it is what is. Love the wholeness of the self. That way you do not acquiesce your power to something outside the self. Become your power, fully. That is to know God, do you understand?*

THE HEALING EFFECT OF SOUND

Vibration, waves of energy, the trembling movement of sound all around us, impacts millions of times on our minds and bodies everyday. No one yet knows the full effects of such chaotic vibra-tions, but many believe them destructive to our health and sanity. Fortunately, there are others who are aware that sound does truly have a profound effect on us.

The use of music and sound for healing was used by the ancient Greeks, Egyptians, Persians, Chinese, Hindus, South American Indians, and other early societies. What did the sha-mans know that modern science is just learning? That sound can heal—both the mind and the body! It is a strange, even wild idea, but one whose time has come—and an idea that Theo repeats continually.

One of the earliest "case histories" in sound or music therapy comes from Pythagoras, who is credited with the discovery of the

musical interval and the diatonic scale. He also developed a phi-
losophy conceiving of the universe as a vast musical instrument.
All things, Pythagoras believed, are constructed on harmonic patterns that can be influenced by purposefully creating resonant or
vibratory effects.

Pythagoras tells the story of a young man who had been jilted
by his sweetheart. In a wild rage he piled wood all around her
house in order to burn it down. One of Pythagoras's students saw
what was happening and realized that talking to the young man
wouldn't do any good. He was literally out of his mind with rage.
The student took out a lute he was carrying and struck a few
notes. The enraged young man stopped what he was doing, lis-
tened for a few moments, and then removed the wood and left.

It is interesting to note that the lute was the calming instrument. Compare that with the fact that modern music therapists
are finding that the guitar is one of the preferred instruments of
disturbed patients. Pythagoras actually wrote that he used the
stringed instruments for healing and therapy. He believed that the
human body was a kind of sounding board that would immediately respond to the vibratory effects of sound.

His ideas are not as strange as they first seem. The idea of
tonal sympathy, for example, is not new and can be easily demonstrated by anyone immediately. If you vibrate a tuning fork and
hold it about an inch or so away from a guitar string that has not
been touched, the string will begin to vibrate up and down its
length. Water glasses placed near church bells can be shattered by
the bells' ringing.

It has even been found that candles can be extinguished by
sound. Considering that every cell in our bodies possesses neuro-
electrical qualities, and that the very nature of atomic matter is
resonance, it becomes less strange to theorize that the sound of a
lute or a mantra can have a profound effect upon our minds or
bodies.

While this is a new science, peculiar facts are beginning to
come out. Research at Kansas State University has demonstrated
that loud noise played around cattle produces a change in their
body physiology, causing animals to produce an undesirable type
of beef called "dark cuttters." With a control group of cattle not
subjected to these "stress sounds," like clanking of heavy equip-

ment, the roar of jet engines, or the playback of normal traffic noise, the cattle produced meat with no "dark cutters."

Research into the effect of sound upon the human body and mind is just now beginning, but even early tests show that sounds produced by instruments like guitars and bass drums dilate the capillaries in the body, increase the heart rate, and cause other physical effects. Dr. Gary Schwartz has written that the pleasant, calming sounds of the mantra or other meditative sounds have a tranquilizing effect. "Psychophysical research indicates that sounds that rise slowly and are resonant can decrease heart rate, inducing relaxation."

The effects of sound on the mind seem just as fascinating. I came across an article on music therapy being used at a California veterans' hospital, where it was found that even the most withdrawn and disturbed psychiatric patients are responding beyond expectations. Retarded, and even brain-damaged children, improve very rapidly using music therapy.

After beginning music therapy, one sixteen-year-old retarded girl with the physical coordination of a three-year-old child began to perform dance movements before mirrors. Her limbs, after almost two decades, were atrophied to some degree, but she then began to learn the basic skills of moving her body. Therapists are finding that musical therapy helps improve muscle activity even in badly crippled arms or legs.

At New York Hospital, psychiatrists have used music therapy on retarded children with very beneficial effects. One doctor found that melancholy music improved the mood of depressed patients, but had the opposite effect on schizophrenic patients. In another experiment the researchers found that the more one likes a piece of music, the deeper one breathes when listening to it. Some doctors suggest their patients listen to symphonies instead of taking drugs.

AN EXERCISE USING SOUND

Using sound, or the body's "vibratory energy," has always played an important part in meditation and spiritual development. Over the ages, the tone and quality of certain sounds and words have been discovered to evoke specific reactions in our bodies and minds. Long ago certain sounds were found to influence the "spiritual" body as well as the physical. Monks in Tibet, India, and China have used mystical sounds, mantras, for centuries to provoke spiritual visions and alter their consciousness. Chanting and singing were also used in the Christian Church for the same purpose. There is little question that particular sounds do indeed have power to stimulate our physical and psychic energies.

Theo most often recommends the sound OM, spoken or sung in a slow, measured exhale. (If it makes using the sound easier, picture it as being spelled A-U-M.) This spelling gives a more precise idea of how the sound is constructed when each letter is specifically sounded during meditation.

During meditations using sound you may focus your mind's eye on one of the chakras, or spiritual centers. For beginners it would probably be best to focus either on the center of the forehead or at the heart. By chanting the OM mantra the energy in these centers will be activated.

Sit comfortably with your feet flat on the floor, your spine straight and head erect. Relax your body completely by focusing on slow, even breathing. When you feel you are relaxed, begin to intone the OM sound softly. With each exhale repeat the sound softly, but quite audibly, seven times. Begin to intone OM slightly louder now, but be sure to stay relaxed and at ease. Repeat this seven more times. Again raise the volume of the mantra while intoning seven more times. Do not strain to be loud or dramatic. This is not a performance; it is an exercise to teach you to feel the different levels of vibrations as your body changes its energy frequency.

You may lengthen the exhale of the OM sound from a normal exhale of a six or seven count to any length that feels comfortable. And this will probably occur as you practice. You will find the body taking over the rhythm, and the sound will become longer and deeper.

To facilitate the energy flow within your body, visualize a bright, intense light as the focal point of your attention as you use the mantra. If you choose to use the heart center, visualize the light as glowing more intensely with each exhale of the OM sound. At some point the light will become brighter and seem to pulse. When this happens, expand its brightness ever farther until it encompasses your whole body. This will activate the other psychic centers in you and raise the energy frequency of your body and mind. This is an excellent exercise to heal your body and mind and integrate all the different aspects of your spiritual self.

THE HEALING ENERGY OF THE MIND

The mind is deeply involved in keeping the body healthy. This is not just wisdom from the New Age prophets, for even modern science has now proved that every change in consciousness resonates in the body. Physical diseases obviously affect the mind— causing hallucinations, delirium, and even loss of consciousness. We all know that emotions or high anxiety can produce ulcers, high blood pressure, and heart disease. More and more, science is ascertaining that emotions and the positive or negative "set" of the mind can influence even pernicious diseases like cancer. In fact, every change of consciousness seems to resonate within every cell of the body.

Since the mind's influence on the body is so powerful, doesn't it make sense to learn thought techniques so you can heal yourself and enhance your body's overall well-being? Sickness may even be a form of "time-out" to repair the imbalances in our system, or the body-mind-spirit's way of "waking us up" to how our life-style is imbalanced. You can help this repair period by improving "where" your consciousness is—that is, by placing your consciousness in the correct *mode* for receiving spiritual inspiration.

According to Theo, a single, fundamental energy changes its vibratory level as it manifests in the physical body. This energy comes from the sea of universal energy around us, and when this energy is used by the physical body, the body lowers its vibratory rate and manifests the energy much like electricity. And it is this same energy, in a different vibrational rate, that is moving the world into the 5th Dimension. The 5th Dimensional energy not only alters consciousness, but the physical body as well. It is a healing energy and will be important for people to learn to use for their own well-being.

*Know that the 5th Dimensionary energy is a vibrational
frequency that is enhancing the physical structures. It is
balancing and healing; it is arcing up that energy in an
electric way, balancing the electromagnetic body, including the left/right brain connections and all the other energies within the body.*

The reason the energy changes rate is that the physical world
vibrates at a slower rhythm, and as you move toward higher levels
of consciousness the rate increases and becomes a more refined
expression of energy. In effect, we live within two forms of energy:
(1) Within a slower physical energy vibration, and (2) also within
a higher, finer energy that exists not only out in space but within
our bodies and all the rest of the physical world. Ultimately it is
only *one* energy that expresses itself in millions and millions of
different rates of vibration. This finer, higher energy rate is what
our psychic centers tune in to and transform for our use in the
physical world.

As Theo tell us, this universal, or God-source, energy manifests itself like electricity in a positive and negative form. Most
people have an imbalance between these negative and positive
energies because their emotional, mental, and physical lives are in
chaos; full of confusion, anger, and innumerable negative emotions and destructive mental attitudes.

People are out of balance and are mostly closed to the healing
influence of this single universal energy source. Once one becomes
attuned to this source, a harmonious balance happens between
the two polarities, and the body and mind are healed.

Too much food, low-grade emotions, and mental negativism
create a negative imbalance in the body, and illness is the inevitable result. But there are practical, simple methods to help you
regain the harmonious balance intended by the God-source.

There are three basic ways in which healing can take place,
all of value.

First, there is the traditional medical treatment by a physician.
Many have recently turned away from traditional medicine, I believe, not only because it is expensive and impersonal but because
it so often fails to help the sick or the person as a whole, concen-

trating instead on treating symptoms. Many doctors may have great skill and wisdom, and I have met some during my stays in hospitals, but few include the ideas of psychic healing in their armory of treatments.

Second, there are physicians and psychologists who see illness as an interaction between the body and mind. This minority has helped to establish a more holistic approach to human illness. They recognize and try to treat sickness as dis-ease arising from emotional confusion, mental disorder, and other subjective conditions. They try to uncover negative attitudes of mind and help to better understand the patient's inner condition as well as bodily illness.

But neither of these approaches goes far enough to fully establish the link between the inner and outer worlds.

The best, most effective healer is your own psychic energy. This is the same energy animating your body, which, if properly used, can correct any affliction.

All illness results from an imbalance of one's psychic energy, and healing takes place as one rebalances this energy through proper use of the mind—in short, by altering the state of consciousness.

To heal is often hard to do for the simple reason that most people don't usually prepare themselves properly. It's a lot harder to heal yourself once you are sick, when you are already weakened by disease, or suffering a high fever, or in intense pain, for you need a clear mind to do the best job. You need to guide your thoughts in order to heal either yourself or others, so never let your energy get so low that you can't use your mind as the cleansing, healing power it was meant to be.

The first step in learning to heal should be taken right now . . . before anything is wrong with you. Start your conscious healing process while you are strong so if an accident or illness should strike, you will be prepared.

Increase Your Healing Energy

There are many techniques for increasing your healing energy, for these practices have developed over thousands of years by many psychics and channelers who have been in touch with the universal, God-source energy. The following are easy methods but highly effective, and they take only a few minutes to practice; however, to build up your energy, they should be done regularly.

EXERCISE: Building Self-Healing Energy

Sit erect or stand with your feet apart and your body weight evenly balanced. Take a deep, slow breath and count to six; relax and exhale for a count of twelve. Repeat this ten or twelve times in a row and as you breathe in and out visualize each breath bringing you a great surge of energy and power. The energy is stored within your body, filling each cell and molecule with power. Visualize the energy as being vital and electric, golden-white and filling every cavity of your being. Keep your mouth and jaws firmly closed, and clench each hand into a fist while doing this exercise. This is so none of the energy can complete a circuit within you and then exit. It will be stored in your body.

After you have finished the exercise, relax. You should notice a great increase in your total energy. Your body will feel stimulated and the energy "high" should last for several hours.

You can perform this exercise several times a day, for there are no bad side effects. But by practicing it at least once a day you will gradually build up your own healing energy. If you do this exercise faithfully, you will find that most of the "normal" diseases that you experienced before will be gone forever. This energy can be used either for healing yourself or others.

Healing Others

To heal another it is important to first build up your own energy. Use the exercise just described, or begin by visualizing psychic energy pouring into your body. Try to actually feel its power. You must strongly *want* this energy to fill you . . . and your purpose must be clear in your mind. Your purpose should be unselfish—a deep desire to heal another.

Fill your consciousness with this healing desire, take a few deep breaths, hold each one to a count of six, and open your hands before you, palms up.

It is best not to diagnose what the patient has wrong. This is a healing, not a psychic reading. Think of the illness as an unknown ailment and that you are simply going to help his or her own body heal itself by "boosting" its energy. You are supplying an extra amount of energy to a weakened system.

Ask the ill person to relax, to calm his or her mind and emotions. Give him or her a visualization, a calm, clear pool of water or a clear pale blue sky. Repeat your energy buildup breathing technique, and center the energy storage near your heart. When you are not healing a specific area, like a headache, a bruise, or strained muscle, etc., then you will release your stored energy into the patient's heart center.

Place your right hand on the left side of the spine between the shoulder blades. Visualize the energy flowing from your heart area, down your arm, and out your hand. It is important to visualize the energy as being continuous. There is no limit to the supply of golden energy flowing through your hand into the patient's body. It will flow unendingly as long as your visualization is clear. The original amount of energy you stored is more like a key to a door within you that opens a floodgate from the universe.

Most healers can maintain a clear visualization for thirty or forty seconds after much practice. When your visualization becomes cloudy or wavers, remove your hand and wait a few minutes. Then repeat the whole procedure, starting with the rebuilding of your own energy.

While this is a physical contact healing, it is often better not to touch a patient physically unless he or she requests it. Then use only a light touch, with your fingertips, never a rubbing or massage.

Often a patient may not want to be touched, or the problem is too tender for touching. In this case you can heal by what is called the radiation method. The entire healing is carried out by use of the mind and heart. If you are in the same room, hold your hands a few inches above the area you want to energize. Use the same visualization method to transfer energy to the patient's body. If you are not in the same room, picture the patient (even if he or she is only a vague outline), and direct your healing force to that location. See the golden light stream to the person, surrounding his or her body with a halo of healing light and filling the patient with its radiance.

Remember that the act of healing is not simply a transfer of energy but an act of love. If you can succeed in feeling love while you are healing, the relief and cure of the patient will be much more rapid. If you find your own energy low after a healing, review all the steps outlined. The error often lies in failing to fill yourself with love, with an open, generous giving of yourself during the act of healing. As Theo says, unconditional love is the energy of the universe.

Psychic energy is the energy of life. When you heal another, you are simply supplying extra energy in order to help the body heal itself. It is all the same energy. Many small problems are helped by this same method of supplying extra energy. Cuts, wounds, and abrasions heal much faster if given this extra "boost" of psychic energy. The same is true of headaches, colds, or other minor ailments.

But again, you must first be healthy and full of psychic energy yourself before you can be successful at healing. Daily meditation is in itself extremely helpful for creating the perfect condition for healing. Another simple meditation often called "A Child of the Sun" is a perfect way to build up your psychic energy.

A CHILD OF THE SUN

Position yourself as before, your feet firmly on the ground. Sit relaxed with your hands clasped in your lap. Visualize a great flaming sun above you. It is bursting with energy and vitality. Picture your consciousness rising from your body and entering the flaming sun. Realize that there is nothing to fear, for this energy is identical to your own consciousness. Let the sun's enormous energy fill your entire being, strengthening and cleansing every particle in you. Do this for at least a full minute and then return to your body. Open your eyes and stand up. Stretch and pull in deep breaths of air, feeling the new power in your body.

This exercise is a good general energizer. Use it as a daily meditation for both visualizing perfect health for yourself and for joining your consciousness with the energy of the God-source.

Visualization: Using Imagination to Heal

In all kinds of meditations, visualization is used to hold consciousness steady, to still the mind noise, not just to fill it with a picture or image. In fact, learning to concentrate by using visualization is a painless way to guide your mind into proper thought patterns. It is using your *imagination and concentration* to create healing visions.

Perhaps because internal visualization is so common, or so easy to create, modern science has underestimated its benefits. Only in the last few years has visualization begun to be appreciated as a powerful tool, both for learning how to guide your thoughts and for healing the body.

One of the most exciting scientific uses of visualization and meditation was developed by Dr. O. Carl Simonton, a radiologist who specializes in cancer therapy. He has become quite famous for creating a meditation technique combining relaxation and visualization for use by terminal cancer patients.

Dr. Simonton's first patient was one of his most dramatic cases and helped convince him of the mind's role in healing the body. The first patient to use Simonton's meditation-visualization technique was a sixty-one-year-old man with advanced cancer of the throat. He had dropped from 135 to 95 pounds. He couldn't eat solid food or even swallow his own saliva. He learned to relax and was able to visualize his cancer, his bodily functions, and immune reaction extremely well. After seven weeks of Simonton's meditation-visualization treatment his cancer had left him. He lived for a number of years with no recurrence. With the advanced state of his cancer doctors had given him a 5 percent chance of surviving two years.

This same patient also suffered from arthritis and impotence, which had been plaguing him for twenty years. Using the same techniques he had learned from Simonton, he managed to relieve himself of his acute arthritis and his impotence. His impotence was "cured" after ten days of meditative work.

Simonton's techniques are similar to traditional visualization and meditation methods—and they are also similar to those that Theo recommends. They are surprisingly easy to learn.

Patients are asked to meditate regularly for fifteen minutes in the morning, at noon, and before retiring to bed. The first few minutes are used for patients to achieve complete relaxation while sitting comfortably. They then visualize a peaceful, pleasant scene. Whatever understanding of their disease is necessary is provided the patients before the meditative sessions begin by using pictures, X rays, diagrams, or verbal descriptions. The patients are also shown photographs of how their own immunological systems work, with pictures of white blood cells destroying cancer cells. They may even be given positive suggestions about the therapy by being shown pictures of other patients with visible cancers getting smaller and eventually disappearing. All of this premeditation education helps create a positive state of mind that will aid the meditator's own body in responding to the visualizations and suggestions.

During their meditation the patients are asked first to visualize their particular lesion or tumor. Then they picture the tumor cells in their body as dead or dying, with the white blood cells swarming over the tumor, destroying the cancer cells, and carrying them off. At the end of the meditation the patients are asked to visualize themselves free of disease and in perfect health.

Theo often suggests meditation and prayer as a way of balancing the energies of the body and mind. Visualization is also recommended by Theo for healing.

Place the hand over the ear—visualize the ear whole and healthy, functioning and clear. Feel the energy of the hand pulling the toxins, the infections, out. Do not negate your positive action with the negative thought that you can't do it. You will have confirmations.

Disease will never find its cure or be erased by our present-day traditional methods for the simple reason that illness does not originate within the material world. Material treatment of the body alone will only succeed in temporarily relieving or masking symptoms. The real cause of illness is conflicts between the soul and the mind. Harmony can be reestablished through altering our consciousness. When our personalities are in conflict with our inner path, the conflict manifests in our lives as unhappiness and disease. When our inner and outer worlds are harmonious, then we experience peace and joy and are in a state of good health.

Everything emanates from the God-source and is expressed in the physical world as action. If we learn to listen to our hearts and to act according to spiritual principles, we can then have true health.

THEO ON HEALING

Many of my channeling sessions have dealt with health and imbalances in people's lives. Theo's answers cover a broad range of ideas and recommendations. Often the questions are repetitious and offer those who have not spoken with Theo an opportunity to identify with other people's health problems and their possible solution. Here are some of Theo's answers to the most commonly asked questions.

Theo, I have a problem with migraine headaches. Is there something I should be doing I am not aware of?

You are too nice. You need to speak out what is in your heart. Ask for what you want. You hold much energy, much stress, in your upper body. Touch your arm by the elbow, in the crease of the upper arm, and you will find a sore place there. When you are having headaches press gently there, and it will release the stress in the upper body, neck, and shoulders. The tension will be released. But know that you must communicate. You are very adept at holding in everything. Allow the emotions to come out.

Theo, when I was two years old I broke my leg in two places. I don't remember anything about how long I was in the hospital or anything about it. Can you tell me what happened?

Yes, you were in traction, but much of the time you were out of your body, existing as your essence. There was great pain, and chemicals were put into your body. The memories are painful, but you will recall the experience within a month's time. It will be part of a clearing of emotions that is about you now. It is the cleansing of emotions brought on by the 5th Dimension changes.

There will be some anger, some fear of abandonment, that come forth. Acknowledge these; do not repress them, understand? For what has been hidden surfaces now during the 5th Dimension. The energy grades of your planet have shifted, and therefore the energy grades of your physical structure have also changed. The old thought patterns, the old forms of acting in the world, will no longer be. And all the fears, all that has been repressed, will surface.

There will be many emotional ups and downs, for the emotional base is where the learning on this planet takes place. Embrace it, acknowledge it, become it fully, and you will feel relief.

I have had gum problems recently. What care should I take?

Know that the energy is shifting within the physical bodies of people during the 5th Dimensional change. The electromagnetic field is being arced up so that the entire body can be in a greater balance with the new energy. Know that when the energy is blocked, when it is stopped at the mouth instead of continuing on up through the crown of the head, then there is discomfort in the gums.

Vibrational shifts made the teeth loose at times. Many others will experience the vibrations of the 5th Dimension shift as a ringing in the ears. Others will feel like they have to eat all the time.

To correct this, visualize the energy going through the entire body and out through the crown of the head, do you understand?

Am I taking adequate care of my physical body?

We will check the body. One moment. . . . There is a weakness in the lower back. Strengthening the abdominal muscles would help the lower back muscles so that they stay in alignment. Sciatic nerve is involved, yes? The drinking of water would assist this. Deep breathing would also help. You breathe too shallowly. Proper breathing is important to health. You hold too much energy in the right side of your hip, in the leg. The adjustment and realignment would help you release it. Vitamin C, B complex, and vitamin E would enhance the nervous system. But proper breathing and drinking plenty of water would be most important.

A meditation would also be helpful. As you breathe in see the energy flow out of your fingertips and the toes and balls of your feet. This will help you in many ways.

You defend yourself quite a bit in your life, do you not? You see the sword in your right hand and the shield in the left, like a warrior. Use the meditation. You will see a release of this defensiveness.

How can I heal my son, Andy?

You will feel areas in the body where there are energy blocks. Feel the temperature changes there, cold and hot. When you find these places that vibrate, hold them. You don't need to say to him, "Okay, now lie down, and I'm going to heal you . . ." Healing can be in a caress, can be in stroking, do you understand?

But how can I feel vibrations in different parts of his body?

You will feel them. At times it will feel as if the area is buzzing.

I have a question about my health. I have been bothered by sciatica, and I'd like to know the root of that problem and what I can do about it?

Your body is very sensitive and when you are under stress your spine twists and then you have a pinched nerve, which creates the sciatica.

Drinking plenty of water would help this because the sciatica has to do with water intake, dehydration. You can

*relieve pressure on this nerve immediately if you take a
small ball, very firm, and sit on it.*

Take a what?

*A small round ball, to stimulate the root chakra. You can
use meditation as well. See the energy come up through
your body. Sit erect with your feet on the floor. See the
energy as a golden light coming up through the balls of
the feet, up through your spine, through all the chakras,
up through your throat, forehead, and crown of your
head. Visualize this as you meditate, do you understand?*

**I am concerned about my health, Theo. Is my body
whole and healthy?**

*Your body is strong, yes. You are aware of the physical
structure. Paying attention to your diet is important. Listen to what the body says to you. Listen to its needs, not
your intellect. Don't pay attention to the intellect or what
others are saying. Ignore the idea of "this book says I
should eat this and that book says I should do this . . ." If
you are hungry for meat, eat it, do you understand? Often
when people crave sugar, it is because their thought patterns are shifting and changing and sugar feeds the brain.
Don't worry about sugars . . . or weight. When weight is
held in the body, it is often held as a protection, as a
storehouse of energy. Remember, one must not judge the
physical structure. It is to be loved in its entirety as the
gift that it is.*

Theo, for some reason I am anxious. Is it my health?

*Yes, it is partly your health. It is necessary to balance the
chemistry within the physical structure. But the energy of
your body is refining itself quite rapidly due to the influence of the 5th Dimension energy shift. Your diet needs
changing, and be more aware of nutrition. A moderate
diet is important. You should eat more than three times a*

*day, smaller amounts each time, do you understand? The
changing energy grids have affected your emotional balance, yes. There is this anxiousness or anxiety because
there is more vulnerability within you. All of the fears
come forth now, to be expressed, as your body's energy
changes.*

Theo, I have been feeling restless. What is going on?

*The refinement of energy here is bringing forth the heal-
ing aspects within your physical structure. Your path is
that of a teacher, a being of light, a facilitator of consciousness in others. What you are experiencing is a refinement
of your energy and a change of the vibrational levels. You
are fine-tuning the creative dimensions of your being.*

**I have been experiencing a lot of despair and skepti-
cism lately, Theo, which isn't really like me. What
guidance can you give me on this problem?**

*The upheaval within your being is caused by the releasing
of old thought patterns. These patterns have served you
well in the past but can no longer be used for your present
life. All that has been structured into your subconscious
since birth are changing rapidly. That is why you feel
chaos inside. And at times you feel as if you are in a void.
That is because it is unknown power and you would grasp
onto the old, the familiar, for it is uncomfortable in the
new circumstances. It can be corrected. Meditate. Breathe
in these new times to keep yourself centered. Know that
this process will bring forth the true essence of who you
are. That is the frightening part, is it not? You ask yourself,
What if I do not like this new person? But you will. Trust
the self.*

**Theo, I have been feeling very depressed and anxious
for the last five weeks. I don't know what is causing it
or what I can do about it. Can you help me?**

This condition has to do with the hormonal balance of your body. The chemistry, you see. The blood sugar levels of the body are also involved. Nutrition is very important at this time. Eliminate caffeine and sugar. The drinking of water is also important to you now. A minimum of eight glasses a day. You will become very thirsty if you do not do this. It will help your depressions.

Theo, a lot of good things have been happening to me this year, but also my blood pressure has gone up quite high, and it is not going down. I don't know what to do about it.

You are going to find that you will be placed in a position where you will need to communicate and speak out. A confrontation comes forth as you try to express your expectations. But as you complete this process of speaking out, the body will adjust itself. The high blood pressure is caused by what has not been spoken, what has been repressed and held in. This experience has begun, and you are in the process of clearing it. You will see the body define itself, become more finely in tune, more refined. You will feel younger, look younger. That is nice, isn't it? You have taken note that medication does not assist your blood pressure, correct? You are aware of jin shin, are you not? Then use it. [Jin shin, along with shiatsu, acupressure, and t'ai chi, is one of several highly beneficial "body-focused" healing techniques from the East.]

Theo, I have a lot of energy, and I'm aware of a healing taking place. Can you tell me what is happening?

There are many questions in your being. The healing you feel is the vibrations coming forth in your experience—as it is with all who are being healed. You are more sensitive to this expression of light that comes forth than others. The energy that is being enhanced here will radiate out through the fingertips. You will become much more attuned to the people you work with.

Clearing the physical structure of the energy that is absorbed from outside the body is extremely important. See this energy flow out of the body. Soaking in a tub of water daily is important. The shifting of polarities within the water allows you to move this energy out. You will feel this discomfort in your own body. It will tell you where the energy is. Do you understand?

Color is going to be a part of this; you will see the energy in color. That is part of advancement of your consciousness.

Color and Healing

Theo, how does color relate to healing? Specifically, what colors are used to aid the teachers on the planet?

Colors facilitate the vibration of the rays of light that each person is enhanced by. It is the colors of the rainbow, you understand. The seven main colors for healing are purple, indigo, green, orange, yellow, red, blue. And the variations of light ranging to the dark, do you understand?

The different colors have positive and negative aspects—as do all the frequencies. You are aware of this, yes? If the energy is from fear, the color is red; but red is also the color of love. Love is also a purple color, as is blue. Blue is also intellect. Blue is also power and can be used as manipulation as a negative power. The purple is spirit, as in the use of spiritual power. But these can also be misused for manipulation, which will bring forth insecurity.

Color should be used in healing. The visualizing of color to heal with is very important—from the healer using the color to the being who is healed. A meditation upon the color assists healing. Green should be used; it is healing. It is rejuvenation, rebirth. Yellow is for the intellect, the use of mental power here. Golden yellow is that of the crown chakra, do you understand? The golden aura for the spirit, for the balancing of the entire body, should be used. It is encompassing. Used in its highest form it can balance all the chakras.

When you say a color "used in its highest form," what do you mean?

Know that there are both sides to using energy—and its colors—positive and negative. When you seek its highest use, it is a positive expression, its most powerful expression. Do you understand?

How can you distinguish the difference between a higher purple or a lesser purple, between a higher red and a lesser red?

The gradients of color do not matter; you mean intensity, do you not? When a color is more on one side than the other, it is a mixing of energy. In this way they blend one into the other. As with green, it is blue and yellow, is it not? So know that the combination of colors is significant.

Can you give me an example of how you would use the color green, say, to heal an injury?

Simply visualize a green aura about the injured area, or about the whole being. Also green is abundance, a new life, do you understand?

Theo, in the 5th Dimension are there colors that we should be aware of?

Colors are important. They are vibrational; they are healing. You have the rainbow, do you not? Those are important vibrational colors. There are variations from light to dark, but know that these colors are frequencies that are a part of the universe. They are spectrums of frequency that when worn on the body, or are looked at or held, allow healing to take place. They create an opening.

Could you suggest some colors for our use?

For you, individually, yes.
The rose quartz held on the left side of the body will be important for you, and a ruby color to help the circu-

latory system. Now and again use amethyst for its purple color, do you understand? The color purple, in varying shades—red, pink, yes? It will be helpful.

I feel comfortable with the color of turquoise. Why is that?

It is a healing color. It is the color of water in many places, is it not? And water is life. It is the flow, it is the shifts and changes; it is a birth, for birth is of the water, is it not? Clarity. And it is of the earth as well. It is grounding.

But all colors have significance. Green is also healing, as well as abundance. Shades of purple as they go out in their frequencies are the color of spirit. Red is the color of passion, and also that of unconditional love. When you let love in, you become radiant with that color.

Theo, are there any suggestions you can give to people as they become affected by the 5th Dimensional energy shifts? How can they enhance their consciousness, their general health and well-being?

Many are experiencing these vibrational changes now. It is good to meditate daily, which allows you to be receptive to the new energy; it allows the being to balance the new frequencies within the self. This is extremely important for all beings. Meditation raises the vibration so that it can easily meld with the God-source. It creates a sense of attunement with the creative powers. It clarifies. A daily meditation is very good for the body, for the physiology of the whole body. It will help relieve stress, enhance the strength of the nervous system.

For good health a regular meditation would be important. Sitting erect, feet upon the floor, allow the energy to come through the balls of the feet, up through the entire body and radiate out to all the cells. Visualize the energy as a golden light, and use the breath to enhance the energy flow. Breathing in and out slowly, you will feel the muscles relax in the body. It is also good to use the vibration of the OM sound, not clipped as a word, but a long, soft humming; either mentally or aloud, whichever is comfortable.

Exercise, the balance of the physical body, is extremely important. Massage, an energy balancing, allows the body to be in proper alignment. It allows healing to take place as well . . . and the release of stress also.

Movement is important to the physical structure in this time of the 5th Dimensional change because the old patterns of thought are leaving; they are shifting and changing. What is held within the cellular structures is being released, and these change the energy, the emotion, and the thought processes.

All of these actions are extremely important for those who are preparing spiritually now for the 5th Dimension changes. But it is also important to seek and ask of the self first. It is important to experience openness to the changes, be fully in the present, to accept new experiences as steppingstones. Accept the self on all levels; this is the way to achieve health and spiritual openness.

III

MEDITATION:

SEVEN KEYS

INTO THE

5TH

DIMENSION

*Each individual is the creator
of his or her own experience.
Each, through thought,
creates his or her own destiny.
This power comes from within
the mind. Meditate more; raise
your vibrations through
meditation.*

11

Key One:
Learning to Use
the Mind's Eye

THERE IS A FABLE ABOUT A MONK
who stops in a wood to listen to the singing of a bird. Its song is
so beautiful that the monk soars on its sound, immersing himself
in its invisible spirit. Sometime later the bird ends its song and
flies off. The monk returns to his monastery only to discover that
he has been away for fifty years.

There is another story about a surgeon who was so engrossed
in an operation that he was totally unaware that a large part of
the ceiling in the operating room had fallen right next to him
during his surgery.

Until the mind-noise (wandering thoughts, emotion-laden
images, etc.) has been quieted, at least to some degree, it is difficult
to try to meditate. For this reason most systems that teach meditation are really methods for developing your concentration. Following a normal, regular, relaxed breathing pattern is, for

example, one of the simplest and most basic concentration exercises and the method most often recommended by Theo.

Concentration is one of the major problems for beginners when learning to meditate, pray, developing focused attention, even relaxation exercises to open the mind for psychic awareness —they all take a certain degree of concentration.

If the mind wanders, gently draw it back to the breath. Allow this, this floating feeling of the body, yes? Use the breath, in and out slowly, to relax the muscles of the body.

When learning to concentrate, and hopefully to apply it to expanding awareness through meditation, it is valuable to remember that there are two basic forms of concentration. One is an emotional form of attention that follows unconscious impulses. The other type of concentration is one in which your awareness is deliberately and consciously directed. With the first kind of concentration you are driven by the "feeling" or emotional part of the unconscious. With the second kind, *you* direct your own thoughts. In effect, you are in control of the direction of your own mind. Theo says, *It is through thought that you build your spiritual being.*

Meditation and its forms of concentration involves a basic condition of our everyday life: focused attention. We can, for example, think clearly only about one idea or one piece of information at a time.

There is a famous tale about the value of concentration. During an archery tournament in ancient India, a wooden fish was set up on a high pole. The eye of the fish was the target. One by one many princes and royal archers came and tried their skill, but each failed to hit the eye of the fish. Before and after each archer shot his arrow, the teacher asked what he saw. All replied that they saw a fish on a pole at a great height with head, eyes, tail, etc. But when the hero of the tale, Arjuna, took his aim and was asked what he saw, he replied, "I see the eye of the fish." He let loose his arrow, which entered the eye of the fish. He was the only archer to hit the target exactly.

Focused attention is intimately connected with our emotions

and memories. A sleeping person may not wake up for even the loudest nearby sounds, but a mother who normally sleeps through the sounds of loading garbage trucks outside her window will wake suddenly if her baby gives a faint cry.

Your attention *can* be guided to obey your conscious will. This is the key to the fantastic power of self-awareness. The meditator is simply learning to focus his or her attention on single points—on simple images, ideas, and sounds within the mind.

Since most of our minds wander at random, a good method for bringing your attention back to focus is to begin to circle the object with your mind. For example, if you are concentrating on an ashtray and your attention wanders, as soon as you decide to bring it back, begin to move your focus around the object in a circle that grows ever smaller until finally you are circling just around the edges of the ashtray. Then bring your focus to a stop on the object and begin to focus your attention again.

An early exercise for learning to focus one's attention is to pin a piece of paper with a simple design on it (a big black dot, a black circle, etc.) on the wall in front of you. Sit comfortably and concentrate on the drawing with open eyes until your eyes tire or tears cloud your vision. Then close your eyes and visualize the picture in detail. Open your eyes again and go through the same process. This exercise is extremely good for steadying the concentration and stops the mind from wandering.

DEALING WITH MIND DIVERSIONS

During *inner mind* experiences (meditation, visualizations, dreams, psychic experiences, channeling, etc.) surprising visions, fascinating fantasies, shocking images or ideas often pop up. When performing the following exercises, you will probably experience impressions that turn out to be psychic, or have visions that turn out to be true, or feel that you have left your body and are looking down upon the world from another reality.

While these experiences are fascinating and sometimes sought after, they can also be a diversion from the more important task of learning how to direct your thought patterns. For thousands of years meditators have complained about these "diversions" when they are concentrating on achieving a mystical union with God.

The cause of these inner mind diversions seems to be a great deal of "crossover" between the various levels of consciousness; one state of consciousness "bleeds" its effects over into another as you reduce the conscious mind's dependency on the external world. In my experience there seem to be no hard or rigid lines separating these different levels, and the constant mixing of impressions one gets in deep meditation often creates confusion or anxiety in the beginner.

It is often harder to ignore these distractions than most people realize. Many of the effects are very attractive. In fact, you can sometimes become wrapped up in watching the unfolding image or vision—like watching an old film once loved but long forgotten.

The best—and simplest—way to avoid the problem is to ignore the diverting image before you become attached to it. Maintain an attitude of detachment, of dispassion, toward the whole process. Disruptive thoughts and impressions will certainly occur. As soon as you become aware that you have been diverted from your goal, gently return your attention to it. If you can maintain an alert, noncritical, dispassionate attitude, you will have created the right state of mind to explore your inner mind and develop the correct thought pattern.

There are some basic, easy, techniques you can use when handling the inevitable and unwanted material floating into consciousness.

As you begin to meditate try to avoid being afraid of doing the "wrong" thing. Do not cling to the idea that everything should be clear, perfect, and easy right away. In other words, do not be judgmental with yourself. Don't be afraid of making mistakes and having to do something over again. A simple, noncritical, nonjudgmental attitude is what you seek—especially in the beginning. Do not waste emotional energy on regret or disappointment over your progress. If you are persistent and patient, you will become more sensitive to the nuances of the inner workings of your mind and your unconscious energies.

You may find that distractions occur with disturbing frequency at first, but as you progress you will be able to recognize them dispassionately and return to your meditation with ever-increasing ease. Complaints to yourself about your "performance" only create frustration and irritation. So whatever happens, simply observe it as it is. In this way you become more and more objective when dealing with your inner thought processes and emotional imagery. As you become more objective in handling this inner world, your ability to move beyond the many miniobsessions will improve.

12

Key Two: Using Silence and Receptive Listening

MEDITATION IS NOT ONLY A METHOD to guide your thoughts. It is also a technique for exploring the true nature of the inner self. One of the most important things to remember is that the traditional secrets of meditation are not beyond the average person. Each individual can travel at his or her own pace.

One of the most difficult things to do is to "let your thinking cease," which is similar to living in silence. Silence is a metaphor for a state of awareness in meditation. It is a metaphor because it exists only as an abstraction, for absolute silence is biologically impossible. A good description of this is an experience of the composer John Cage:

> . . . try as we may to make a silence, we cannot. For certain engineering purposes, it is desirable to have as silent

a situation as possible. Such a room is called an anechoic chamber, its six walls made of special material, a room without echoes. I entered one at Harvard University several years ago and heard two sounds, one high and one low. When I described them to the engineer in charge, he informed me that the high one was my nervous system in operation, the low one my blood in circulation. Until I die there will be sounds.

This is not unlike the chamber I was placed in at Maimonides Hospital's dream laboratory in Brooklyn. It reminded me of a meat locker with its thick walls and heavy metal door.

During the experiment I was seated in a reclining chair with electrodes attached to my wrists and forehead. I had headphones clamped on my ears through which the researchers could speak to me. They asked me to begin to meditate so I relaxed and immediately became aware of the inner sounds of my body. My breath was a loud sighing, and my heartbeat pounded in my ears. I was even aware of the sounds my digestive system was making.

Yet, it is inner silence, as incomplete as it is, that meditation techniques consider important to the process. But in meditation silence is much more than the mere ending of noise. For example, early in meditation there comes a point where the quiet external surroundings are far less important than the quiet of the mind. And even though inner sounds can bubble up from the internal workings of our bodies, the quiet mind of meditation eventually succeeds in filtering out these inner sounds. One of the simplest methods is the mantra, a tone sung either internally or vocally that overwhelms the more subtle inner noise of the body. Theo often recommends this method for particular people who seem to need the focusing power it gives.

Theo also recommends visualizations for those who are "visionaries." Theo often describes people in terms of their natural way of perceiving—most often either as visionaries or sensory perceptors.

In fact, any consistent and patterned stimulus, like white noise in the background, or the steady rhythmic sounds of an ocean or waterfall, seems to organize itself into a nonsound by becoming part of the background, which we tend to ignore when concentrating. There is a constant filtering of perceptions going on during our waking and sleeping hours. We often sleep right through sounds from the street, wind, even storms and sudden heavy rain.

External quiet does not ensure internal silence, but an external noise can be ignored so thoroughly that it in fact becomes silence. As a meditator, you must first learn to disengage yourself from external noise by tuning out. The easiest way to do this is by finding the quietest place you can to meditate in. After a while you can meditate anywhere.

Then you can begin to learn to deal with a whole set of new sounds: *mind-noise*. The nonstop activity of the mind does not seem to be a problem—in fact, many consider constant mental activity to be a virtue—until you attempt to control it.

Once the meditator starts trying to control his or her mind noise, it will become clear how little control one has over what goes on in one's head. This is why most early exercises in meditation stress learning to guide your thoughts and handle the innumerable images, ideas, words, and fantasies that flash through our everyday consciousness. This early stage of "thought guiding" helps the beginning meditator understand the difference between the conscious mind and its contents. Most of us tend to view the conscious mind as the sum of its contents. Yet since we are not fully conscious of the mind's total nature, we tend to confuse the everyday mind-noise with the mind itself.

The silence sought in learning to meditate is not to simply sit in a quiet place. Meditative silence is something that happens when there is an absence of mind-noise or uncontrolled mental activity. At this point the mental noise quiets down and the conscious mind *becomes* a part of the "silence."

One of the most common types of silent meditation is prayer. This is because the effectiveness of prayer depends more on the spirit and involvement than on the form (or words) followed. If one loses sight of a prayer's purpose, following the form of the prayer becomes a hollow exercise, a simple chain of words or images.

When I began meditating seriously, I did not think of meditation as prayer. Prayer was what I did in church. I thought of it as most other people did—as the "Our Father" prayer, or grace at the supper table. Most of all I did not think of meditation and prayer as similar. Eventually it began to dawn on me that both are natural processes. Meditation is a natural extension of consciousness moving inward, of thought directing one's inner life. I also realized that prayer is not just asking, but also a receptive listening. Finally, it occurred to me that both meditation and prayer had many things in common—but most importantly, *silence* came to seem the most significant common denominator. I realized that silence was a gentle bridge between the inner and outer worlds over which we all can travel.

"Be still and know" is the clear scriptural command to let the mind rest from its own activities and to quietly wait for the Infinite to reveal itself.

But these ideas of silence and learning to remain quietly open and receptive to the spiritual dimensions of life are not easy for the activity-oriented Westerner. There are automatic escapes in our culture that most people use. The television or radio or stereo is snapped on as soon as we are alone. It rarely occurs to us, in our fast-paced, action-dominated lives, simply to enjoy the solitude.

People constantly ask me how to open themselves to the spirit of the 5th Dimension, or how they can become a channeler, or how they can become more psychic, and when I mention silence and becoming quietly receptive, they seem lost. I think this is because our culture has not educated us to the beauty and subtlety of inner experience, just as it has not allowed us to open ourselves to experience without judgment or critical evaluation.

In fact, in our society *silence* and its spiritual cousin, *solitude,* are often seen as negatives. When prisoners in a penitentiary are punished, they are put in solitary confinement. Children are punished by making them stand alone in the corner or sending them to their room. These attitudes do not allow us to be sympathetic to the positive role of solitude and silence. Being open to the spiritual dimensions in solitude and silence are not taught to us as virtues, as a positive experience that can enhance our inner life. But the individual who dares to confront the silence within and who understands the value of solitude is well on the path toward self-truth.

Moments in the life of Christ, as well as in the lives of other spiritual leaders throughout history, can be interpreted as symbolic of the common person's possible spiritual growth through using solitude constructively. When Christ went into the desert, His ordeals of temptation and loneliness became the pattern for everyone. Yet, in surviving the dangers of solitude, Christ was rewarded with the gift of truth. His truth involved rejecting three kinds of illusions: power, reputation or fame, and great wealth or obsessive security. Learning these truths, which are among the spiritual lessons of the 5th Dimension, can become your truths if you have the courage to survive solitude and the temptations within your own temperament. The freedom that comes from learning such great lessons cannot be had without experimenting with the self. As the 5th Dimension energy touches you, new opportunities for self-reliance, self-exploration, self-examination, and self-modification become possible.

RECEPTIVE LISTENING

Silence, once learned, can establish new dimensions of reality for you—*5th Dimensional reality!* One California psychologist found that most people communicate with closed-ended questions calling for brief yes or no answers, instead of open-ended questions exploring ideas. This psychologist avowed that people rely so heavily on verbal reactions to the world, they talk *at* other people with a kind of "verbal crowding."

It is typical, for example, for people to respond so quickly in conversation that there is no pause. We've all experienced this. One person launches so quickly into his or her own "verbal crowding" that there is no time at all to see if either person really understood the other's viewpoint. In effect, silence is sacrificed along with any opening to the other's mind. Naturally this prevents good communication.

What normally happens is the victims of verbal crowding become frustrated because they feel they have not been understood or that their thoughts have been misinterpreted. They then begin to speed up their own speech patterns in order to get in as many words as possible in the shortest time. Soon the conversation is a race among frustrated people who cannot properly communicate or understand one another.

I, on the other hand, responded differently to verbal crowding.

I had always felt overwhelmed by this barrage of words and had to learn to be direct and ask the person I was trying to communicate with to please fully listen to my words. I suspect many people who instinctively shy away from the conflict and competition within our society react the same way. For these people receptive listening techniques offer a way to deal with the loud, nervous, and aggressive personalities we encounter every day.

By learning to pause, to allow a few seconds to elapse between someone's statement and your response, a reflectiveness develops both around the other person's ideas and your own understanding. This small silence that I call receptive listening can at first throw off other speakers who expect the normal rapid-fire speech pattern. But, interestingly, it takes very little time for people to sense that you are dealing more seriously with their ideas. In response they seem to give more consideration to your answers because the small silence reflects your own attempt to take the idea under discussion more seriously. It is, in short, like telling the person you're talking with that you have heard him or her and are letting what he or she says filter through your own mental and emotional systems. It is showing your empathy and your honest attempt to grasp the idea in the other person's mind.

The more you listen the more you hear. Receptively listening with an open, nonjudgmental attitude eventually will help you move beyond your own limiting patterns, for you won't be constantly referring everything you hear to your own prejudices or preconceived ideas.

In a meditation experiment conducted by Dr. Karlis Osis of the American Society for Psychical Research, the high point of the week's meditation experiment for one subject was the realization that he had stopped talking *at* someone. It was, he said, "an awesome thing . . . to feel oneself on the verge of the possibility of really knowing another person." In effect, this is vulnerability, an opening of the self to others.

In the 5th Dimension energy know that all humans are experiencing an opening of the heart and a coming together, not the separation of selves. New communication is coming forth that brings wholeness, sharing in all relationships, acknowledgment of the truth of self. In allow-

ing truth and vulnerability to be in the world, there is a
fuller expression of the totality of being, which enhances
your relationships on all levels, do you understand?

Such a feeling is possible only when the silence shared with others becomes meaningful and you develop an empathetic communion. Receptive listening can be used in everyday life without elaborate work or preparation. Norman Cousins, the former editor of *Saturday Review,* uses similar techniques all the time. Cousins had been impressed with how the former United Nations Secretary General U Thant used receptive listening in his work. "Most of my visitors wish to leave me with a message," U Thant once said, "with a deeply felt belief or an idea. In order to receive and fully understand what my human brother has to say to me, I must open myself to him. I must empty myself of self."

U Thant is right. People can learn so much, Cousins said, "by simply opening themselves to others, by lowering the barriers of their self-sufficiency. . . . It is perhaps the clue to serenity in our bewildered, complex world."

Silence is a doorway into the 5th Dimension, and can be used in a number of ways: from a mental silence in meditation to psychological methods for better communication. However, learning to use receptive listening and silence in communication is more than just gaining control over your own verbal habits. You also have to develop the ability to empathize beyond the self: As Theo says, *To listen receptively is to listen nonjudgmentally.* To truly open oneself to another's point of view is to listen mind-to-mind without prejudice, critical dissection, or harsh judgment.

When you acknowledge the self unconditionally, and
love it without judgment, you become whole. That is lov-
ing the positive aspects of the personality as well as the
negative. God created energy, a positive and negative bal-
ancing of forces, not to be thought of as good or bad. It is
what is. It is a balance, a wholeness, that each person
seeks to achieve within his or her being.

If you make a judgment or have a negative thought,
that is not bad. (Do not judge yourself, either.) It is what
is, is it not? Love and accept that. Do not relinquish your

power to another. Become it; become your own power fully, and do not diminish it by loving only the negative. Become your own power fully, and that is to know God. Understand?

13

Key Three:
Breath Control

*Sit quietly in a quiet place.
Begin with deep breathing in and out. Slowly. You will
feel the vibrations within the cellular structure of your
body with the breath. If the mind chatters, draw it back
gently to the breath.*

Of all Theo's many recommendations, nothing is more basic,
more necessary for human life, than air and breathing. For most
of the meditative religions, breath and breathing is not simply the
act of taking in oxygen and exhaling carbon dioxide. Breath is
considered a life force, prana, as it is called in Hinduism. Theo
emphasizes the same thing, constantly referring to breath as "energy," or a life force. Sometimes it is even called "light."

Most of us tend to think of breathing as an automatic action,
something we do unconsciously. And this is as far as we go. But

actually breathing is a dynamic process related to our complete physical and psychic wholeness. For example, short, uneven, shallow breathing often accompanies fright, neurosis, and physical illness. The breathing of the average person changes dramatically according to stress, tension, and the bewildering number of situations experienced every day. Learning to guide the breath for even a few minutes can help one turn away from these irritating sources of negativity and stress.

Guiding your breath can be practiced almost anywhere at any time . . . with incredibly good results: like waiting in an office, or any place you have free time. A good place to try out a little breath control is on the subway, train, or bus. If you find crowds and the tensions of the day difficult, you can do a breathing exercise, and the person sitting next to you will probably not notice. Simply close your eyes to block out the more glaring distractions and quickly inhale. Hold the inhalation for a second or two and then exhale slowly. As you find yourself relaxing, inhale more slowly until your breathing is deep and regular. If you concentrate on the inhale-exhale rhythm of your breathing, you will be surprised at how quickly your tensions will be reduced and your energy level raised.

To practice more controlled breathing and develop the ability to move on to more advanced exercises, an easy beginning exercise is simply to inhale for four seconds, retain your breath for four seconds, exhale for four seconds, hold the exhale for four seconds, and begin the cycle again. The idea is to breathe deeply and reduce the number of shallow breaths per minute. No one knows just how many breaths one ought to take, but eighteen breaths a minute is common for the average person in a relaxed state. For the practiced meditator taking only four or five breaths a minute is common.

There are more advanced counting methods using first one nostril then the other. The counting varies and may be used in a series of 2–8–4 or in a series of 3–12–6, etc. The numbers in sequence refer to inhale, hold, and exhale, respectively. In practice you can count according to any form you wish. You can use beads, mentally count your heartbeat, snap your fingers, touch the thumb to each of your fingers, etc. But the one-to-ten count and a halving of the "holding breath" are the most common methods.

To halve your "holding breath," you simply reduce by half the number of seconds you inhale and exhale. If, for example, you inhale for eight seconds, you should hold for four, then exhale for eight seconds, and hold again for four. Then repeat the cycle.

> **Theo, I have been experiencing a great deal of despair recently, which really isn't like me. Is there something going on with me, just all the energy in general, and is there any guidance you can give me?**

> *In general, yes, there is an upheaval in your being, a releasing of old thought patterns that have served you well in the past but can no longer be in your present. There is chaos inside, and at times you feel as if you are in a void. Those things that have been structured in your subconscious since birth are changing and moving rapidly now. This is the time of the 5th Dimension, is it not? Breathe in these times to keep yourself centered, and know that this process will bring forth the true essence of who you are. Trust the self.*

These breathing techniques are Theo's most frequent suggestions for helping people during times of stress; they help to focus the mind, heal the body, or even lift the vibratory activity of the body's cells. Theo says that breathing clears the toxins from the physical body. The breath is even used as a metaphor for inhaling the new and exhaling the old. It is a focusing point for each of us that will help us make transitions in our own lives less painful and confusing. Accept the breath as an expression of the rhythm of your life, and as you alter your breathing pattern, you can alter those negative elements that are causing you pain or difficulty. Accept the metaphor and use it.

> *There is a death here, yes? There is the dying away of the old . . . so there is the necessity of breathing this out. Allow the breathing; allow the change; allow the expression of whatever comes from this emotional upheaval. It is an acknowledgment of the fuller energy of being, the totality of the self.*

14

Key Four:
Simple Techniques
for
Reducing Stress

How do people start to prepare spiritually for the coming of the 5th Dimension?

Daily meditation, on a regular basis, allows the being to balance in the new energy, or the new frequency, that is coming about.

To prepare for this change, one should perform a regular meditation, sitting erect, feet upon the floor, to allow the energy to come through the balls of the feet, up through the entire body, radiating out into all the cells. Visualize the energy as a golden light coming through the balls of the feet, using the breath to enhance this energy flow.

Breathing in and out slowly, directly, feel the relaxation in the muscles of the body with the movement of the

breath. Use the vibration of the "AUM" [OM] sound, not
clipped as a word, but as a sound. Do this either verbally
or aloud, whichever is most comfortable psychologically
and emotionally.

Theo often uses the natural rhythms of breathing as a simple
but effective way to relax.

From long habit we condition ourselves subconsciously to go
through many tensions when we concentrate—we clench our
teeth, tense our hands, tighten the muscles in our necks and
shoulders. It's no wonder we are a nation of migraine sufferers, a
nation of many small but nagging ailments, most of which can be
traced to stress.

I had a girlfriend who lived next door to me who would
always stick her tongue out of the side of her mouth when she
was concentrating. My mother would always ask me whether I
was frowning or making a face when I concentrated and how I
would like it if I froze like that. When I saw my friend do it again,
I thought how funny it would be if she actually did freeze like
that. Unfortunately, many of us are frozen in our stress responses.
And that's why meditation is so necessary.

Here is a simple, basic technique for relaxing *all* your muscles
that can be used when preparing for meditation and for quick and
effective stress reduction. After you learn this simple, basic
method, you will be able to relax your body in less than a minute
merely by focusing your attention on specific areas of your body.
But in order for it to be effective, it is necessary to learn the
technique thoroughly.

Begin by consciously slowing down the rhythm of your
breathing, and with every exhalation either think or say out loud
a calming word such as "peace" or "be tranquil." Any word that
quiets your fast, tension-oriented rhythm will work. As you think
"peace," exhale and continue to slow down your breathing. Do
not slow down your breathing so much that it becomes uncomfortable, for you will only build up further tensions. A reasonable
time at first is to count six slowly for both inhale and exhale. Then
lengthen to eight and ten counts. The more advanced breathing
exercises should only be undertaken after you have some experience. If you know where your tensions tend to build up, focus

your calming word on that area of your body. Most people, for example, get tense between the shoulder blades where the neck and spinal vertebrae meet. Focus your attention on that spot, and with every inhalation picture the air coming into your body to flow directly to that spot.

Let your mind flood that area with the air you breathe in, while you think your calming word at the same time. When you exhale, envision the tensions in that area leaving your body with your exhalation, again repeating the calming word. Repeat this process with each area of tension in your body. Cover your whole body in this way.

Other simple aids to relaxation Theo has talked about include a gentle rocking while sitting in a meditation posture, humming quietly, or—easiest of all—going over each part of your body individually, first slightly tensing and then releasing that particular group of muscles. Starting from the feet and moving to the head, the body is generally completely relaxed by the time you reach your face, neck, and scalp.

> *The use of meditation daily fine-tunes the being and releases anxiety and stress. Also ask for confirmation to be brought forth in your meditation. Ask for signs to be given in your outer world activity so that your conscious mind can be in agreement with the spirit. . . . The 5th Dimension energy is that of enlightenment and light, and you have chosen to be here, have you not?*

BECOMING SERENE

Another simple technique for reducing stress and relaxing is a meditation on being serene. This simple meditation uses both physical muscle-group relaxation and word-repetition focusing.

Relax all your muscles and nervous tensions. Breathe slowly and rhythmically. Visualize your face and body in a serene condition. See your face with a serene smile. *Believe* yourself to be serene.

Think about serenity and what it means to you. Think about its quality, its value and use, especially when you are faced with a normally tense situation. Praise serenity in your mind; affirm its effectiveness; concentrate on feeling it in your body and mind. Evoke it directly by feeling it in specific places in your body. Feel it in your heart, and feel it slowly expand in peaceful waves like the gentle ripples moving across the surface of a placid pond. Feel its waves expand throughout your chest, into your neck and shoulders and head; down into your stomach, hips, legs, and feet. Feel the tension and tautness leave your muscles, tendons, and nerves as it radiates throughout your body.

Repeat the word "serene" over and over again in your mind, or use some other word that appeals more to you, such as "peace," "calm," "tranquil," etc. If you wish, you can repeat a phrase or sentence from a book that appeals to you. Any positive, suggestive phrase will do.

My favorite affirmation is: "Divine love is doing its perfect work in and through me now." It works beautifully for me. I can feel those words penetrate every cell, warming them like sunlight and relaxing me completely.

A variation on this meditation is to insert a visualization in which you picture a hostile person confronting you in anger; or place yourself in danger; or see yourself surrounded by rapidly moving events to which you must respond—and then picture yourself calm and serene in the midst of them all. Visualize yourself facing and dealing with the hostile person calmly and with patience.

Before you conclude this meditation you might suggest to yourself strongly and repeatedly that you will remain serene throughout the day regardless of what happens. Determine within yourself that you will radiate serenity and be a living example of peace and calm.

15

Key Five:
Using Your Energy
Wisely

THE HEART OF ALL SELF-CHANGE IS
a redirecting of mental energy, of altering attitude and changing
thought patterns. This results in a balancing of internal energies
. . . and using your energy properly is one of the keys to successfully living in the 5th Dimension. From Theo we get the clear
advice: Become sensitive to your own energy patterns, and learn
to use them for self-change.

*You must understand that thought is the creative force in
your universe. It is the energy within and around you. It
is electric and comes into the thinking processes of your
conscious mind; it is the energy form of your being.*

*God created energy, a positive and negative balancing
of forces, not to be thought of as good or bad. It is what*

is. It is a balance, a wholeness that each person seeks to achieve within his or her being. It is the whole of the self.

Our normal everyday energy seems to be wasted in three basic ways: (1) stress and unconscious muscle exertion; (2) negative emotions, such as anxiety, fear, and negative fantasies; and (3) mind-wandering.

Mind-wandering, however, is not always wasteful; sometimes it is creative, as in daydreaming. But until you learn to relax and use your energy wisely, you will not have full, creative use of your mind and body. By adjusting your internal energies you eliminate the effects of stress, negative emotions, and mind-wandering.

And how do you redirect your mental energy and alter these powerful thought patterns that have dominated your life since childhood? As you read through the following ideas, remember Theo's prescription for thought guidance: *It is the immediate that is important. Thoguht creates reality. Energy follows thought.*

The energy is there, understand? Visualize the opportunity; affirm it. You create the opportunity by the energy of your thought. Then there is the shifting of energy and of consciousness.

First, learn to use your energy wisely; then learn the following exercises, and you will be pleasantly surprised at the change in both your mind and body.

LEARNING TO USE YOUR ENERGY WISELY

Imagine the three types of energy loss (stress, mind-wandering, and negative emotions) as a three-story building, with each floor devoted to a particular energy use. The ground floor is for our physical work, the second where we carry on our emotional life, and the top floor where we experience our intellect. When we are working on any one of the floors, the others are frequently involved. For example, when we are using the ground floor of our physical life, it is not necessary to have the lights turned on all over the house. And even while this is obvious, we indulge in this kind of waste all the time in our daily lives.

These three sources of fatigue and energy loss can be corrected by a few simple techniques.

1. Handling stress. The first principle of using energy properly is to be conscious of its loss, to be aware of physical, emotional, and intellectual energy waste. Once you become aware that you are fatigued because of anxiety or excess physical tension, try to notice the specific muscles involved at that instant of recognition. You will probably find that you are sitting in a tense position, your legs crossed like a strung bow. Your neck and shoulders are probably two or three inches higher because the muscles are bunched up in a knot. If you consciously think "relax" to these shoulder and neck muscles, you may be surprised to find them literally drop several inches. This means that the lights are on in your ground-floor physical life when you are sitting and should be relaxed. The cure for this obvious fatigue-creating problem is to turn off the lights by allowing the conscious mind to guide the situation and relax the body. Since your body, probably through long habit, has learned not to shut itself down when, say, you have just finished running for a train, you must teach it to hang loose.

2. Mind-wandering. Letting your mind wander and thinking aimlessly, often for unrecognized emotional reasons, are wasting energy and creating fatigue in the top floor of your life's house. Everyone has these experiences, but the easy techniques described in the exercises I have devised for this book can give you the control to turn off the lights when you don't need them. Just as with your physical body, you must first learn to catch your mind wandering. (Following the exercises in Key One and Key Six will be extremely helpful for this.) At first it may seem tiring and even unpleasant or unspontaneous to bring your mind back from a daydream. But remember that when you have learned to do it, you can also bring it back when it is involved in an emotional, exhausting, and unhealthy recounting of the day's problems or irritations.

3. Negative emotions. To develop an awareness of what your body, mind, and emotions are doing is the first step in eliminating the problems preventing you from fulfilling more important life goals. All it takes is learning to *remember* to do it. Once you are convinced you are creating your own exhaustion, use the testing and relaxation techniques, such as tensing and relaxing muscle groups, all over your body in order to "turn off" the unnecessary lights. When your mind wanders, have a positive sentence (compose one yourself), an "affirmation," that you can concentrate on and repeat over and over to yourself until all the irritations of the day, all the energy-absorbing fantasies about what you should have said or done, or what you should do tomorrow, are quieted.

The English poet Shelley wrote, "We look before and after and sigh for what is not." In fact, we do much more than simply look and sigh: We exhaust ourselves unnecessarily. By relaxing your body and repeating an affirmation, you can convert this wasted energy into energy savings. Those who practice these simple methods—and those who follow—will find themselves with more energy than they need in a very short time.

16

Key Six: Ten "Focusing" Exercises for Beginning Meditators

As EACH OF US MOVES INTO A fuller experience of the 5th Dimension energy shift, we will be challenged to change ourselves in constructive ways. To accomplish this, several fundamental points must be worked on: to open oneself to the universe, to feel honestly and directly ourselves and the world around us, and to raise our consciousness to the highest level we are capable of. The following ten exercises have been created to allow the average person to guide—and elevate—his or her awareness. They are graded in difficulty and cover a wide range of different elements in learning to focus your mind and, ultimately, expand consciousness.

The basic, general advice for practicing these exercises is to fix the mind on some object either in or out of the body and to keep the attention there steadily for some time. It will, as with all things relating to growth, need daily practice.

1. Ask a friend to show you some playing cards. Immediately after being shown a card, describe it in detail. Give the number, name, color, etc. This is a great help in building concentration and learning how to focus your mind.

2. Read two or three pages of a book and then close it. Now think about what you have read and abandon all distracting thoughts. Focus your attention carefully and allow the mind to associate, classify, group, combine, and compare what you have read. If you concentrate carefully, you will receive a clear, strong impression. In addition to practicing focusing and concentration, this exercise helps you develop your memory as well as comprehension abilities in reading.

3. In a quiet room, sit in your favorite meditative posture about one foot from a watch. Concentrate on the tick-tick sound. Whenever your mind runs away, try again and again to hear the sound. See how long your mind can stay fixed continuously only on the sound. Practice this exercise until you have improved your original length of concentration.

I remember the first time I tried this exercise. After five seconds I thought to myself, This isn't so hard. I've already concentrated for five seconds. Of course, I then realized that my ego had interrupted the exercise.

4. Sit in your favorite posture and close your eyes. Close your ears with your thumbs, or plug them with cotton or wax (make sure the wad is large enough to pull out easily).

You will hear various sounds of the body like your heartbeat, etc. These are the "gross" sounds of the body described in the section on Receptive Listening and Silence. Listen to them for a while and then try to hear only a single sound among all the others, a sound underlying the others. Try to isolate this "special" sound from the others and concentrate on it. If the mind runs away, you can shift it back and forth between the gross sounds of your body and the subtle single sound. You will often hear sounds mainly in your right ear. Occasionally you will hear them in your left ear also. Let this experience happen, and try to retain the sound in one ear or the other. Shift the sound from one ear to the other. In this way you will also develop one-pointedness of mind. Yogis say that this is an easy way to capture the wandering mind because the mind is enchanted by the sweet sounds, just as a snake is hypnotized by the notes of a snake charmer.

5. Keep a candle flame in front of you, and concentrate on the flame. When you are tired of this, close your eyes and visualize the flame. Do this for half a minute (approximately) at first, then increase the time to five, ten, fifteen minutes, or longer, depending on your preference. This exercise moves the meditator into deep altered states of consciousness.

6. In a supine posture, concentrate on the moon (or a star, or even a spot on your ceiling). This is an excellent exercise to do out of doors—for example, on a camping trip, or even in your back-yard. Whenever the mind runs away, bring it back time and time again to the image. This is a very beneficial exercise for calming the emotions.

7. Sit by the side of a river where you can hear its subtle sounds. Listen to the overall sound the rushing water creates. Sometimes it even sounds like the "AUM" (OM) sound. Concentrate on that sound as long as you like. If you don't live near a river, choose a special piece of music you enjoy and listen to it over and over again, following every rise and fall of tone, volume, and quality of sound. Listen to the music as many times as you can. You shouldn't become sick of it if you are listening properly. You should literally try to identify with the sound so thoroughly that when it moves, you "feel" the action—the music seems to become a part of you, and you a part of it. You should not become tired of that piece of music any more than you would become tired of a single mantra sound if you are concentrating properly.

You can also use environmental tapes, such as whale sounds, ocean sounds, wind sounds, and so forth. Any quiet, rhythmic sound of nature is helpful.

8. Lie in the open and concentrate on the blue, expansive sky above, or concentrate on clouds. If you live in a city, or it is

inconvenient to lie outside for other reasons, try to position your-self near a window so you can lie down and look out of it. As you concentrate on the blank, blue depths, your mind will expand. Think of the sky as an expression of the infinite nature of the universe and the inner self.

9. Sit in a comfortable posture, and concentrate on any one of numerous abstract virtues such as mercy, kindness, understand-ing, gentleness, love, forgiveness, etc. Concentrate on this idea for as long as you can, and repeat the exercise as often as you can.

10. Take any piece of furniture and use it as the object of concentration. This means getting full, detailed knowledge about the object. If you are concentrating on, say, a chair, notice the type of wood, its construction, workmanship; imagine yourself sitting in it, and establish its degree of comfort and whether the parts need polish or not.

These exercises, if done regularly, can enhance the expansive-ness of your mind. Meditation becomes easier, and other thought-guiding techniques for relaxation and stress reduction become a natural extension. And the ultimate goal of achieving higher states of consciousness is tantalizingly close.

17

Key Seven: A "Flow" Meditation for Higher Consciousness

OF ALL THE MEDITATION OR thought-guiding techniques used for moving on toward the higher states of consciousness, none have all the special ingredients of this "flow" meditation. Literally, if practiced regularly, this meditation can help one to flow into higher states of awareness. The single most important piece of advice when practicing this meditation is to think of the experience as a unification of the mind and nature, of the self and the universe.

The meditation begins with the body and progressively moves on to the fuller use of the senses, and ultimately to using the mind fully as both a device for visualization and a free-moving point of awareness. It is an invaluable exercise and will help anyone to achieve a higher state of consciousness.

Lie or sit in a comfortable position. Make sure your arms, legs, body, trunk, neck, and head are in an extended relaxed position.

Move through your body with the standard tensing of each muscle group for a few seconds, and then relax them. Pay particular attention to the chest, neck, and shoulder muscle groups. Take a deep breath, and hold it for five or six seconds. Release the air and let your breathing become deep, easy, and normal. Picture the breath as a fluid energy connecting your body and consciousness with the world outside your skin. Concentrate on the ease with which these two worlds communicate on the pathway of your breath.

Next, think about your blood circulating throughout your chest; feel your heart beating, pumping blood through your veins up to your head, out to your shoulders, arms, and down through your stomach, hips, pelvis, legs, and into your feet. Feel it flow in each of these places; feel it flow through your face and into your toes.

After you have traced the blood pulsing throughout your body, relax even more and feel it softly moving in your chest. Join the rhythm of your heartbeat; tune in to its resonance and regularity.

Now relax and feel the multiple rhythms of your body. Visualize your body as a whole. You are a single, total being, mind, body, and spirit. Your mind and consciousness are an electric, alive part of this rhythm. See your body as an alive, vibrant electrical being. Each cell, each small blood vessel, each fiber, is alive with pulsing blood, with electrical energy that extends out from your body in all directions. Watch the patterns as the energy flows out of your body into the space around you. Visualize an enlarging electrical field that extends beyond the room, beyond the house, beyond the earth and into the sky, in all directions.

As you watch these lines of energy rhythmically extend from your body into infinity, feel your conscious awareness expanding along with the energy; allow your consciousness to be moving out on the electrical lines beyond your body and the room or building you are in. Imagine yourself floating higher and higher until you can see the earth below for miles in every direction. Rise still higher until you can see the slight curve of the earth's horizon, until you see the towns and cities beneath you.

Envision the earth turning slowly as you float higher into the sky. Be aware that the sky and earth are touching and that your body is still in contact with the earth through vibrating lines of energy.

There is no anxiety in this floating, for you are a part of both the earth and sky, with the gentle rhythms connecting all your awareness can encompass. See the stars glittering in the sky around you, the moon in the distance slowly changing its shape as it floats around the earth. As the moon changes its shape, see its gravitational pull on the great bodies of blue water on earth. Feel the warm energy of the sun as its rays join the many other particles rhythmically passing around and through you.

Feel yourself move still higher, passing beyond the orbits of the solar system's planets. Your own body continues to radiate lines of particles that mingle with the constant energy of the universe buzzing around you. You are an integral, perfect part of all that is happening. Not only do you still feel comfortably connected with the earth, but now you are intimate with the moon, the sun, and the planets. As you float outside of the solar system, join in its graceful cycle. And as you move farther into space, watch the solar system become smaller and more distant until it slowly dissolves into just another bright, blinking star.

Now you are a bright light of consciousness, of radiating light, just as all the other stars are. As you extend your particles of energy to all the stars around you, you receive waves of light from them. Let yourself be bathed in their streaming lines of undulating particles of energy.

Visualize yourself as being on the edge of the immense Milky Way galaxy, looking toward its distant center, which is an intense point of light many times brighter than the sun. Watch as the Milky Way turns slowly and majestically in its circle and you float out beyond its rim, beyond all the bright stars, toward other galaxies, beyond other slowly turning galaxies of milky light shifting their colors all across the spectrum.

As you move farther and farther into the universe, realize that all the planets and stars within the galaxies are alive and breathing, a pulsing part of the whole universe. Be aware that each galaxy is circling slowly on its own axis, yet is spinning in relationship to all the other galaxies. Realize that all this movement throughout the whole universe is identical to your own body back in that small room on that distant planet; it is identical to your heartbeat, your soft regular breathing, and the electrical rhythms of your mind and brain.

Feel the unity within this vast, unending being you call the universe. The universe is alive, yet calmly, rhythmically, unendingly functioning just as you are. Feel the immense calm throughout the universe, within all the dark spaces between the galaxies. Feel this peace within your own mind and body. There is a calm underlying all the pulsation around you: Identify with it and let it embrace you. Become aware of this calm inside you. It is beyond alteration and sustains all the activity around you. Feel yourself a part of this universally sustaining peace, and allow yourself to float in its immense, unending comfort.

When you are ready to return to Earth and your body, begin to visualize the particles of energy intensifying, moving faster and faster. Feel the quickened pace of the vibrations in your mind and body. If you feel like remaining in that immense universal peace, remind yourself that it will always be there for you to return to. You have a body to enliven and utilize.

Visualize the vibrations becoming so intense, they form cloudlike groups and interact with your physical brain and body. These particles are highly energized, and they form the basis for organic life. Visualize these cloudlike particles entering the cells of your body. Feel the billions of cells in your body interacting with one another to form the organs of your body. See the particles and cells pulsing in your heart as it pumps blood to your lungs, stomach, neck veins, brain, legs, arms, feet, and hands. Feel each of these cells filling your body with energy. Feel your bones and muscles being filled with these energetic cells; feel them spill over in their rush to energize your body and skin.

Now relax and feel the many rhythms of body and mind working together. Feel your body working in unison with the billions of cells sending energy and vitality throughout your body until your skin seems to glow with its strength. Listen to your heartbeat, your regular breathing.

If you are sitting, trace all the surfaces of your body that are being touched by something. If you are lying down, do the same thing. Allow yourself to breathe regularly, and feel your whole body in relation to its surroundings. Feel your body and mind rhythmically working, and feel your relation to the room, the house, the neighborhood, the city or town, in which you live. You are a part of a community of beings, a community of living beings. Relax and simply feel your body-mind and its contact with the world around you. When you are ready, move your body very easily, slowly. Gently stretch your muscles and tendons as you get up. Retain that feeling of unity with the world as much as you can throughout your day.

Since this is an advanced meditation, you may want to read it through several times to get the sequence and images clear in your mind before using it. It might be easier for you to read the meditation slowly into a tape recorder and play it back during your meditation, which will allow you to follow it exactly and effortlessly.

CONCLUSION

FOR GENERATIONS WE HAVE ASKED
ourselves what is the meaning, the purpose of life. In a peculiar
way I think the very pressures and extremes our polluted and
war-threatened world is suffering brings us to a point of decision:
It's almost a condition of "change or die."

The answer to the question of what is the purpose of life has,
at least for me, become fairly simple. The purpose of life is to
preserve our planet from the polluters, the manipulators, all the
destructive energies, that are buzzing around our heads. In the
process we must work on ourselves; so, in essence, we are saved
the more we work on the problems of humankind as a whole.

The themes of unity, of a family of humans, of spaceship
Earth, to use an old phrase, all become real and less abstract as
we turn our attention to the task of saving our world. Out of this
labor of love comes world unity, care, and nonjudgmental affection for our fellow human beings, and a renewed commitment to
self-growth.

Each of us then becomes a peacemaker; we become responsible for our own actions first. Then we must act in a way that
enhances the life of our planet and the role of peacemaker—both
in our personal and social life. We cannot change the world's

279

system overnight. That's a task for the coming decades. But what we can do immediately is create specific, healthy realities in our lives that will have an impact on our society.

We cannot solve our personal problems, or the problems of our world, by living with a subservient attitude toward any power we allow to reign over us—that is irresponsibility. On that path we neatly avoid holding ourselves accountable for our actions. We can neatly say "He did it" or "She did it. . . . They made me do it." But we also cannot change ourselves or the world by placing responsibility for everything on the shoulders—no matter how loving—of a god or *entity* (no matter how neatly channeled or packaged) that appears to be more enlightened or whole than ourselves.

If we traverse that path, somebody else—a guru, a religious leader, one of the many gods worshipped around the world— becomes the authority for our actions. That is a clever way to avoid responsibility for our own lives, but a terrible way to grow up! And that's why every cult whose members exalt the guru to divine status is ultimately destructive to the disciple.

The power is, as it always has been, in our own hands. We must first learn to recognize the nature of our foolishness and then take corrective action. Only by being responsible for ourselves can we become responsible citizens of the world.

All beings are totally responsible for what they create in their experience.

Using the insights of an enlightened teacher like Theo should not result in giving over your power to someone else. In fact, the opposite should happen. Theo, aware of the problems human beings have in avoiding responsibility by placing authority on others, constantly urges seekers to become whole, to recognize the power of their own selves. That, I am sure, is the path to fulfillment, to growth, and ultimately, to spiritual enlightenment.

Do not relinquish your power to another. Become it; become your own power fully. And that is to know God, understand?

broach

Br o a ch

brō ch

brō (long o)